Thirteen Million Tons of Allied Shipping . . .

. . . that was the toll the U-boats took in the last war.

This is the complete story of how they did it—written by a man who was on the staff of Admiral Dönitz and who saw it all from the inside.

From the very beginnings, when Hitler reconstituted the German Navy in 1935-1939, through the start of war and the U-47's sinking of the *Royal Oak* inside Scapa Flow, through the terrible dark days of 1942 when American and British convoys were horribly decimated, right through to the turning of the tide, this book presents the dramatic facts—clearly and thoroughly—as the enemy saw them.

Some experts think that if Hitler had had fifty more U-boats in 1939, he would probably have won the last war.

The Sea Wolves shows how close he came.

"Exciting reading. . . . It is told in the crisp style of a professional sea hand." —*Chicago Sunday Tribune*

THE GERMAN U-BOAT OF THE CONVOY BATTLES

1. Bow torpedo tubes—torpedo officer, torpedo mechanics and mates
2. Bow compartment with crew
3. Reserve torpedoes
4. WC
5. Chief POs' mess
6. Officers' mess
7. CO's cabin
8. Hydroplane cabin, with operator and second watchkeeping officers
9. W/T cabin
10. Battery compartment
11. Bridge
12. Conning tower, with CO at attack periscope, helmsman, and torpedo director rating
13. Control room, with the engineer officer, diving rudder operators (with sky-searching periscope above), the coxswain, navigating chief PO and one rating
14. POs' mess
15. Galley
16. Diesel engine room with chief ERA and three ratings
17. Motor room with chief electrical artificer and three ratings
18. Stern torpedo tubes with two torpedo ratings
19. Diving rudders
20. Steering rudder

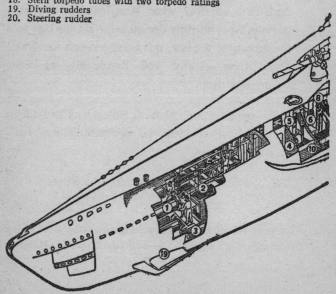

WOLFGANG FRANK

The Sea Wolves

Translated by
Lieutenant Commander R.O.B. Long,
R.N.V.R

Foreword by
Vice Admiral Leland P. Lovette,
U.S.N. (Ret.)

BALLANTINE BOOKS, New York

ISBN 0-345-29504-8

This edition published by arrangement with
Holt, Rinehart and Winston, Inc.

Manufactured in the United States of America

First Ballantine Books Edition: April 1958

Sixth Printing: April 1981

CONTENTS

FOREWORD

Most of us remember that in two World Wars the German U-boats came perilously near controlling the major sea lanes of the Atlantic. Such control would have changed the course of the war; the eventual outcome would most probably have been an Allied defeat. In World War I German submarines destroyed more than five thousand ships amounting to 11,000,000 tons. The lesson appears in the light of history to have been forgotten both by the United States and Great Britain, for between the wars it was generally believed here and in England that the convoy system with improved anti-submarine devices had taken away much of the sting from underwater vessels. Prior to World War II, Hitler and some members of his military staff also greatly underestimated the strategic value of submarines, officered and manned by highly trained and determined men. Some experts think that if Hitler had had fifty more U-boats in 1939, he would probably have won the last war.

The saga of the extraordinary exploits of the German submariners is admirably told by Wolfgang Frank in THE SEA WOLVES. Their successes and failures are set forth clearly and frankly. High policy controversies between the German war lords with special accent on the struggle of Admiral Karl Dönitz to get more ships and men are reminiscent of Grand Admiral von Tirpitz's troubles in World War I. But it was never the job of the seagoing submarine service to reason why; its task was to keep the seas and destroy enemy shipping. "Sink ships" was their brief but dangerous mission, as it was for our courageous submariners in the Pacific.

It should not be forgotten that although freighters and tankers cannot win a war at sea, the lack of them can perhaps lose one. "We must regard this struggle at sea," so Churchill said, "as the foundation of all the efforts of the United Nations. If we lose, all else is denied us." The British Prime Minister also wrote: "The U-boat attack was our worst evil."

This "evil" spelled success for the German Sea Wolves as they rampaged over ocean areas they called the "Golden West." One of their most successful attacks was on Convoy PQ 17 (July 1942) enroute to ice-free Murmansk with British and American aid for beleaguered Russia; of 33 ships in convoy, 22 were sunk, including 5 American. If the tide had not turned soon after such staggering losses of men, ships, and cargo, it is quite probable that the convoy system would have been discontinued until greater escort strength could be secured.

All this the Germans knew. As the author of SEA WOLVES states: "He (Admiral Dönitz) continued to press hard his point that the main objective was to sink ships faster than the Allies could build them." One recalls how at that time ship production was the No. 1 priority of the American industrial effort. And only in May 1942 did new ship production exceed current tonnage losses. Slowly but surely the Allies were winning the first round in the Battle of the Atlantic. However, the Sea Wolves maintained the attack with unabated fury.

In brief, how did the Allies gain a reasonable control over our underwater enemy? (1) By scientific development of highly technical equipment such as special radar in airplanes, effective sonar devices, the new sono buoy, de-magnetization of ships, towing dummies or "Foxers" in order to divert acoustic torpedoes, and 1,000-pound "Killer" depth charges. (2) More efficient operational techniques such as improved convoy-escort and anti-submarine tactics, and development to a fine point of the famous "hunter-killer" groups which utilized to a high degree the respective offensive capabilities of aircraft carriers and fast surface craft. (3) By the tremendous cargo ship production of the United States.

Never to be forgotten was the incalculable human factor: intrepid Allied naval and merchant service personnel, unsung heroes, who waged the long and bitter Battle of the Atlantic. They believed that the only good U-boat was one on the bottom and full of water.

In 1943, the Germans lost 30 per cent of their U-boats at sea; and by 1944 the submarine crews all knew "that only three or at the most four boats out of every five could expect to return." This period marked the end of the wolf packs and thereafter submarines proceeded singly to assigned areas. By the summer of 1943 U-boats had the schnorchel, but it was then too late for them to be a decisive factor in the war.

The Battle of the Atlantic, fought often in gales and ice, marks one of the most momentous periods of sea warfare, because on its outcome largely depended victory or defeat for one or the other implacable foe. To read the thrilling story of these courageous men of the sea who stood by their posts to the last, while knowing for some time that the fight was really lost, accentuates the deadly aggressiveness of unrestricted submarine warfare. Will it happen again?

At this writing, the *U.S.S. Nautilus,* first atomic submarine, driven, lighted, heated and air-conditioned by atomic energy, has successfully completed trials. And since from a consideration of power the *Nautilus* can proceed indefinitely at submerged depths, there is cause for much speculation on the great but yet undetermined strategic value of this new type. With the British Navy concentrating on modernization of anti-submarine and anti-mine forces; and the Soviet Navy embarked on a vast building program, with special emphasis on the most modern type of schnorchel submarines, there is clear indication that the control of the sea lanes has become one of the prime objectives in the current military planning of the world's most powerful nations.

Leland P. Lovette
Vice Admiral, U.S. Navy (Ret.)

I

THE GROWTH OF THE OFFENSIVE
1939-1941

1

THE BIRTH OF THE SUBMARINE

(1624–1919)

> They write here one Cornelius-Son
> Hath made the Hollanders an invisible eel,
> To swim the haven at Dunkirk
> And sink all the shipping there.

Ben Jonson put these lines into the third act of a comedy which he wrote in 1624.[1] It was a topical reference to the feat of one Dr. Cornelius van Drebel, a Dutchman and personal physician to the King of England, who had invented a machine in which, if contemporary reports are to be be-

---

[1] *The Staple of News*, Act III, Scene 1.

lieved, he had traveled under water from Westminster to Greenwich.

This was the first recorded occasion on which man had successfully navigated beneath the surface of the water. It was inevitable that others should follow in van Drebel's footsteps. Ben Jonson makes it clear that even in those days men were searching for an antidote to the maritime weapon of blockade. The search was keenest in those countries which, unlike Great Britain, did not possess great navies. Among those designing and developing submersible vessels in the eighteenth and nineteenth centuries were the Americans Bushnell and Fulton, the Frenchman Gustave Zédé, the Swede Nordenfeldt and another American, John P. Holland. In 1804 Fulton managed to interest Mr. Pitt, the British Prime Minister, in his inventions; and the designs for his *Nautilus* submarine and his "electric torpedo" were carefully considered by the British Admiralty. The First Sea Lord at that time was Sir John Jervis, later Lord St. Vincent. It is not difficult to imagine the impact that this tremendous new creation must have made on the mind of the great seaman. He was quick to perceive the potential danger and instinctively he tried to ward it off.

"Don't look at it," he said. "Don't touch it! If we take it up, other nations will, and that will be the strongest blow against our supremacy on the sea that can be imagined."

His warnings were ignored and, with Pitt's full approval, Fulton was allowed to make his experiment. On October 15, 1805, the hulk of the old Danish brig *Dorothea* was moored in Deal Harbour below Walmer Castle and Fulton "attacked" it with his "electric torpedo." The infernal machine exploded with terrific force, splitting the *Dorothea* in two and hurling wreckage high in the air. St. Vincent was highly critical of the whole proceedings. "Pitt is the biggest fool that ever lived," he declared roundly. "He has given encouragement to a form of warfare which is not desired by those who command the sea and which may well deprive us of our supremacy." Six days later the victory at Trafalgar ended Napoleon's hopes of invading England, and Great Britain ruled the waves more surely than ever. As far as she was concerned, all thoughts of submarine warfare were allowed to fade into oblivion.

Elsewhere, however, the ideas evolved by Fulton and others were further developed. In 1863, in the American Civil War, a semisubmersible vessel, fitted with an explosive charge on the end of a spar, made a partially successful attack on the Yankee battleship *New Ironsides,* which was blockading Charleston. In the following year at the same place the hand-propelled submersible *Hundley* succeeded in sinking the corvette *Housatonic,* but the explosion also caused the loss of the attacker, with all hands. It was the first and only instance before the First World War of a successful submarine attack on a warship.

The next important development was the production at Fiume by the English engineer Whitehead of a self-contained torpedo, driven by compressed air, the potentialities of which were soon appreciated by all the maritime nations. They began to build fast torpedo-carrying ships, and thus were born the flotillas of torpedo boats and destroyers that were an integral part of the fleets in the First World War. Yet the submarine was the ideal carrier for a torpedo.

Meanwhile France began to show a lively interest in the possibilities of the submarine and by 1901 had built no less than twenty-nine models of electrically propelled submersibles. At this time the main obstacle lay in finding a reliable method of propulsion under water. The earliest inventors relied entirely upon electricity or compressed air since it was not thought possible to introduce an internal combustion engine into a submersible craft. In 1893, however, the United States Congress called for designs for an underwater boat and eventually awarded the contract to a young schoolteacher of Irish birth, John P. Holland. After several initial failures, he finally produced his "Holland Number 9," which was accepted in 1900 by the United States Navy. This vessel may fairly be described as the first of the modern submarines. A revolutionary feature of its design was the installation of a 50 hp. gasoline engine for surface propulsion and an electric motor for use when submerged—essentially the same system is is used today. The U.S. Navy ordered six more of these boats, while the British Admiralty gave an order for five; soon afterward every maritime nation had either placed an order or purchased the right to build them under license.

Germany had watched these developments with the closest interest, but for a long time the German Admiralty hesitated to commit itself. It remained for Frederick Alfred Krupp, the great armaments manufacturer, to take the initiative at his own risk, and in July, 1902, work commenced on his 16-ton *Forelle.* This tiny vessel, barely 40 feet long, was built for experimental purposes only. She proved an immediate success and after the Kaiser had shown his interest by inspecting her, she embarked Admiral Prince Henry of Prussia as her first passenger on September 23, 1903. The following year *Forelle* was delivered to Russia as the prototype of three larger boats ordered for the Czar's Navy.

The initial success of the *Forelle* finally convinced the German Admiralty of the need for such a vessel and in September, 1904, Krupp received his first order for a submarine for the German Navy. Admiral von Tirpitz, then Secretary of the Navy, called for a boat displacing 237 tons and some 120 feet in length, which could develop a speed of 10.8 knots on the surface and 8.7 submerged. In other words, von Tirpitz wanted an ocean-going submarine. While *U 1* was still building, the Navy Yard at Danzig started work on a submarine of the Admiralty's own design. In July, 1912, Germany started to equip her U-boats with diesels in place of gasoline engines.

By 1914 the "submersible" was fully fledged—the direct descendant of van Drebel's device, of Bushnell's *Turtle* and Fulton's *Nautilus*, of the inventions of Holland and Lake in America, of Nordenfeldt in Sweden and Zédé in France.

The outbreak of war in 1914 gave the "submersible" its baptism of fire. Its war potentialities were completely unknown, for the world was still thinking in terms of fleets of battleships, whose big guns alone would decide the issue at sea. Germany entered the war with a total of forty-two U-boats, some in commisson, others still being built. Eight hundred and eleven more boats were destined to be laid down in the course of that war, but relatively few of these had been put into service by the time it ended. Their chief function was to attack shipping, but a violent difference of opinion soon arose as to the best way of using them for this purpose. No provision for this form of warfare had been made in the articles of international law, for the clauses relating to war at sea applied only to surface vessels. The submarine's concentrated offensive power, together with its extreme vulnerability, had never been the subject of study by international lawyers; as a result it was expected to wage war in a way which made nonsense of its raison d'être. The existing rules of war required it to fight like a surface raider, which meant that U-boat commanders had to call upon every merchant ship to heave to before sinking it, even if the ship was obviously bound for enemy port. They were obliged to search every neutral vessel for contraband, yet this method left the highly vulnerable U-boat an easy prey to the merchant ship's guns. Also, before sinking any ship, the U-boat commanders were to take steps to safeguard the lives of the crew, but the submarine did not have space in which to house the survivors. What the U-boat needed was the legal right to sink without warning any ship that entered a previously declared danger area.

The blockade of Germany brought the issue of "sinking without warning" to a head. Anxious to evolve a direct countermeasure to the blockade, the German Navy demanded unrestricted U-boat warfare against all ships within a prescribed area round the British Isles. But Chancellor von Bethmann-Hollweg's Government wanted to spare all neutral shipping, and could not be dissuaded from this attitude despite persistent representation from the German Admiralty, in particular from Grand Admiral von Tirpitz. The U-boats had to fight with one hand tied behind their backs. Thus they were not allowed to develop their full capabilities, whereas the enemy was given time to build up powerful antidotes. When all restrictions were at last lifted in February 1917, it was too late; the U-boats were no longer in a position to win the war, for the enemy had grown too strong.

The sinking of the cruisers *Aboukir, Cressy* and *Hogue* on September 22, 1914, by Lieutenant Weddigen in *U 9* gave the British a terrible foretaste of the new submarine's tremendous power of destruction. In little over one hour 28 men in a 400-ton U-boat had destroyed British warships displacing altogether 40,000 tons, carrying 2,265 men, of whom scarcely one third were saved. The world stood aghast at this new weapon; would it spell the end of Britain's supremacy at sea? The loss of the three cruisers and the first attacks on her merchant shipping quickly brought home to Britain the importance of the new menace, and she was not slow to draw the correct conclusions. The situation called for a new type of combined naval and political warfare: one that would deprive the U-boat of its right to attack unseen, and at the same time force it to expose its vulnerability to counterattack because of its lack of defensive armament.

Time was needed to create and develop the naval counter measures—the most extensive and costly in England's maritime history. But political countermeasures could be commenced at once. Northcliffe placed his enormous propaganda machine, with its world-wide connections, at the disposal of Britain's politicians and launched an unparalleled press campaign to bring the U-boat war against Britain's merchant shipping into world-wide disrepute. He achieved his aim, but it was clear for all to see that for the first time in her history, Britain's very survival was threatened. In April, 1917, the figures of shipping losses were rising week by week. The U-boat was quickly eating away not only the life line of the British Isles but the whole foundation of the Allies' strength. The danger of complete collapse lay dark and menacing on the horizon.

In November, 1917, a balance sheet of the forces engaged on either side, which the head of the Anti-Submarine Warfare Department of the Admiralty drew up for Admiral Sir John Jellicoe, showed that ". . . on the German side there were about 178 U-boats. Against these the British were using 277 destroyers, 30 corvettes, 49 steam yachts, 849 trawlers, 687 drifters, 24 mine sweepers (paddle boats), 50 small dirigibles, 194 aircraft, 77 Q-ships . . ." and well over 100,000 mines as well. It was not until 1918, when the effect of the convoy system made itself felt, that the number of sinkings began to drop. Radio communications had not progressed sufficiently in those days for whole groups of U-boats to be launched in concerted attacks against convoys. As soon as ships ceased to sail independently and destroyer-escorts and A/S[2] defenses grew stronger, the tide began to turn. Admiral Scheer's great new U-boat building program never had time to materialize before the war ended.

Thus in November, 1918, there were those who maintained that the U-boat, which at times had alone borne the brunt of the war, was outdated. In the final result, or so it seemed, the convoy system and the improved anti-submarine methods had shown themselves superior to their adversary. Yet it was hardly surprising that the submarine was among the weapons which Germany had to renounce for all time, by the terms of the Versailles Treaty.

[2] A/S: this abbreviation for "Anti-Submarine" is used throughout the book. The term "A/S ship" is a general designation for all types of vessels equipped with depth charges and other devices for hunting and destroying submarines, and embraces destroyers, frigates, corvettes and trawlers.

2

MANIFEST DESTINY

(1920–1935)

The passage of the years softened the memories of the submarine nightmare, the anguish and terror of the war under the seas. Thousands of new ships again moved peacefully and safely upon their lawful occasions. War had been outlawed and people no longer spoke of it; but the British had not forgotten their "greatest hour of trial," as Admiral Jellicoe had epitomized the U-boat menace. At the naval conferences British delegates used every possible argument to persuade other maritime powers that the convoy system had rendered the submarine obsolete, that it could no longer stand up to antisubmarine weapons, and that in future wars it would be destined to play a quite subordinate role. Germany took no part in these negotiations for she no longer ranked as a sea power. Her little *Reichsmarine* consisted of a few obsolete surface ships. The accumulated knowledge of her shipyards in building submarines—the most extensive experience in the world—lay fallow.

Yet in these years a small number of Germans were working away in the drawing office of a Dutch shipbuilding firm. All of them had been engaged in the development of U-boats during the war, and now they were applying that experience to the creation of new designs. Their building plans went out all over the world—to Sweden, Finland, South America, to Spain and Turkey. The plans embraced a variety of U-boat types, all bearing the signature of Techel and Schürer, men who had achieved fame in the Great War. It was these same men who designed the nucleus of the new German U-boat Service, the prototypes of the Sea Wolves that were destined to sweep the seas in the Second World War.

Two boats were built for the private account of that Dutch firm—a 250-tonner at Abo in Finland, which was later delivered to the Finnish Navy, and a 500-ton boat built in Cadiz which the Turks took over. German engineers, dockyard experts and naval officers helped to supervise their construction. Small groups of men—never more than half a dozen at a time

—traveled incognito to Spain and Finland. Naval officers of the executive and engineering branches and naval constructors, posing as businessmen, students, fitters or employees of the Dutch company, went there to relearn the technical problems of U-boat handling. Their teachers were two veterans of the war—"Roberto" Bräutigam and Papenberg, who later gave his name to a range-finding device familiar to all submariners.

On June 25, 1933, a handful of officers and about sixty petty officers and men assembled at one of the barracks in Kiel-Wik. The barracks were cleaned and repaired and on the first of October work began in the offices of the newly established command. The sailors' cap ribbons showed that they belonged to the "Anti-Submarine School." Officially, this school was organized in order to develop an up-to-date system of anti-submarine defense, but the school also provided a preliminary instructional course for future U-boat commanders and ratings. The officers, petty officers and men were given plans and models to study so as to familiarize themselves with every detail of their future activity.

In the spring of 1934 the international trains between Trelleborg and Stockholm carried a number of young men northward, traveling singly or in pairs. Nobody showed any curiosity about them and for their part they kept silent. After all, lots of German tourists go to Sweden and Finland for holidays. All through that summer, however, those young men were engaged in taking the U-boat to sea from Abo for systematic diving and armament tests before it was handed over to the Finnish Navy. Then they returned to Germany. Meanwhile a series of mysterious, heavily guarded sheds had sprung up inside the *Deutscher Werke* and *Germania* shipyards in Kiel. Nobody was allowed inside without a special pass, which was closely scrutinized.

In the early part of 1935 London became the setting for a political event of the first importance—England and Germany concluded a naval agreement. The rise of the old Imperial Navy had been regarded by England as a challenge to her supremacy at sea, and had been a factor in bringing about the First World War. The 1935 agreement was designed, as far as Germany was concerned, to show beyond doubt that German rearmament plans did not aim at a naval armaments race. Everyone was resolved that never again must there be a war between the two countries and the naval agreement was to be tangible proof of this resolve. The strength of the German fleet was voluntarily restricted to 35 per cent of the British, which constituted no danger to Britain, for even the French fleet was allowed to build up to 60 per cent of the British. Among a number of other clauses the agreement allowed Germany a submarine fleet equal to 45 per cent of the relatively small British submarine arm, and under certain circumstances this could be increased to 100 per cent. Thus the Versailles Treaty, which for more than ten years had so severely restricted the German Navy, was replaced by an agreement freely entered into, which seemed to exclude any possibility of a conflict between the two countries. The Commander in Chief of the German Navy, Admiral Raeder, could at last initiate plans for a small but well-balanced navy, to be completed within about eight years.

In June, 1935, one wall of the mysterious sheds in the Kiel shipyards was pulled down. A powerful floating crane, *Long Henry*, came into action and carefully lifted the first postwar German U-boat into the water. On the twenty-eighth of June, *U 1* was commissioned with due ceremony, to be followed at intervals of only a fortnight by another eleven U-boats. These were 250-tonners, replicas of the one built in Finland: small, nimble craft, easy to steer and handle, which were popularly known as "canoes." It was in the first of these boats, *U 1* to *U 6*, that the young U-boat commanders and crews now learned their seamanship and the practical side of all those theoretical studies that they had crammed in the barrack schoolrooms on the Wik. Germany had had no U-boats for fifteen years. All these new officers had been children when the First World War ended and they had to be taught everything from the ground up.

Orders were now issued for the creation of the first operational U-boat flotilla, and the name of Dönitz was mooted for the command of it. At this time he was a *Fregattenkapitän* (junior captain) in command of the cruiser *Emden,* then on her way back from an extensive foreign cruise which had taken her around Africa to India. He had hoped to retain his command and take the ship on another voyage as soon as possible, for the cruise had been a success as political propaganda besides providing valuable experience. Dönitz and the captain of the cruiser *Karlsruhe,* also newly returned, were summoned to report to the commander in chief. Admiral Raeder listened carefully to their reports, then addressed the captain of the *Emden.* "I appreciate your desire to remain as captain during the next cruise of the *Emden,* but I have decided that you are to command the First U-boat Flotilla."

That evening, Dönitz's thoughts traveled back over the past eighteen years, for this new assignment to the U-boats had revived every detail of his war memories. On one of his first patrols his U-boat had been rammed while submerged, and dived out of control toward the bottom. They did not regain control until she had reached 150 feet, and when they managed to bring her to the surface, they found the upper deck had been torn open, the gun overturned, the conning tower battered and the periscopes twisted out of shape. For the next ten days they had to navigate "blind," and every time they surfaced, they risked finding themselves in the middle of a bunch of A/S ships with depth charges at the ready. He thought too of his first command—*UC 25*—in which he had crept toward the jetty in Port Augusta, Sicily, to sink the British repair ship *Cyclöps*. His last action had been in command of *UB 68*, which was notoriously difficult to control when dived. On October 4, 1918, he had made a surface attack on a Mediterranean convoy, torpedoing one ship which had dropped astern. He then steamed to the head of the convoy in readiness for a further submerged attack at dawn. He started a normal dive when suddenly the U-boat stood on her head and went down like a stone toward the bottom. As the depth-gauge indicators swung toward the danger mark, the first lieutenant switched off the lights so that the crew could not see how deep they were. When two reserve air tanks burst under the excessive pressure, Dönitz realized that only one thing could save the U-boat from sinking beyond recall. He blew all tanks and, still out of control, the boat now shot to the surface, popping up like a cork right under the guns of a cruiser and some destroyers. Shells began to burst all round him, but as he shouted orders to dive again, the reply came, "All air-bottles empty!" The enemy had found the range and one shell pierced the conning tower. Dönitz and his crew scuttled the U-boat and abandoned her. They were picked up by a British destroyer but when the survivors were mustered, there were several men missing, including Jeschen, the chief engineer, who had gone down with the U-boat after carrying out the order to scuttle.

The little group of survivors reached Malta in a British flotilla leader, and from there they started the long journey to England. There followed endless months of life in prison camps in Scotland and England, where the popular clamor was to "hang the U-boat commanders." Dönitz began to plan his return to Germany by the only possible means—the repatriation of such prisoners as were considered medically or mentally unfit. Steadily and conscientiously he feigned insanity, playing childish games with biscuits tins and little china dogs that could be bought in the canteen, until at last even his first lieutenant was convinced that the captain had gone crazy. Then came the day when he was moved to a hospital reserved for serious cases. He was greeted by another U-boat commander, Lieutenant von Spiegel, with the words, "It won't help here, playing daft; they've all tried that. Can't you have something else wrong with you, Dönitz—malaria or something?" And so, added to "insanity," he came to be labeled as suffering from "a recurrence of an old tropical ailment." At last, tied to a stretcher, he heard the English doctor's diagnosis, for which he had worked so hard. "Typical case for repatriation. Put him on the list."

Home at last—and how different everything was! He had reported to *Korvettenkapitän* Schultze, his erstwhile superior in the Mediterranean U-boat Command, who now had the task of recruiting officers with whom to rebuild the tiny postwar German Navy. "Will you join us, Dönitz?" he asked. On Dönitz's answer depended the whole of his future career. "Shall we ever have any U-boats again?" he asked. "Yes, I am sure of it," replied Schultze, "in a few years, certainly." At Schultze's reply he made up his mind. He would continue to serve his country as a naval officer.

And now in 1935, as this prophecy came true after so many years, it was Dönitz who was chosen to supervise the revival of the U-boat Service. Seen thus in perspective, his new command seemed predestined. The First *(Weddigen)* U-boat Flotilla was formally commissioned on September 27, 1935.

3

REBIRTH OF THE U-BOAT ARM

(1935–1939)

The nucleus of the new U-boat Service consisted of the depot ship *Saar* and three small U-boats commanded by Lieutenants Grosse, Loos and Freiwald. Dönitz established two fundamental principles: firstly, that all training must be based on the conditions of real war, and secondly, that officers and men must acquire enthusiasm for their boats and must work with unselfish devotion. The rightful place for U-boats was *on* or *under* the water, in all weathers and as far out to sea as possible, for long periods. Indeed, the *Saar* and her three little satellites were seldom to be seen in port.

While at sea, Dönitz moved from boat to boat, teaching the young commanders the ABCs of U-boat handling. While he was on the bridge, his flotilla engineer officer moved from the control room to the engine room and from there to the motor room, putting the engineer officers, the engine-room artificers and the stokers through their paces until they knew their way through the U-boat blindfolded. This was "Papa" Thedsen, who had started as an ordinary stoker in U-boats and rose to be engineer admiral.

The three boats grew to six. From working independently they began to operate in groups, practicing attacks on a convoy as represented by the *Saar*. Dönitz was not content that the commanders should merely be trained in theory and practice; in submarine warfare invisibility is the key to success, so he taught them to develop an instinct as to when an enemy would see them on the surface and when not. Training under conditions so akin to war inevitably brought danger in its wake, even in peacetime. In November, 1936, *U 18* was rammed and sunk in the Gulf of Lübeck while attacking a moored target. A year later *U 12* had a hair's breadth escape when the whole flotilla was practicing deep dives. But risks and even losses had to be accepted, provided that they contributed to efficiency in war.

On the day that the German Army was ordered to occupy the Rhineland in what the U-boat men called the "First Punic War," the U-boats were exercising as usual near Moens-Klint, in the Baltic. They received a signal to break off the exercises and return immediately to prepare for war. From Kiel they sailed through the canal to Brunnsbüttel where they loaded torpedoes and left again at 4 A.M. with orders to take up positions against "the enemy." Two days later the operation was canceled. Unimpeded and amid the cheers of the inhabitants, the German troops had completed the reoccupation of the Rhineland; the "First Punic War" was over.

New boats arrived as training went on. The First Flotilla branched off into the Third; the Second was reconstituted; there followed the Seventh and the Ninth. After the "canoes" came the Type VIIs of 500 tons, and the first large boats, nicknamed "sea cows." [1] All the flotillas, whether in actual commission or still only in the planning stage, bore the name of U-boat "aces" of the Great War—*Weddigen, Saltzwedel,*

[1] See Appendix 2 for details of U-boat types.

Emsmann, Wegener, Hundius, Loos. The problem that Captain Dönitz had to consider was the type of boat with which these flotillas should be equipped. Whereas the German Admiralty was thinking in terms of 2,000-ton U-boats, Dönitz was strongly in favor of much smaller vessels which, he argued, would be handier against shipping and less vulnerable to anti-submarine attack. He maintained that in war it was better to have two smaller U-boats occupying two positions than one larger boat covering one position; the chances of success were thereby doubled. In short he aimed at a basic type of operational U-boat with a displacement not exceeding 740 tons, carrying spare torpedoes in watertight containers outside the pressure hull and possessing a large radius of action. Eventually he had his way, for this conception formed the basis of the Type VII U-boat which was to prove so effective against convoys in the Second World War.

He also worked out an entirely new set of tactics. In the Great War, U-boats had worked singly and independently in prearranged areas; but in future, thanks to progress in radio communications, it would be possible to counter the convoy system by massing U-boats, summoned by radio, for a coordinated attack on the convoy.

The U-boats were given their first real test in the Naval maneuvers of 1937. Some twenty boats were to "attack and destroy" a convoy of transports equipped with every known A/S device, en route from East Prussia to Swinemünde. The ships were located and attacked and, despite every countermeasure, they were adjudged completely eliminated. Later the exercise areas were extended beyond the Baltic to the North Sea and even into the Atlantic. In the spring of 1937 German U-boats participated in the international control organization during the Spanish Civil War.

In May, 1938, Dönitz addressed a special memorandum to the commander in chief. The press had published an official British statement to the effect that Britain was fundamentally opposed to the concept of a Greater Germany. He submitted to his superior that the German Navy would be incorrect to assume that *under no circumstances* could England and Germany be in conflict; consequently he maintained that it was vital to accelerate U-boat building without delay.

The reply to this memorandum reached him a few days later; no change was to be made in the plans for a "balanced" fleet or in the number of U-boats. In service circles only Admiral Densch, the Flag Officer commanding Scouting Forces, came out in support of Dönitz. "We ought," said Densch, "to build U-boats on every river, in every meadow in green-camouflaged sheds." But neither his opinion nor that of the newly promoted Commodore Dönitz prevailed. The belief was general and deep-rooted that another clash between the two great nations could only lead to misery and ruin for the whole world; it must never be allowed to happen.

The Sudeten Crisis or "Second Punic War" in the autumn of 1938 caused the U-boats to be brought once more to a state of war readiness. Although the commodore was away on leave, all preparations went forward smoothly and the U-boats sailed the same evening. But as they were passing through the Kiel Canal the news of the Münich agreement was broadcast; the "Second Punic War" was over before it had begun. A sigh of relief and gratitude for the preservation of peace swept through Germany. Nevertheless Dönitz continued to remind the German Admiralty of the need to expedite U-boat construction within the limits of the naval agreement. His request for depot ships to accompany the U-boats on shakedown cruises abroad was granted, but no change in the building program was conceded.

About this time an engineer named Walter, who had invented the hydrogen-peroxide gas turbine, came to see Dönitz at Kiel. He demonstrated the value of the "Aurol" fuel for underwater propulsion and asked for Dönitz's support, explaining that the German Admiralty, to whom he had offered his inventions, did not seem to appreciate their significance. He claimed that a boat built to his designs should be capable of maintaining a submerged speed of 23 to 25 knots over a long period without difficulty.

Dönitz at once realized the possibilities of this invention and pledged his fullest support.[2] Knowing only too well how memoranda ended up unanswered in filing cabinets, he determined to speak his mind to the commander in chief at the first opportunity. When at length he was able to do so, Admiral Raeder listened attentively but rather skeptically. He pointed out that, while Walter did not lack support in the appropriate departments of the Admiralty, the amount of time required to develop such a revolutionary process would

[2] After the war, Dr. Walter and other German scientists were brought to Great Britain and worked for several years at Vickers-Armstrongs Ltd. at Barrow-in-Furness, where HMS *Explorer*, the first British submarine to use hydrogen-peroxide propulsion, was launched on March 5, 1954—nearly twenty years after Walter's first experiments.

not be economical. Dönitz retorted that even if Walter's claims should not be completely realized in trials, the effort would still be justified.

Before long, Walter was again complaining that the German Admiralty still showed indifference to his designs and again Dönitz brought pressure to bear, for since that day in May he was by no means so sure that *under no circumstances* would there be a clash with England. This doubt prompted him to plan a "war game" based on imaginary hostilities with England. The area he chose for it was the Atlantic and the imaginary tactics were those of "U-boat packs" against escorted convoys. In January, 1939, he forwarded a detailed report on the exercise, concluding with a revolutionary request, couched in these words: "I need at least 300 U-boats, otherwise I cannot achieve decisive results in war, no matter how well the individual boats perform. With the number of boats at present in commission or building, I could accomplish nothing more than a series of pinpricks." This proposal fared no better than its predecessors.

The Memel Incident—the "Third Punic War"—in the spring of 1939 merely afforded the U-boats some practical exercises in the Baltic, off Swinemünde. Then came the German fleet's spring cruise to Lisbon, Ceuta and further into the Western Mediterranean. It provided an excellent test for the twenty-odd U-boats that took part. Between Cape St. Vincent and Ushant the boats attacked a force composed of supply ships and escorts of the fleet, and once again the results justified Dönitz's belief in his own theories of tactics and training. After the severest analysis he was satisfied that the "pack" tactics had accomplished, and in wartime would accomplish, all that was expected of them; and that the U-boat Service, small as it was, had developed into a keen-edged, serviceable weapon.

In mid-July, 1939, Grand Admiral Raeder attended an exercise in the Baltic of all the U-boats, after which he addressed the assembled officers at Swinemünde. "People are talking about war every day and every hour," he said, "but I can state that the Führer has told me personally that under no circumstances will there ever be war with the West. Such a thing would mean *Finis Germaniae*." Raeder had elicited this assurance from Hitler after a somewhat bombastic speech that the Führer had made to his generals. Once, in a private interview, Hitler had said to him, "I have three ways of keeping a secret. First, by a private conversation alone with someone; secondly, the thoughts which I keep to myself; thirdly, the things that I do not even allow myself to think about." There was evidently some hidden advice in his words; he meant, "Only believe what I tell you in private. Don't be misled by what I say in public." Raeder remembered this advice, and his conviction that Hitler did not intend war was rooted in those private talks.

Commodore Dönitz was so impressed by the way that Raeder had repeated Hitler's remarks that he did not hesitate to take a much-needed spell of leave. Yet in the wardroom a little later he was heard to say, "One thing is certain. If war should come, England will be against us. Make no mistake about that."

During August, international tension quickly rose to a climax. Reports showed that the British and French navies were taking precautionary measures. Dönitz, summoned back from leave by telephone, also received his orders, and as a result the little fleet of U-boats sailed in the middle of the month from their North Sea and Baltic bases to take up prearranged positions in the Atlantic and North Sea, with orders to remain unobserved as long as there was peace.

As August gave way to September the boats remained at their stations. The weather was mild, almost balmy, and the routine at sea went smoothly through watch after watch. On the afternoon of Sepember 3, a U-boat commander was leaning on the bridge rail chatting with his chief engineer, when suddenly the sound of bugles came from the radio loudspeaker below. Feet clattered on the conning-tower ladder and the flushed face of a young rating appeared through the hatchway. "Captain, Sir—just heard it on the radio. War with England!" A few minutes later a signal from the German Admiralty confirmed the news. "Commence hostilities against England immediately." It was timed 3:40 P.M. on the third of September.

Just before the outbreak of war Dönitz had moved his headquarters from Swinemünde to a barracks on the outskirts of Wilhelmshaven. Here on the morning of September 3, while in conference with his staff officers, an "immediate" teleprinter message was handed to him. It contained an intercepted British signal sent in plain language to all warships and merchant ships, consisting of the two words "TOTAL GERMANY," which denoted that England had declared war. Dönitz sprang to his feet and began to pace the room in agitation. "Damnation!" he cried, "do I have to experience this all over again?" Abruptly he left the conference room and crossed over to his own study, where for nearly half an hour he remained alone with his thoughts while his staff officers were drafting the necessary orders for transmission to the U-boats at sea.

When he returned he had recovered from the initial shock and his officers were conscious only of his energy and determination to do what was needed. "What steps have you taken? Show me your draft signals. . . . Very well, make it so." Having approved the orders to the U-boats he went to the huge chart which covered one wall of the room, showing the coastline of the North Sea, the British Isles and the Eastern Atlantic. In the course of the next five years this chart would be progressively filled in and enlarged until it embraced nearly all the oceans; it would claim his unceasing attention. Now, watching the duty officer pinning up the little numbered flags indicating the latest positions of the U-boats at sea, he reflected bitterly on his frequent and fruitless efforts over the recent years to expand the U-boat Service. Had they listened to him, he thought, he could at this critical moment have deployed another thirty boats against the enemy.

4

EARLY SUCCESSES

(September—October, 1939)

The outbreak of war found the U-boats at the western approaches to the English Channel in relatively calm seas; but where previously there had been a constant coming and going along the shipping lanes, there was now nothing—no streamer of smoke, no sign of a masthead. Vainly the lookouts searched hour after hour in every sector of the horizon. Then on September 4 the world's press burst into sensational headlines. The British s.s.*Athenia* had been sunk by a mysterious explosion on the first day of the war. At first nobody knew the cause of the disaster. "German U-boats!" cried the British press. "Sabotage!" retorted Dr. Goebbels from Berlin, "sabotage deliberately organized in England so as to provoke another charge of frightfulness against Germany." Telephones rang and tape machines clattered as questions and answers shot back and forth between the Admiralty in Berlin and the U-boat Command. In the absence of any U-boat report, both authorities declared in all good faith that no U-boat had been involved in the sinking of the *Athenia*.

The U-boats had indeed gone to action stations but search as they might, throughout the night of the third and during the whole of the fourth of September they sighted nothing. It was only on the morning of the fifth, as the "canoes" were sowing their mines round the coasts of England, that *U 48* encountered a steamship heading for Scotland. Lieutenant Schultze was careful to make sparing use of his periscope while approaching, but he kept it long enough above the waves to see that the target displayed neither flag nor neutral markings.

"Stand by for gun action! Radio room, report to me immediately if the ship starts to use her wireless. Surface!" The war at sea really began as *U 48* emerged from the depths. Heedless of the heavy waves breaking over the decks, the gunners rushed to their stations and sent the first shell screaming over to the ship almost before they had been given the order to open fire. Tall white columns of water shot up round the target, which turned sharply away and hoisted the British ensign. The next moment the Morse signals sounded loud and clear in the headphones of the U-boat's radio operator. "Captain, Sir, the ship is signaling! *Royal Sceptre* chased and shelled by submarine, position xyz."

That clinched the matter. The first warning shots had been fired across the target's bows, but in using radio to call for help she had committed a "hostile act" in international law. Despite the heavy seas breaking over the gun position of the plunging U-boat, shot after shot went howling through the air and with every hit the gunners felt a sense of achievement. When the ship's crew began to swing out their boats, the U-boat ceased fire until the boats were in the water and had begun to pull away from the ship. "Control room!" called the radio operator, "tell the captain the ship is still signaling." He could plainly hear the message: *"Royal Sceptre* chased and shelled by submarine. Abandoning ship. Position xyz."* Clearly the enemy operator was a brave man doing his duty to the last, as ordered by the British Handbook on the Defense of Merchant Ships in Wartime. "It can't be helped," said the U-boat commander, "we'll have to waste a torpedo on her." At thirty-eight minutes past one *Royal*

Sceptre was sunk, the first of 2,603 ships which, as the Allies were later to admit, were destroyed by U-boats in the Second World War.

Meanwhile *Royal Sceptre's* radio call for help had evoked a lively response. Radio stations in France and England and along the Irish coast were sending out urgent calls: "Warning to all ships. U-boats in positions xyz." Once again those terrible signals filled the air to disturb the peace of seafaring men: "Pursued by U-boat" . . . "chased and shelled by U-boat" . . . "SOS—U-boat."

When radio operators in peacetime heard those three letters "SOS," it was a signal for all wireless traffic to cease while every station, whether on ship or on shore, listened for further messages from the afflicted ship. But from September, 1939, a new call was heard—"SSS"—"Submarine, submarine, submarine." *Royal Sceptre* and *Bosnia* were the first ships to announce their own destruction in this way; they were soon followed by the *Rio Claro* of 4,086 tons, the *Gartavon* with 2,900 tons of ore for Glasgow, the 5,055-ton *Winkleigh* and the *Firby* from Hartlepool. Lieutenant Herbert Schultze, later to win the oak leaves to his Iron Cross, sent a signal to the British Prime Minister about this last ship: "CQ—transmit to Mr. Churchill. Have sunk British s.s.*Firby* in position xyz. Please pick up the crew."

Apart from this grimly humorous message, which achieved a mention in Parliament, more and more calls for help came from ships in the North Sea and Atlantic which were being fired on as they sent their frantic messages. On September 6 came a signal from the 7,200-ton freighter *Manaar*, which even in those early days had been fitted with a gun aft, and which was sinking after trying to resist. On the seventh of September two more ships were heard calling for help before they disappeared forever: the 5,809-ton *Jukkastan* which had tried to ram her assailant and the tanker *Olivegrove* of 4,060 tons, sunk after making use of her radio and trying to escape. On September 8 there were signals from the British tanker *Regent Tiger* of 10,176 tons and the s.s.*Kennebec*. And so it went on day after day, night after night, and always the same cry for help: "Save us—U-boats!" the s.s.*Neptunia*, the *British Influence*, the tanker *Vermont*, the *Yorkshire* of 10,200 tons, the Danish *Vendia*, the Finnish *Martti Ragnar*, the Swedish *Gertrud Bratt*, the Norwegian *Takstar*—each one was sighted, forced to heave to, examined and then sunk for carrying contraband or for using radio. After them came many more.

Ever since 1918 the British had maintained that the submarine had been rendered obsolete by the convoy system and by A/S weapons. Many naval authorities in different parts of the world, including Germany itself, also believed that the day of the submarine was over. But the U-boats' answer to this was 175,000 tons sunk in September 1939, 125,000 tons in October, over 80,000 tons in November and 125,000 tons in December. On the day that Britain declared war she instituted a total blockade of Germany; in fact she did exactly what the German Naval Command expected. The British were beginning just where they had left off in 1918, arming their merchant ships with guns, fitting them out with depth charges, and ordering them to avoid search by taking evasive action, by opening fire on the U-boats or by trying to ram them. At all costs they were told to signal their position by radio and ask for help.

U 29, commanded by Lieutenant Commander Schuhart, was lying in wait on a shipping lane west of the English Channel. While the crew were having their morning coffee, a steamship came in sight, moving at high speed on a zig-zag course—a passenger ship of about 10,000 tons flying a red-colored ensign. As the captain watched her through his periscope, trying to make out her nationality, a black spot suddenly swam into his line of vision. It grew larger and larger as it flew over the liner's stern—an aircraft! This surely meant that the ship was carrying troops or munitions. He gave the order to the torpedo room to stand by, but before he could fire, the target changed course, showed her full length and turned away. Schuhart abandoned his plan to attack and dived to 120 feet; he would have to wait until the ship was out of sight before surfacing to give chase. Meanwhile there was time for a cup of coffee and a sandwich.

At last the moment to surface had come and he cautiously raised his periscope for a quick look around. Suddenly he saw a cloud of black smoke to port. He wiped the eyepiece and looked again—and then it dawned upon him that this was no cloud of smoke but an aircraft carrier heading toward him! The range was still too great to pick out any details but already he could discern the masthead of an escorting destroyer. The picture became clearer in his mind. That aircraft hovering over the liner had belonged to the carrier. He knew full well that a carrier would not be at sea like that without air escort, and he began a careful search of the sky. No aircraft were in sight. "Slow ahead both, Chief," he muttered, "keep her steady at this depth. The big ships are coming up now. Pass the word—aircraft carrier in sight, be prepared for depth charges and bombs."

At moderate speed, keeping a constant lookout, Schuhart closed his prey. Still no air or outer surface escorts were visible. He could see the close escort now—one destroyer ahead, one astern and one on either side of the carrier as she held her westerly course. Suddenly two planes appeared, flying in irregular sweeps round the ships. The range was still too great and the U-boat had to steer parallel with the carrier, which at times zigzagged right away from her. Then, as the carrier turned through almost 70 degrees, the captain seized his opportunity and fired, relying largely upon guesswork because, as he wrote later in his log, "the vast size of the target upset all normal calculations and in any case I was looking straight into the sun."

The sweat was pouring down Schuhart's face as he stood in the control room with his cap back to front. Through the periscope he could see the port-side escorting destroyer moving smoothly through the water at about fifteen knots and only some 500 yards ahead of him. His torpedoes were running—it was time to dive to safety. He had barely started to go deep before two explosions echoed through the boat, followed by another big detonation and several smaller ones. He had hit her! "The explosions were so heavy," wrote Schuhart later, "that I thought the boat had been damaged. There was jubilation among the crew although we were all wondering what would happen to us next. In the meantime we had gone down to 180 feet and as we appeared to suffer no harm at this depth, we went cautiously deeper." It was the first time they had taken their boat so deep; after *U 12*'s narrow escape, 150 feet was the maximum depth permissible in peacetime on strict orders from the Admiralty; they had no idea whether, on reaching 250 feet, their pressure hull would stand up to the tremendous pressure.

While tensely watching the pressure gauges they heard the sound of rapidly approaching propellers. They needed no hydrophones to pick up these noises, which grew louder and louder until they sounded right overhead. Then as they began to die away, four heavy explosions smashed into the silence. The boat staggered as though struck by a giant's fist. Schuhart saw the conning tower tremble, but quietly and apparently unmoved he continued to pass orders to the diving officer; his steadiness set an example for the whole crew. The destroyer came up again and dropped a fresh pattern of depth charges right over the boat.

"The third pattern," ran the log, "fell some distance away . . . attacks continued until eleven o'clock that night, sometimes close and sometimes further away . . . at 2340 propeller noises grew much weaker and bearings were no longer obtainable. I surfaced." The next day the BBC announced that the Admiralty regretted to report the loss of the carrier *Courageous.*[1] The news spread like wildfire throughout Germany. "It seems that we have U-boats again," people were heard to say, and suddenly the long-dormant faith in this weapon was reawakened. Schuhart's attack on the *Courageous* had struck a chord in the memory of the German people.

On one of the last days of September, Commodore Dönitz stood at the lock gates at Wilhelmshaven, watching the return from patrol of *U 30*, commanded by Lieutenant Lemp. Seagulls were wheeling and screaming over the harbor; a band began to play as the boat came slowly into view.

At length the U-boat captain stood before the commodore.

"I beg to report, Sir, *U 30* has returned from patrol."

The commodore held out his hand. "Well, Lemp, what was it like?"

But still keeping his hand to the peak of his cap the young captain answered gravely, "Sir, I have something else to report. I sank the *Athenia.*"

"WHAT?" said the commodore in a stunned voice.

"I sank the *Athenia,*" Lemp repeated. "I mistook her for an auxiliary cruiser. I only realized my mistake when it was too late."

"Here's a pretty kettle of fish. You've certainly given us a headache over this, Lemp."

"I realize that, Sir."

"I shall have to court-martial you."

"Aye, aye, Sir."

"Above all, this must be kept strictly secret. Tell your crew that."

"I've already done so, Sir."

[1] HMS *Courageous* was sunk by *U 29* on September 17, 1939, in the Western Approaches with the loss of the captain and 518 of her crew. She had been hit by two of the three torpedoes fired by Schuhart. Her duty was to provide a measure of protection for shipping in these waters, to make up for the shortage of escort vessels and shore based aircraft. Only three days earlier HMS *Ark Royal* had narrowly escaped an attack by *U 36* in the same waters.

"Good."

Now the telephone wires began to hum. Lemp was ordered to report immediately to Berlin, where the last ounce of information was extracted from him. Eventually the German Admiralty proved to its own satisfaction that it was indeed owing to a mistake that he had sunk the *Athenia*. An order was issued forthwith that the matter was to be regarded as top secret. As Lemp had acted in good faith, no court-martial was considered necessary. On his return to Wilhelmshaven, Dönitz put him under nominal arrest for one day to improve his acquaintance with ship silhouettes, and the affair was then regarded as closed. At the same time a new directive was issued that in no case were passenger ships to be attacked, even when sailing in convoy or without lights.

This order had a curious outcome. During the first weeks of the war there was plenty of activity in the English Channel while the British were transporting their expenditionary force to France. For political reasons all attacks on French shipping were forbidden. As it was impossible to distinguish French from British ships at night when all were steaming without lights, several fully-laden transports crossed before the torpedo tubes of German U-boats in complete safety. The order was later rescinded, though the German Naval Command still insisted upon adherence to international law; it was only when the British Government, on October 1, ordered all merchant ships to ram U-boats on sight, that the German Government, on October 4, sanctioned unrestricted attacks on armed enemy ships. This however was preceded by two events. On the twenty-sixth of September the British First Lord of the Admiralty had announced that very soon every British merchant ship would be armed, and two days later the German Government issued a warning to all neutral countries that their ships should avoid any suspicious action, either by the use of radio on sighting German warships or by steaming without lights, by zigzagging, failing to stop on demand, sailing in convoy or any similar measure. "The German Government would very much regret," ran the note, "if the property of any state were to suffer damage through failure to comply with these instructions. Equally the Government requests neutral governments to warn their nationals against traveling in British or French ships."

5

OPERATION SCAPA FLOW

(October, 1939)

In September, 1939, one of the "canoes" operating east of the Orkneys found herself off the Pentland Firth, the passage between Scotland and the Orkneys. A strong westerly current caught the boat and swept her through the turbulent narrows. Finding that his engines were not powerful enough to pull him free, the captain, making a virtue out of necessity, carefully surveyed the movement of ships and the defenses in the area. On his return he made a detailed report to Dönitz, who at once saw the possibilities of a special operation. After much deliberation he ordered one of his best young officers, Lieutenant Günther Prien, to report on board the depot ship *Weichsel* at Kiel.

As Prien entered the commodore's cabin he found Dönitz in conference with his own flotilla commander and Lieutenant Wellner, the captain of the "canoe." Charts lay spread on the table before them and Prien's eye was immediately caught by the words "Scapa Flow." The commodore addressed him.

"Do you think that a determined C.O. could take his boat into Scapa Flow and attack the ships there? Don't answer now, but let me have your reply by Tuesday. The decision rests entirely with you, without prejudice to yourself." It was then Sunday. Prien saluted and withdrew, his heart beating fast. He went straight to his quarters and settled down to a thorough study of the problem. He worked away hour after hour, calculating, figuring, checking and rechecking.

On the appointed day he stood once again before the commodore.

"Yes or no?"

"Yes, Sir."

A pause.

"Have you thought it all out? Have you thought of Emsmann and Henning who tried the same thing in the First World War and never came back?"

"Yes, Sir."

"Then get your boat ready."

The crew could make no sense of the preparations for their next patrol. Why were they unloading part of their food supplies and taking so little fuel and fresh water with them? Apart from giving essential orders, the captain was uncommunicative, and on the appointed day the U-boat slipped quietly through the Kiel Canal into the North Sea. The nights were dark, the seas running high. While on passage the crew watched their captain closely; although funnel smoke was sighted several times he never attempted to attack. At last, early in the morning of October 13, the Orkneys were in sight. Prien gave the order to dive and when the U-boat was resting easily on the sea bed, he ordered all hands to muster forward. "Tomorrow we go into Scapa Flow," he began, and went on talking quietly, making sure that every man knew what he had to do. Then he ordered every available man off watch to turn in; they would need all their strength when the time came.

At four o'clock in the afternoon the boat came to life again and the cook served a specially good meal. Jokes were bandied about and Prien wrote in his log, "The morale of the ship's company is superb." At 7:15 all hands went to diving stations, and the chief engineer began to lift the boat off the bottom; the ballast pumps sang and the boat began to move as the motors stirred into life. Prien took a first cautious glimpse through the periscope. All clear. He gave the order to surface. The wind had dropped but the sky was covered with light clouds; although there was a new moon, the northern lights made the night almost as bright as day.

As they moved into the narrows, a powerful tide rip suddenly caught the boat, just as Prien had expected. He needed every ounce of concentration now and a good deal of luck. The rudder was swung from port to starboard and back again, with full use of diesel engines, to keep the bow steady against the stream. At one moment he had to go full astern to avoid colliding with a blockship. Then he suddenly bent down and shouted through the hatch, "We are inside Scapa Flow!" [1]

At this point his log read, "I could see nothing to the south, so turned away along the coast to the north. There I sighted two battleships and beyond them some destroyers at anchor. No cruisers. I decided to attack the big ships." As the U-boat crept closer still, he could make out the details

[1] The entry into Scapa Flow was made through Kirk Sound, which was inadequately blocked.

of the ships. The nearest to him was of the *Royal Oak* class. He went closer, until the bow of the second ship appeared beyond the first. She looked like the *Repulse*. He gave his orders. "Ready all tubes! Stand by to fire a salvo from Numbers one to four!" Endrass, his first lieutenant, was taking aim; the forecastle of the *Repulse* [2] came into the cross wires. "Fire!" He pressed the firing key.

The U-boat shuddered as the torpedoes leaped away. There was a moment's agonizing pause. Would they hit? Then a tall column of water reared against *Repulse's* side. But *Royal Oak* lay motionless as before. A miss? Impossible. Defective torpedo? Unlikely. Minutes went by but the silence of the bay remained unbroken. Had the ships been abandoned? Was the whole of Scapa still asleep? Why no counterattack from the destroyers? It is almost impossible to believe what happened next. Calmly deciding to make a second attack, the captain took his boat in a wide circle round the anchorage *on the surface*, while the spare torpedoes were being loaded into the tubes. For nearly twenty minutes he cruised round the main base of the British fleet while down below the sweating hands pushed torpedo after torpedo into place. As though the situation were not tense enough already, Prien suddenly noticed one of his junior officers, Sublieutenant von Varendorff, calmly walking round the deck. "Are you crazy?" hissed the captain. "Come up here at once!" Once again Prien moved to the attack—this time at closer range—and once again the torpedoes raced toward their target.

Thunderous explosions shook the area. Huge columns of smoke and water towered into the air while the sky was filled with falling wreckage—whole gun turrets and strips of armor plating weighing tons apiece. The harbor sprang to life. Morse signals flashed from every corner, searchlights probed and swept, a car on the coast road stopped, turned and flashed its headlights on and off as though signaling, then dashed back the way it had come.

"Emergency full ahead both!" ordered Prien. "Group up motors. Give me everything you've got!" As the water bubbled and boiled beneath the U-boat's stern, he saw a destroyer coming swiftly toward him, sweeping the water with

---

2 Prien mistook the old seaplane carrier *Pegasus* for *Repulse*, which was not in Scapa Flow. Only *Royal Oak* was hit in both attacks. For the next five months the Home Fleet had to use remote anchorages on the west coast of Scotland, until the defenses of Scapa Flow had been put in order.

her searchlight. She began to signal with her Aldis lamp; Prien bit his lip as the bridge beneath him shuddered to the vibration of the screws. His wake showed up all too clearly, yet he could not afford to reduce speed. Suddenly the miracle happened; the destroyer dropped astern, turned away and disappeared. A moment later he heard the crash of her depth charges in the distance. The U-boat scraped past the end of a jetty and then—"We're through! Pass the word, we're through!" A roar of cheers answered him from below. Prien set course for the southeast—and home.

During the long hours of waiting before the attack, the crew had passed round a comic paper; one of the cartoons in it showed a bull with head down and nostrils smoking. "Harry Hotspur," someone had said; that was also their name for their captain. Now, on the way home, Endrass had an idea. Armed with paintbrushes and some white paint, a small working party clambered onto the casing, and limned on the side of the conning tower the boat's new crest—the Bull of Scapa Flow.

While crossing the North Sea they listened to the wireless. "According to a British Admiralty report," said the announcer, "the battleship *Royal Oak* has been sunk, apparently by a U-boat. British reports say that the U-boat was also sunk." The men in *U 47* smiled. In the afternoon came an official announcement from the German Admiralty; "The U-boat which sank the British battleship *Royal Oak* is now known to have also hit the battleship *Repulse* and to have put her out of action. It can now be announced that this U-boat was commanded by Lieutenant Prien." For the first time the name of Prien was heard by the German people. Prien in Scapa Flow—where twenty years before, the German High Seas Fleet had gone to the bottom!

As the U-boat made fast to the jetty Dönitz could be seen standing next to Grand Admiral Raeder, the corn-flower-blue lapels of his uniform clearly visible. The grand admiral came on board to congratulate the crew; offering his hand to each man he conferred upon every one of them the Iron Cross, Second Class, while the captain was awarded the First Class of the order. "Lieutenant Prien," said Admiral Raeder, "you will have an opportunity of making a personal report to the Führer." Turning to Dönitz, he then announced before them all that the commodore had been promoted to rear admiral. Henceforth he would be the flag officer commanding U-boats. That same afternoon Prien and his crew were

flown to Berlin. Hitler received them in the Reich Chancellery and conferred upon the captain the Knight's Cross of
the Iron Cross.

6

A U-BOAT ACE IN THE MAKING

(Winter, 1939—1940)

In the early months of the war the U-boats, operating singly,
went in as close as possible to the coast of Britain. They
crept by night into estuaries and harbor mouths, into bays
and creeks, laying their mines in the channels. Lieutenant
Frauenheim penetrated the Firth of Forth as far as the
great Forth bridge and laid mines which damaged the
cruiser *Belfast*.[1] The battleship *Nelson* ran on a mine laid
by Lieutenant Habekost in Loch Ewe.[2] Several other attacks
made at the same time, however, were spoiled by defective
torpedoes. In November a U-boat fired three torpedoes at
close range at *Nelson* west of the Orkneys. The torpedoes hit
but failed to explode.

Nevertheless the successes mounted. Lieutenant Herbert
Schultze of *U 48* was the first captain to sink more than
100,000 tons of enemy shipping, which won him the Knight's
Cross; he was soon followed by Lieutenants Hartmann in
U 37 and Rollmann in *U 34*. Winter came all too quickly
with its heavy storms and bitter cold. Boats that had gone
out looking smart and trim in their fresh gray paint would
come limping back with battered conning towers, their paint
stripped and streaked with rust after being subjected to weeks
of pursuit and hours of depth charging. It was an exceptionally severe winter. The creeks in Kiel Bay froze over as
did the Kiel Canal and the river Elbe itself. Every outbound
and inbound journey meant an unending battle with ice.
They tried fixing protecting sheets of steel plate over the
bows and the torpedo caps but this did not always avail, and
sometimes they would have to turn back with buckled bow
caps and damaged hydroplanes and propellers.

[1] HMS *Belfast* had her back broken by a mine in the Firth of
Forth on November 21, 1939.
[2] HMS *Nelson* was seriously damaged on December 4 by a mine in
the entrance to Loch Ewe. The mines had been laid five weeks earlier.

When *U 49* returned from patrol in the early days of December, 1939, her captain, von Gossler, brought back an important piece of information. During a depth-charge attack, his boat had plunged out of control to 450 feet without sustaining any damage. When in the First World War U-boats went down only to 240 feet, their rivets would be forced in; nowadays the hulls were no longer riveted but welded. It was some comfort to the crews to know that they could go so deep and survive, and thereafter it became the usual practice in an emergency.

Early on a bitterly cold morning one of the "canoes"—*U 19*, commanded by Lieutenant Schepke—sailed westward on patrol. With each day at sea, however, the cold grew less; when the centigrade thermometer showed only five degrees below zero, the crew began to feel almost at home, and when the mercury shot up to five degrees above, they felt really comfortable. As they were nearing the enemy coast on the surface, a long, low silhouette appeared which proved to be a destroyer. Schepke decided to attack; a torpedo leaped from its tube—but missed astern and blew up with a roar on the rocky beach. Anxiously Schepke peered across at the destroyer, which must surely have sighted him. Yes, she was turning now, her bow wave growing higher with every second, her searchlight sweeping the sea. Schepke crash-dived, ordering the crew to go forward so as to add weight in the bow. The U-boat plunged sickeningly—then without warning her stern dropped and she started to surface again. All ballast tanks were flooded in a desperate attempt to get down and at last the boat began to sink once more; she hit the bottom with a violent jolt. As the men began to recover from the shock the destroyer came thundering overhead and there followed the heart-shaking crash of the first depth charges. The whole boat leaped, shook itself free from the bottom, then crashed back again. Paint stripped off the bulkheads, gauge glasses cracked and splintered, the lights flickered on and off and leaking compressed-air leads whistled piercingly.

In the comparative silence that followed, Schepke, endeavoring to appear at ease, glanced at his watch. Something was needed to distract the crew's attention. "Cook, issue a bar of chocolate to every man." It was really mealtime and all realized that they were in for a long period of waiting.

There was the destroyer overhead again, suddenly and without warning. Involuntarily the men ducked their heads; then came three tremendous explosions right over the starboard engine room and the boat was pushed bodily and violently sideways, as though she had been rammed. Men were thrown in heaps on the deck; they could plainly see the bulkheads being forced inward, as from giant hammer blows. The pressure hull groaned and creaked, the inner lining cracked, the leaking air pipes whistled shrilly. "Hurry up, Chief," said Schepke urgently, "let's get out of here. I don't care for it." "Neither do I," replied the chief with a grin, wiping his face with oily fingers.

Slowly and painfully the boat was raised from the bottom and started moving. The stern planes were stiff and hard to move, groaning and creaking, and the propeller shaft had an unhealthy sound like a dentist's drill on a hollow tooth. Surely the enemy up top *must* hear that noise? Slowly the crash of the depth charges grew fainter and in the *U 19* breathing became easier. At dawn, as the U-boat came to periscope depth, nothing was to be seen save a couple of windows on shore, reflecting the early light. The boat surfaced to commence charging batteries, and the men gratefully drew the fresh air into their lungs, sniffing appreciatively at the smell of coffee, eggs and bacon coming from the galley. Knives clattered on plates, cooks hurried to and fro. Life was not so bad after all!

Some hours later the chief engineer, sweating through a mask of grease, reported all damage repaired and the batteries fully charged. In the tiny radio room the operator's pencil was flying over the signal pad. The U-boat Command was ordering *U 19* to proceed to a fresh operational area. Schepke read the signal, then gave the helmsman a new course to steer.

The new area lay along the eastern edge of a British mine field and here Schepke vainly patrolled up and down for two days. At length, tired of inactivity, he decided to penetrate the mine field. Having confirmed that high tide that night would be at ten o'clock, he left orders to be awakened at that time and climbed into his bunk. After nightfall the boat turned on to her new course and began to creep slowly into the mine field. By morning she was through it and the coast lay flat and menacing ahead of her. To starboard some badly dimmed lights shone red, white and green.

"Evidently trawlers," hazarded the officer of the watch, "but they're getting bigger."

"Too fast for trawlers," replied Schepke. "Let me see . . . those two to port—they're merchantmen! Action stations! Stand by to go to periscope depth!" As the periscope rose above the waves Schepke could clearly see the leading ship

—a 3,000 to 4,000-tonner, not fully laden for the red paint of her bottom coating showed above the water. Schepke fired his first torpedo and immediately went deep. When he came up again the whole forepart of the ship was standing up out of the water and a lifeboat was being hastily launched. The heads of some men swimming showed up like little black dots dancing on the water. Slowly Schepke moved his periscope round; the next ship had turned and was coming right into his cross wires. She was bigger than the first—long, black and deeply laden. The torpedo hit her amidships and a huge column of flame, smoke and water shot skyward. As the curtain of spray came splashing down again, Schepke could see that the mortally wounded ship had already taken on a heavy list, and even as he watched, she leaned still further over and sank. A small Norwegian freighter, her national colors brightly painted on her sides, stopped to launch a boat and began to pick up the survivors.

Two days later the U-boat made fast in the inner harbor at Heligoland; she had sunk four ships totaling 20,000 tons —not bad for a mere "canoe" which carried only five torpedoes. Schepke was later to rank among the greatest of the U-boat commanders.

Well over a hundred ships of more than half-a-million-gross registered tons fell to the U-boats in the long winter of 1939–1940, not including those unknown losses caused by German mines. Yet the Germans, too, had their losses. Many who went forth full of confidence were never to return. In vain the radio summoned them. "*U 53*, report your position . . . *U 53*, report your position. . . ." At length an asterisk was put against her number in the list at headquarters, followed after a further interval by a second asterisk. Then with a heavy heart the commodore would take up his pen to write the letters of sympathy that were always sent to the bereaved —the wives, the parents and the sweethearts.

7

BLUNTED WEAPONS

(Spring, 1940)

Early in the spring of 1940 Admiral Dönitz was ordered to report to the commander in chief in Berlin. On arriving at the *Tirpitzufer* where the German Admiralty was located, he was received by the Senior Operational Staff Officer, Captain Wagner. From him Dönitz learned that as early as the beginning of October, 1939, the Allies had been contemplating the occupation of Norway as part of their strategy of encircling Germany and cutting off her supplies of ore from Scandinavia. Reports from Admiral Canaris' Intelligence Service and from the German Naval Attaché in Oslo, said Wagner, showed that Allied military officers had been active in Norway for some months past, while it was known that the Norwegian shipowners had placed about one million tons of tanker space at the Allies' disposal.

On April 5, the day on which the Allies began to lay mines in Norwegian territorial waters, Earl de la Warr declared in London that neither Germany nor any neutral country should expect England to handicap herself by always adhering literally to international law. Subsequently a secret British operation order was captured, dated the sixth of April, which referred to "preparations for the occupation of the North Swedish ore fields from Narvik."

It was the period of the "phony war" on land. The German Army lay waiting in its concrete dugouts and, apart from patrols and sorties and an occasional artillery duel, there was little fighting. In the early days of April, 1940, however, various German warships and naval transports began to assemble in the North Sea and Baltic ports. One night under cover of darkness they embarked arms, ammunition and supplies of all kinds. When the next day dawned, the jetties were clear of ships; Operation *Weserübung* had begun. Norway and Denmark were occupied by German troops, their arrival forestalling the Anglo-Franco-Polish Expeditionary Force by only a few hours, due to the fact that the latter's departure was postponed from the fifth to the eighth of April.

In order to cover this operation to seaward, some U-boats were dispatched with sealed orders which were not to be opened until they were off the Norwegian coast. Within a matter of days the U-boats were in contact with the Allied invasion forces and carried out several attacks on enemy ships. Nearly every U-boat captain, however, reported that his attacks had unaccountably failed. Torpedoes had been fired at battleships, cruisers, transports and destroyers but not one of them had caused any damage. They might, as one of the U-boat captains put it later, have been fighting with blunted weapons. Even Prien, the hero of Scapa Flow, had no better luck than his colleagues.

On April 15, the flag officer, U-boats, signaled: "We must reckon with enemy landings in Gratangen and Lavangen. *U 47* is to reconnoiter and report." Prien reached his new position in the early dawn. Through his periscope he sighted two small coastal steamers and a small group of fishing vessels, all apparently lying stopped. Softly and silently, like a pike that lurks in the shallows barely moving its fins, *U 47* stayed watching throughout the day, unobserved by the destroyers patrolling the fjord in irregular sweeps or by the armed trawlers which ran ceaselessly up and down. Realizing that so much activity must signify something, Prien waited patiently. Late in the afternoon, just as he was about to surface and look for a place to recharge his batteries, a series of strange new metallic sounds echoed through the boat. With the utmost care Bothmann, his diving officer, brought the boat up so that not more than a couple of inches of periscope peeped above the surface. Prien held his breath as he looked. Right ahead of him were three large transports, a French cruiser, another cruiser and three merchant ships! "Pass the word," he said, his voice barely under control, "there's a whole fleet above us. The noises we heard must have been their anchor cables running out. My lads, there's more here than there ever was in Scapa Flow!" Using every care, he continued to watch and soon found his expectations proved to the hilt. This was where the troops were to be disembarked. Fishing boats were shuttling to and fro, between the transports and the shore. They went off laden with mens, arms and supplies and came back empty.

Prien began his attack, while below him his men moved like clockwork. Four torpedoes left their tubes; the men in the U-boat could plainly hear their engines running. Prien kept his eye glued to the eyepiece. If he could sink these ships, the British and French troops of the Norwegian Expeditionary

Force would be left stranded on the rocky coast without food or supplies. The effect on the campaign would be incalculable. The torpedoes must hit, he thought, they *must!* It was child's play, firing at great ships at anchor like that. Below, his men watched and waited, while the coxswain counted the seconds out loud. Now . . . now . . . it must come now. Prien almost danced with impatience—but nothing happened. How was it possible? Feverishly he checked over his calculations with Endrass. He interrogated the torpedo gunner's mate. As far as was humanly possible the torpedoes had been accurately adjusted. It was shattering that at such a moment, when the opportunity of upsetting the whole invasion was being offered to them on a plate, the targets should still be floating—that four torpedoes should fail simultaneously!

Prien knew that his men were utterly reliable; the fault could not lie with them. He forced himself to review the matter calmly, as he steamed away to a secluded spot where the batteries could be recharged and the spare torpedoes loaded. Day was breaking as he surfaced to make a fresh attack. Again he fired four torpedoes, the one with air propulsion going straight for a cruiser, while the others, driven by electricity, ran unseen. Suddenly he saw the air-driven torpedo curve to the right and go off at a tangent of ten degrees. And the others? All missed again. For a moment he was overcome with desperation, but pulled himself together and ordered, "Course x degrees!" The helmsman calmly echoed his words and the U-boat began to turn. Then came a grinding noise as she ran aground. This is the end! thought Prien. Here I am, in growing daylight and perfect visibility, high and dry in front of them all—and over there are the guns of a cruiser. At that precise moment one faulty torpedo struck the rocky beach and blew up with an ear-splitting roar, throwing a column of water high in the air. Now it would only be a matter of seconds before the cruiser sighted the U-boat and shelled her to pieces. Only a lightning decision could save them.

"Stop both! Full astern both! All available hands on deck!" Prien rattled out his orders, hoping to roll the boat off the reef—a last, despairing hope. A young officer dashed past him to prepare the confidential books for destruction. A couple of ratings set demolition charges to prevent the boat from falling into enemy hands. On deck Endrass was giving orders to the hands off watch. "To port, quick march! About turn, quick march!" And back to port and back again to starboard. Below decks Bothmann was ringing the changes on the motors, full astern on one and slow ahead on the other. At the same time he was blowing the torpedo-compensating and trimming tanks to lighten the boat, and alternately flooding and blowing the main ballast tanks. There was a confusion of shouted orders, the trampling of feet, the hiss of compressed air, the spitting and shaking of whirling diesels, the bubbling of water from the vents and the turbulence of foam beneath the stern.

All of a sudden a fishing boat began to flash signals to them. "Shall I answer with something to confuse them, Sir?" asked a quick-witted signalman. . . . "Yes, for God's sake do. Perhaps they'll think we are English, or a lighthouse!" Prien himself never thought it would work, but he had lived through so many strange experiences that nothing now seemed impossible.

Inch by inch the U-boat worked herself loose. The screws bit deeper and deeper into the water; the compressed air was coming out in huge bubbles from the forward vents. Then suddenly there was a jerk—and they were free again. At that moment there was a loud crash and the starboard diesel cracked up. "Starboard motor half-speed astern, port engine half-speed astern, all hands below except for the bridge watch!" The U-boat was floating easily now as though nothing had happened. The men went sliding like weasels down below decks. Prien made a sharp turn into deep water, dived, ran out of the fjord and did not surface again until he was well out of sight of the enemy; he stood well out to sea before starting to repair his damaged engine. The next day he received orders to return to base and began the long and painful voyage home, frequently interrupted by dives to escape enemy aircraft.

After endless investigation, Dönitz's torpedo experts discovered the real cause of the trouble. The so-called non-contact pistol with which the torpedoes were fitted was designed to detonate at the precise moment when the torpedo was under the keel of the enemy ship, where the explosion would do the greatest damage. Provided that the torpedo was running at its correct depth setting, it would pass just under the keel, where the pistol, being subjected to the maximum magnetic influence, would explode the warhead. But should the torpedo be running a few feet deeper than intended, the pistol would not fire.

During the Norwegian campaign the U-boats had spent many hours submerged, which often raised the air-pressure above that of the atmosphere, since there were always slight

leaks from the compressed-air system. The excessive pressure
affected the balance-chamber mechanism of the torpedoes,
which therefore ran deeper than intended. In addition the
British had demagnetized many of their ships; but at the time
of the operations in Norway, neither of these factors was
known to the German Naval Command.

8

THE HUNTERS AND THE HUNTED

(May–June, 1940)

In May and June, 1940, the German Army broke out of the
Siegfried Line and smashed its way through Holland and
Belgium to France. The German Navy took no part in this
campaign as it was still heavily committed to the Norwegian
area, but it was soon apparent that the fall of the Low Countries would make a vast difference to U-boat operations, for
it meant that the southern portion of the North Sea was at
last freed from enemy domination.

The end of the Norway campaign also brought relief for
the U-boats. This operation, which Sir Winston Churchill
acknowledged to be one of the finest chapters in the history
of naval warfare, was brought to a successful close with fewer
losses than had been anticipated. Moreover, possession of the
Norwegian ports now meant that the U-boats could take a
safer and shorter route to the Atlantic; and the enemy was
unable to fence the German Navy in behind vast mine fields
as he had done in the First World War.

As soon as they could be released, the larger U-boats were
once more switched to the Atlantic, where the trade war had
been abandoned during the Norwegian campaign. Only the
"canoes" were left to keep a standing watch on the sea routes
between England and the Dutch and Belgian ports. This was
the dawn of the "First Golden Age" for U-boats in the
Atlantic. For the most part they were still operating independently of each other in prearranged areas; the time was not
yet ripe for several boats to cooperate against convoys, as
most of their actions took place so close in to the coast that
the U-boat commanders had no time to summon their colleagues for a joint attack. There were many weak points in

the enemy's defenses; the British destroyers and A/S vessels were either in dock, repairing the damage they had sustained in Norway, or were disposed along the south coast of Britain which, since the disastrous evacuation of the Allied armies from France, was threatened with invasion.

The log of one of these larger boats—*U 37*— was typical of the period. Her captain was new to the boat; his predecessor had been given a shore appointment after winning the Knight's Cross. The crew still laughed when they recalled the first captain's expression on receiving the news of his new post. "Are they mad? Me—of all people—in a staff job? Condemned to death by suffocation with paper work?" When he left he gave a farewell party—and what a party it had been! They had crawled back on board on hands and knees.

It was early morning when, in the new captain's first patrol, they sighted their first ship, a motor vessel of some 5,000 tons. The skipper was ordered to come alongside in his lifeboat and show his papers. These revealed the ship to be the Swedish *Erik Frisell* of 5,066 tons, ostensibly carrying a cargo of grain to Ireland "for further orders." It was clear enough to the U-boat captain that "Ireland" in this case was only a cover name, and that in fact the grain was destined for Britain. His course of action was clear; the Swede had been found in a prohibited area and was carrying contraband. The Swedish crew were ordered to take to their boats and the *Erik Frisell* was sunk by gunfire.

The next entry in the log describes how for four days the U-boat chased an elusive and mysterious ship, the *Dunster Grange,* which eventually escaped; they never discovered whether she was a Q-ship or simply commanded by a very quick-witted captain. Two days later they torpedoed a merchant ship which sank quickly after her boilers had exploded, but they were unable to discover her name. There was no mark on a life belt floating among the wreckage and two survivors clinging to a raft refused to divulge it. Forty-eight hours later the captain recorded the sinking of the 10,337-ton French ship *Brazza,* which was escorted by a torpedo boat. The *Brazza* was followed by a small coastal tanker, which was shelled and set on fire and finally sunk with a torpedo. The next entry, however, shows that when the captain attacked a small, armed merchant ship, the enemy returned the fire so accurately that *U 37* was forced to dive and make good her escape.

When the captain had fired his last torpedo and turned for

home, he added up his "score." He had sunk 39,000 tons of Allied shipping on a single patrol.

One of the "canoes"—*U 9,* commanded by Lieutenant Lüth—ran into trouble off the Norfolk coast very early on the twenty-fifth of May, 1940. In calm weather Lüth sighted a small cruiser or single-funneled destroyer, which he decided to attack on the surface. He gave the usual orders to flood the torpedo tubes and open the bow caps but, just as the range was closing very rapidly, the bow caps jammed shut. Lüth had to crash-dive to escape; from being the hunter he had suddenly become the quarry. As five depth charges exploded close alongside the steeply diving boat, everything shook and quivered, and her hull seemed to sag. The lights went out and water spurted from the smashed gauges; Lüth wondered whether he had sufficient depth of water beneath him to escape. To be on the safe side he ordered the escape gear to be issued. One man lost his nerve and floundered in a panic toward the conning-tower ladder. Lüth caught him by the nape of the neck and hit him hard. "Control yourself, man!" That did the trick. The man looked round as though dazed, then subsided. The rest of the ratings began hastily pulling their escape gear out of the packs.

Five more depth charges burst very close to them; Lüth ordered all noise to be stopped and the boat slid along at silent-running speed. "Destroyers approaching again!" Six more explosions, very close. The U-boat lost buoyancy and began to crunch heavily on the sea bed. It was 4:30 A.M. That meant that daylight would be breaking overhead; it was far too dangerous to surface until darkness fell again. By six o'clock all hands were squatting in the diesel compartment, to compensate the forward trim of the boat. Both motors were noisy and the port one was producing a piercing whistle.

"Can't we use the pumps to lighten her, Chief?" asked Lüth. The engineer officer shook his head. "Even before the attack started, the blowing and trimming pumps were too loud. If they can hear anything at all up top, they'll certainly hear *that.*"

The chief engineer was gazing at the scene of devastation around him and trying to sum up the situation. Except for the main motors, all the electrical gear was out of action. The bow planes had partly seized, the steering rudder was clattering, the periscope mirrors were unusable and every compartment was piled with smashed equipment. Gyrocompass, engine telegraphs, wireless—all useless. In fact this was more a wreck than a warship, yet it still floated and was still under control.

As the hours passed they tried repeatedly to elude their pursuers by making sudden alterations of course, but the enemy remained in close contact. Finally the U-boat dropped down onto the sea bed as though weary of the fight. Lüth mustered his crew; "We shall feign death in the hope of deceiving the enemy. Our only chance lies with the darkness. Somehow we've got to last out until nightfall. Above all, we must conserve our air supply. Every man is to lie down at his diving station and get some sleep, for when you sleep you use up less air." Oxygen masks and potash cartridges were issued to all hands and they tried to sleep as ordered. From time to time more depth charges exploded near them.

The hydrophones were now out of action but they were not needed, for every man could distinguish the destroyer's propeller noises with the naked ear. Lüth and his officers took turns in keeping watch in the control room. At noon each man was given a packet of chocolate. Overhead the destroyers circled and searched, probing the water with their sound gear. Suddenly came a clanking noise forward, which brought the men to their feet, looking anxiously at their captain. Lüth stood as calmly as ever in the control room, wearing his breathing mask, his cap back to front. "They probably think we're dead," he said, taking his mask off for a moment. "They're dropping buoys to fix our position. They may try to raise us later on." There were more noises up by the bows, as though a metal weight were being dragged over the hull.

Slowly the day wore on, every minute filled with tension. From time to time a solitary depth charge exploded and a destroyer could be heard moving slowly overhead. From time to time, too, the chief engineer released a little oxygen into the boat to refresh the air. Midnight came at last; they knew that at least there would be no moon. The navigator had worked out the bearings of a few stars in advance, so he could snap a sight quickly on surfacing. Another destroyer came on the scene, listened, dropped a charge, then moved away again. Now was their chance!

"Surface! Blow the midship and for'ard tanks!" Afraid to use the noisy machinery that raised the periscope Lüth brought his boat to the surface like a cork, pulled open the hatch and had a quick look round as he drew his first deep breath of fresh air. Three hundred yards astern lay the dark shape of an A/S vessel, motionless. The night was dark and cloudy but the water streaming off the U-boat's sides shone with a silvery phosphorescence. Then, "Slow ahead on both motors, officer of the watch and helmsman to the bridge." The brightly shining bubbles of air alongside the hull began to die away and the U-boat crept forward. As Lüth was taking another cautious look round, the interior lighting suddenly came on again and sent a stream of light through the conning-tower hatch. With an oath he kicked the hatch door shut. On the port quarter the destroyer's searchlight was sweeping the horizon. The polestar appeared from behind a cloud just long enough to get a check on the compasses. Yard by yard they increased their distance from the enemy, turning so as to show him their narrowest silhouette. Ten minutes elapsed before Lüth dared to switch over to the diesels. An hour later the U-boat was passing through the British-declared mine field; three days later she was home.

Admiral Dönitz was on the jetty as Lüth brought *U 9* slowly in. "Where have you come from?" he asked, "I thought you were all dead. The British claim to have sunk you." . . . "Then the British spoke too soon," answered Lüth drily. "They even dropped wreck buoys right over us—but they won't find us there now." [1]

Three years later Lüth, still an operational commander, was awarded the highest decoration—the Knight's Cross with diamonds. Having survived all the perils of the war, he perished from a stray bullet fired by a German sentry in the dark days of the capitulation.

9

ACTION IN THE ATLANTIC

(July–August, 1940)

The heat of the summer sun was beating down on the U-boat Headquarters at Sengwarden and the scent of hay was wafted through the open windows of the Operations Room. Faint sounds of martial music drifted in from a nearby room, then broke off suddenly. The flag officer, U-boats, was stand-

[1] The attack on *U 9* described above occurred on May 25, 1940, off the Norfolk coast inside the British mine fields. The destroyers in the hunt were *Jackal, Javelin, Gallant* and *Jaguar,* but they made no claim to have destroyed the U-boat.

ing in front of the big chart. He already knew it by heart, but used it as a sort of mental sheet anchor. His U-boats appeared as pinheads in that vast expanse of water. Even when he sent them in as close as possible to the enemy coast, their ranges of vision still did not overlap; there were enormous gaps which he could not bridge. If he brought them closer together, the enemy would sail round their flanks; but if he spread them out, the enemy would sail right through them.

Captain Godt, the Chief of Staff to Dönitz, remarked that the possession of the Biscay ports would save the boats those long transit routes which until now had severely limited their operational endurance. The admiral nodded. "France's capitulation has come like a gift from heaven and we can't be too grateful for it. Britain's sea communications are now, so to speak, on our doorstep, which means that our boats can devote nearly all their time to operations. This will multiply our chances of success and will compensate to some extent for the catastrophic shortage of boats. A hundred boats, Godt! If only . . ." He swept the thought aside. "When do the first boats arrive at Lorient?"

"They will be able to use the Biscay ports for repairs and supplies when they return from operations in July," [1] Godt answered. "We are sending workmen from the *Germania* yards and advance parties from the flotilla commands are already on their way."

"Good," said Dönitz, turning to gaze abstractedly through the window at the flat green landscape, where the cattle were browsing in the shade. "You know that Britain's declaration of war came as a shock to me," he continued, "for at that time we were not really strong enough to offer battle, nor had we a sufficient land mass under our control to survive a total blockade by her. Now, however, the area under our control"—and he turned to the operation chart as he continued—"includes all this!" His hand swept over Poland, Norway, Denmark, Holland, Belgium and Northern France. "So for the first time I now believe victory to be within our grasp, since we cannot be harmed by such a blockade. Provided we fully control and exploit these new territories the fortress of Europe can survive a very long war. But to ensure this we must permanently prevent the enemy from penetrating into these areas, and we must maintain control of the air over them."

[1] The first U-boat to use Lorient was *U 30*, which arrived there on July 7, 1940.

The lookouts on the bridge of the inward-bound *U 34* sighted a faint blue-gray line on the horizon; it was the French coast. They gazed eagerly toward it as the U-boat steered between fleets of small fishing vessels with their brightly colored sails. A German minesweeper hove in sight and signaled, "Welcome to France"; how strange that sounded! As they drew nearer the harbor of Lorient they could see men in German uniforms waving to them, their cheers for the returning U-boat carrying across the water.

The advance guard of the flotilla staff had moved into the French Naval *Préfecture* at Lorient. They had plenty of booty—uniforms, footwear, equipment—some of it bearing the names of British and American firms and the date 1918; there were piles of tropical kits, arms, ammunition, food, and a thousand and one items which the enemy had had no time to destroy. The town itself showed hardly any signs of damage. It was a typically unlovely provincial Breton town with untidy houses badly in need of repair, huddled together in dirty narrow gray streets. But there were palm trees in the *Place d'Armes* and behind the high walls surrounding the better-class houses. Prisoners of every branch of the French Army and Navy, both white and colored, were moving through the streets, guarded by men in field-gray. They looked in friendly fashion at the U-boat men. They were well fed, for their country was rich; to realize that, you only had to look in the shop windows or enter the restaurants and *estaminets,* which had everything in superabundance. And now the flotilla depot was there, with everything one's heart could desire—transport, fuel, money; only the sanitary arrangements left something to be desired, but that was soon rectified.

Admiral Dönitz came by air from Sengwarden for a visit of inspection. Restless as ever, he carried out a detailed schedule, saw everything, talked to the men, inspected the yards and the arsenal, listened, questioned, gave advice, made notes. "Write that down, Fuhrmann . . . Make a note, Fuhrmann . . ." The flag lieutenant jotted everything down in his notebook and off they went again by car to Bannes, where the Junkers plane was awaiting them. "In the autumn, Fuhrmann, we will move in here," said Dönitz as the car rolled over the bridge. "I want to be close to my men, to keep in touch with them and their problems—everything depends upon that."

As the days passed, there was a continual coming and going of U-boats. Arriving with fuel tanks and torpedo tubes empty, they repaired defects, rested, filled up and put to sea again.

The tale of their successes mounted steadily. Something of the general picture at this time may be gathered from the signal log of *U 34*. While outward-bound, she intercepted signals from other U-boats, entering them, as was the usual practice, in this log. From one U-boat came: "All torpedoes expended, 35,000 tons sunk, am returning to base"; and from another, "Am pursuing fast troop transport"; from another, "Battle-squadron in sight"; and another, "26,600 tons sunk, one torpedo defective." The following morning she heard one of the larger U-boats reporting from the southern Biscay, "Three ships sunk. Nothing left in this area. Request permission to move to another position." At the same time another boat was reporting the sinking of 11,000 tons, another 32,000 tons "and a probable 6,000 more," a third that she was north of the Shetlands, a fourth that an enemy convoy was heading northward in the Bay of Biscay. This U-boat kept reporting the convoy's position at short intervals; meanwhile still another was reporting weather conditions. Orders from the U-boat Command followed and then a second boat came within range of the convoy. "Convoy in sight," her captain reported, while a third boat signaled, "Have sunk two ships of 16,000 tons and another of 7,000; two days ago torpedoed an *Orion* class but did not see her sink." Then came a signal from a homeward-bound boat, "Nine ships of 51,086 tons sunk." And again from the U-boat attacking the convoy, "At least twenty ships. Course southwest. Escort weak. One ship sunk." And another, "Attack periscope out of action. Am returning. Three ships of 15,000 tons sunk. Torpedoed tanker *Athellaird* but did not see her sink." Lieutenant Commander Rollmann, from whose log these extracts were taken, himself sank 22,800 tons of shipping, the destroyer *Whirlwind* and a naval tanker, while another commander sank 30,000 tons and the big boat in the south got 23,600. And so it went on, with the boats ceaselessly pursuing and attacking. The "First Golden Age" of the U-boats was in full swing. As Dönitz had predicted, the shortened routes were paying dividends.

One U-boat sortie, lasting only eleven days, which the admiral later described as an "exemplary and particularly successful mission," was typical of those days. Let the U-boat remain anonymous.

On a windy, rainy morning the crew were mustering in their olive-green sea kits on the square in front of the *Préfecture* at Lorient. The cries of French children playing round the old bandstand almost drowned a farewell address to the crew by the admiral, who happened to be there on one of his lightning inspections. He knew these men well, and had seen them leave before. They had six patrols to their credit and several of the petty officers who now stood stiffly before him had served with him as young initiates in the prewar days of the "canoes."

Punctually on the stroke of nine the U-boat cast off and disappeared in the rain squalls, following the pilot-boat. She carried a crew of forty-one, eleven torpedoes, eighty rounds of ammunition, food for seven weeks and a full load of fuel and lubricating oil. Her diesels humming as she rolled and pitched in the oblique swell, she stood out to sea to face further battles. The captain leaned on the periscope socket. "Keep a good lookout, lads. Your poodle-faking days are over now. Back to business! All hands down below except the bridge watch."

In the evening the chief engineer appeared on the bridge. "This French lubricant we've taken on is too thin, Sir. The temperature of the water in the cooling system has been well above normal for some time. We've tried adding some old German oil to it but it doesn't help; consumption is still far too high."

"Very well," said the captain, "what now?"

"It means a considerable reduction in our top speed over long distances."

"How much can we do?"

"Not more than thirteen knots, Sir, in my estimation," said the chief, shrugging his shoulders apologetically.

"Curse it! Perhaps you'll be able to think of something."

"Afraid not, Sir, we've tried everything we can think of. That's why I've come to you."

The captain smothered another oath. "Oh well," he said at last, "that won't help. Better make a signal to headquarters."

The night passed without incident; as the first suspicion of light loomed in the east, the officer of the watch called down the conning tower, "Tell the captain that dawn is breaking. Shall we do a trial dive?" At the same moment the lookout on the northeastern sector reported smoke on the horizon. "Call the captain—smoke bearing eighty degrees!" The news ran through the U-boat like wildfire, and men who a few moments before had been sound asleep sprang fully awake from their bunks. A few strides took the captain through the control room and conning tower up onto the bridge. The U-boat altered course and increased speed. Two ships gradually appeared above the horizon, steering west. The U-boat turned on a parallel course, dead into the wind and sea. The spray came whistling over the bridge as the day dawned gray and cold; dew was falling and visibility was only moderate. On the horizon ahead of them, a forest of slim streamers of smoke suddenly appeared, rising until they formed one large cloud.

The U-boat kept contact at long range and as mastheads and funnels began to appear, the picture gradually became clearer. It was a big convoy of ships in open formation. Every four or five minutes they altered course precisely and expertly, and the U-boat altered with them. "We must have patience," said the captain, whose black cigar had gone out. "If you want to steal a child out of its cradle you must first find out where its mother is." Even as he looked again, he saw two long low fast warships and a couple of trawlers with tall thin funnels ranging round the convoy like sheep dogs.

Soon after midday, the U-boat had attained a position ahead of the convoy. The captain kept up a running commentary for the benefit of the men below decks. "All the ships are armed . . . their average size is seven to eight thousand tons, including one large liner, several tankers and some big freighters. Most of the ships are in ballast . . . the merchant ships have paravane gear on their bows. . . ." The men below listened to the quiet voice of their captain and unconsciously drew strength from it. "I am attacking the liner," said the voice. "She is at the head of the outer column. She's a modern ship painted in three colors. Armed with . . . I can't see all her armament . . . one funnel, two masts. I presume she is an auxiliary cruiser. If she were a passenger ship she would be in the middle of the convoy. . . ." In between the captain's words they could hear the low hum of the periscope motor and the chief's muttered orders. "Up five degrees forward, bring her up! . . ." Clearly now, without hydrophones, they could hear the noise of several propellers, while from above them came the captain's voice again, "I have got through between the two leading escorts . . . I'm approaching the leader of the third column . . . now I'm between the second and third column . . . stand by torpedoes! . . . salvo from Numbers one two and three . . . fire!"

The seconds ticked by. "All torpedoes running," reported the hydrophone operator. Were they going to run forever? At last came the sound of an explosion echoing through the U-boat. The captain described the scene. "The torpedo hit exactly amidships . . . now the left-hand fish has hit a ship just beyond the auxiliary cruiser. Splendid! The second ship was hit right aft. Range about two thousand yards." There was another dull crump.

"Was that the third, Sir?"

"No, that was the first ship again, her boilers are evidently blowing up. She's listing heavily to starboard, there's a lot of damage amidships, her lifeboats are out of action, she's going down by the stern. She's about five hundred fifty feet long, probably about eighteen thousand tons. The second ship might be a blue funneler—I'd say seventeen thousand tons. Her stern is down below the waterline."

The captain had no time for further colorful reportage, for he had to concentrate on the next attack. He was right in the middle of the convoy now, with ships signaling to each other all round him. In every direction he could see short white puffs of steam coming from their funnels as their sirens sounded. A tanker came within range and he fired, but his target turned sharply away and the torpedo ran past it into the void. No time to cry over that, for already two large freighters were bearing down upon him from the next column. Down periscope and dive to 60 feet! The rumbling and thumping of the propellers sounded right over their heads, then died away again. Up to periscope depth again. What a pity, nothing but the rearmost ships were left now, but there was still a chance of evading the enemy hydrophones by closing the stragglers! As the captain ordered "Full speed," the pitch of the motors increased to a high note.

"Reload the tubes!" Cautiously using his periscope at short intervals only, the captain could see the escorts circling round the spot where he had fired his first torpedoes, slowing down to listen and hoisting the red "Z" pennant before they ran in to drop their depth charges. As the crash of their explosions boomed through the water he could see the ships of the convoy increasing speed, while their crews were putting on their life jackets and manning the guns. The two damaged ships were lying helpless in the water, listing more and more. One hour after being hit the giant auxiliary cruiser wearily lifted her bow, dropped heavily on one side and sank. The other one followed her a few minutes later.

Down in the bow compartment the men were toiling and sweating to get the spare torpedoes into the tubes. The bunks on either side of the tubes had been lashed up out of the way and now the heavy torpedo-lifting gear was being lowered over the torpedoes. Chains rattled and trolley wheels clanked as naked muscular arms manhandled the torpedoes into position. Thickly smeared with grease and accompanied by many a pious wish, the torpedoes disappeared into their tubes. Late that same afternoon, steaming once more on the surface, the U-boat renewed contact with the convoy. A flying boat was describing wide circles above it. But although the captain waited until darkness fell, it was still too light to make a surface attack even at one o'clock in the morning; on the other hand, it was too dark to make an attack submerged. He would have to await the moon.

By the light of the newly risen moon, the captain dived to deliver his next assault. He could see little through his periscope, for faulty maintenance work at base had rendered it almost useless for nightwork; but the loom of huge silhouettes and the sound of propellers thrashing the water above him were sufficient guide. "I'm going to attack the leading ship of the third column," he said, thinking aloud as usual for the benefit of his men. "She is a big freighter, perhaps eight or ten thousand tons." In the darkness the ship looked like a moving mountain, filling two thirds of his field of vision. The torpedo was running now. "Twenty-one . . . twenty-two . . ." The coxswain in the control room was counting the seconds out loud. "Torpedo has hit abreast the after end of the bridge," said the captain and at the same moment an explosion boomed through the U-boat. The big ship quivered, lost speed and began to sink by the stern. Morse signals flickered across to the escort vessels, and the deck lighting shone out as her crew rushed for the boats. Beyond her, two ships showed up as an overlapping target—a tanker and a freighter. "Number one . . . ready . . . fire!" But nothing happened, for this time they had missed. The next torpedo also missed, but eight minutes later the first lieutenant was scribbling at the captain's dictation, "Fifth attack made on a large tanker showing a light on the bridge, estimated speed six to eight knots . . . have hit her for'ard . . . estimate her size at nine thousand tons." And again, "Twenty-two minutes after the first attack the convoy is widely scattered. The escorts are trying to reassemble them with orders passed by searchlight."

The game was over and the time had come to return to Kiel. The crew were jubilant. "Forty-two thousand tons sunk, six thousand damaged, all in eight days!" they were saying. "We've nothing to be ashamed of when we reach Kiel. And there's still one torpedo left. We're sure to find a target for it before we get home." And they did. Six days after they had started for home their log read:

1817 sighted a small streak on the horizon like a mast or peri-

scope. At 1819 dived and identified submarine, heading straight
for us on a NW course, as British *Sterlet* class. . . . 1904:
closed the range at high speed and fired torpedo which hit
forward. Very heavy explosion, target sank in a few seconds.
1906: surfaced and approached the spot but could find only
one survivor, whom we took on board at 1910. At 1908 large
air bubble came to the surface, practically no oil to be seen
but a lot of wooden wreckage. Submarine was *Spearfish*,[2] survivor's name Able Seaman Pester, William Victor.

That evening they were all quiet and thoughtful. Able Seaman Pester sat among them, the only survivor of a submarine
crew, a man like themselves but now a prisoner—and all the
others dead. One or two of them tried to say a few words in
English—"Good fellow . . . sorry." They dried out his clothes,
gave him food and chocolate and allowed him to go for a
smoke in the conning tower. They respected his bewildered
silence. Poor devil, they were thinking, it can all happen so
quickly—in a couple of seconds . . . and who knows whether
it won't be our turn next?

10

U 47

(August, 1940)

On August 17, 1940, within a year of the outbreak of war,
Germany at last met the British blockade with a counter-
blockade. The declaration of this was of special significance
for the U-boats, for it gave them the right to sink ships without warning in an area which corresponded almost exactly to
the danger zone which President Roosevelt had barred to all
American ships on November 4, 1939. Since that date the only
formula for trade with the USA was "cash and carry." Anyone
was welcome to trade with the Americans as long as he used
his own ships to take away the goods he had bought. The
German declaration of blockade also reflected the change in
the balance of power which had come about since the war
began—for Poland, Norway, Denmark, the Low Countries and
most of France were now in German hands; on land there

---

[2] HM Submarine *Spearfish* was sunk by a U-boat on August 1,
1940, in position 58°28′N, 1°6′E.

was no fighting and Great Britain—a sea power—was the only adversary.

The increasingly violent measures adopted by the British had been copied by the Germans only after much hesitation—but now the gloves were off. The two adversaries were in the early stages of the frightful conflict that was destined to prove fatal to one of them; Britain's sea power was still intact, while Germany could deploy no more than a handful of U-boats. Henceforward the U-boats were free to swoop in and attack anywhere in the great sea spaces round the British Isles and far out to the west, destroying everything they found except hospital ships and a few neutrals moving along agreed routes, such as the "Sweden Route." No more would be heard of "war according to the prize regulations," of stopping ships and examining papers, of search parties and contraband, of U-boats exposing themselves to the danger of Q-ships. This did not mean that every restraint was to be cast aside, for there remained what Grand Admiral Raeder termed the "natural precepts of soldierly honor"—the humane feelings for the ghastly position of survivors in lifeboats and the desire to help, so long as the U-boat itself was not endangered. There remained the realization that in the enemy ships too, men were serving their country faithfully and unselfishly. The enemy is still the enemy, and to damage him, to kill, to destroy him, is still the pitiless rule of war. It's you today, me tomorrow—nobody knew that better than the U-boat men. But the beaten enemy, the survivor in the water, in a lifeboat, on a raft or a piece of wreckage, is just a poor devil who has lost his ship—a fate that might overtake either German or Briton at any moment.

This was the law obeyed by the commanders—those in the U-boats and those in the British destroyers. They fought with everything they had, but they did not fight the defeated survivors. They were men of war, not murderers.

In June, 1940, *U 47* was patrolling to the west of Scotland, still commanded by Lieutenant Prien, the "Bull of Scapa Flow." The weather was calm and mild, the nights so light that one could read a book on the bridge at midnight.

Early one morning the haze lifted to reveal a ship—their first target for days. Just as *U 47* altered course to attack, the target turned too and came straight down at her. Prien lowered his periscope and dived as fast as he could to 180 feet, while the ship rumbled unwittingly overhead. Almost at once he surfaced again, ordering the gun's crew to their stations; but as they were closing up round the gun, an after lookout suddenly reported more smoke astern of the U-boat, and Prien realized that a convoy was approaching. He abandoned his original plan and, after sending out a hasty sighting report to head-quarters, he submerged again.

As soon as *U 47* was running smoothly at periscope depth, he took a quick look through the lens as it broke surface for a few seconds. He could hardly believe his eyes. Forty-two ships were steaming majestically toward him in open order, seven columns of six ships of all shapes and sizes, escorted by two ancient-looking destroyers and three modern ones. For three hours, still submerged, Prien tried to close the convoy, but his boat was too slow; steadily he lost bearing on the ships, until they were out of periscope sight. He started to surface but al-most immediately a trawler hove in sight and he had to dive; at his next attempt a Sunderland zoomed out of the sun like a fat bumblebee and forced him below again. Prien now realized that to catch up with that convoy he would have to chase it for at least ten hours, and by then it would be so close to the coast that he would never get near it for aircraft and surface escorts. As he sat weighing his chances and scanning the hori-zon, masts and smoke suddenly appeared to port and a strag-gler from the convoy came hurrying along zigzagging violently. So he stayed below the surface, and everyone kept deathly still, as if the U-boat herself were holding her breath like a living thing. "All tubes ready!" Every man was standing tensely at his post. Suddenly the ship turned away; with a curse Prien called for the last ounce of power from his motors as he stood after his prey. "Number five, stand by . . . fire!" Some seconds later there was a clanging crash. "We've hit her near the fun-nel!" called Prien triumphantly. "She's the *Balmoral Wood*.[1] Look and see how big she is, I'd put her at five or six thousand tons." As the water closed over the sinking ship, all that could be seen on the surface were a few large crates, some of which had burst open to reveal aircraft wings and fuselages. "Well, *they* won't be dropping any bombs on Kiel, anyway," com-mented one of the crew.

All next day Prien carried out a searching sweep on various courses but sighted nothing. "The Atlantic seems to have been swept clean," he wrote in his log. But his luck changed with the dawn of the following day, for a 5,000-tonner without lights came steaming past, barely 5,000 yards away. Despite the growing daylight, Prien tried to approach on the surface but he was soon forced under by a Sunderland; however he was determined to get in an attack and once again he surfaced.

[1] This ship was torpedoed and sunk on June 14, 1940.

This time his first hasty look round revealed warships ahead
and merchant ships astern of him; quickly he sent out a sighting signal and dived again, realizing that he had chanced upon
the meeting place of a convoy with its escort. He moved in to
attack but soon saw that the twenty ships in convoy were
screened by at least four escorts of the *Auckland* and *Bittern*
class, while a Sunderland flew above them. His original plan
of attack would be of no avail against such a strong escort, so
he waited awhile before surfacing and then made a wide sweep
round, so as to try his luck from the other side. As night fell,
he closed in, once more at periscope depth, and began to look
for a likely target. The weather was favorable; white caps of
foam on the waves would make it difficult for the enemy lookouts to spot his periscope, and although the sky was cloudy,
visibility was good.

Despite all this, it looked as though the U-boat had in fact
been sighted, for one of the escorts turned toward *U 47* and
came down like a pointer sniffing into the wind for game. The
range dropped quickly—300 yards, 250, 200. Prien was
tempted to fire at the escort, but she suddenly turned away and
disappeared on a parallel course to the U-boat. With a sigh of
relief Prien ordered, "Number one ready . . . fire!" His target
was a great tanker, deeply laden, which had caught his eye
earlier in the day. He did not wait to see the torpedo hit but
turned immediately to his next victim, which was slightly
nearer—a ship of about 7,000 tons. "Number two . . . fire!"
While the U-boat was still swinging, Prien suddenly saw a
column of water spouting up alongside a ship he had not aimed
at. There had been a slight mishap in the torpedo compartment; the torpedo artificer had been thrown off his balance by
the movement of the boat and had saved himself from falling
by catching hold of the firing grip. As a result Number three
tube had fired a fraction after Number two—but the torpedo
had hit a second tanker.

Fifteen minutes later the U-boat surfaced and Prien sprang
up to the bridge; it was not yet quite dark and the sea was
getting up. Over on the port quarter lay the big tanker with a
heavy list, her bows well below the surface, her decks awash.
Prien sent for the silhouette book and soon identified the battered wreck as that of the tanker *Cadillac*, 12,100 tons.[2] The
other ship, of which nothing could now be seen, was presum-
ably one of the *Gracia* class of 5,600 tons. The third had also
disappeared. Now for the rest of them!

[2] Probably the tanker *San Fernando*, torpedoed and sunk on June
21, 1940.

But it was not to be; a storm blew up and after two days' fruitless search Prien realized that he had lost the convoy. A day later, however, he sighted and sank the Dutch tanker, *Leticia,* 2,800 tons,[3] bound for England from Curaçao with fuel oil. Late that night in a freshening sea, yet another tanker was sighted and Prien ordered the gun to be manned, having decided to stop the ship with a couple of well-placed rounds and then sink her at his leisure.

"Only five rounds of ammunition left, Sir," warned the gunner's mate.

"Never mind, we'll use them just the same."

Time passed but there was no sign of the gun captain.

Prien called down the hatchway, "Control Room! Where's Meier?"

There was the sound of running feet below, then the voice of the control-room petty officer. "Meier is lying in his bunk, Sir, and says there's absolutely no point in trying to aim a gun in this weather."

Prien could hardly believe his ears; the bridge watch did their best to hide their amusement. "Give him a direct order from the captain to report immediately on the bridge!"

When Meier at last appeared he did not trouble to hide his feelings. "In *this* sea, with only a couple of rounds?"

"They *must* hit, Meier!"

"Aye, aye, Sir."

Indifferently he moved toward the gun and Prien gave the order to open fire. The tanker turned sharply away as the first shells screamed toward her, but two of them hit her; Meier was excelling himself. "Hit her in the engine room!" ordered Prien. Another hit—but the target was still moving away. The last of the five rounds went into the breach, and this time the shell burst was followed by a cloud of gray smoke and a yellow flash. Soaked to the skin, Meier returned to the bridge; the tanker had stopped and the crew were hastily abandoning ship. Throwing a quick word of congratulation to his still impenitent gunner, Prien brought *U 47* into a good firing position and let go a torpedo. His log reads: "The torpedo hit and the ship began to sink. Despite the gunfire and the torpedo hit, her radio operator continued to signal, '*Empire Toucan* torpedoed in position 49°20′ north, 13°52′ west' and later 'Sinking rapidly by stern.' Finally he jumped overboard with a flare and was seen swimming away from the ship." Prien immediately

[3] Sunk on June 27, 1940.

steered toward the flare but when he reached the spot, there was nothing to be seen. A brave man had died.

Weeks went by as Prien and his brother captains hunted and sank, watched and waited, shadowed the convoys and "homed" other boats on to them, in fair weather and in foul. When at length the U-boats returned to France for repairs and provisioning, their crews were sent to the new rest centers at Carnac and Quiberon near Lorient, where they could relax on the beach, bathe, ride and do exactly as they pleased. Here they could let the world go by, as they took the pretty daughters of France by storm and quaffed the local wines; all too soon they would once more be at sea, the perpetual thunder of the diesels around them and the waves foaming and crashing on their decks.

Prien too was soon back at sea. One dark and rainy night he and half-a-dozen other boats encountered a convoy, which they attacked from all sides at once. This was one of the earliest organized wolf-pack actions of the war, and will go down in history as the "Night of the Long Knives." Torpedo after torpedo raced from its tube to detonate against some ship's side. Ten thousand tons of petrol went up in a fiery ball of white-hot flame a thousand feet high; an ammunition ship exploded with a deafening roar and literally disintegrated; all around was nothing but the bright glow of flames. Some ships stood on end before finally disappearing, some listed heavily and turned turtle, others broke apart, to die a painful death. Everywhere, like a pack of wolves, the U-boats were at the convoy. With all his torpedoes gone, Prien reckoned up the tonnage he had sunk by identifying his victims from the "picture book." Then he took a signal pad and wrote, "Have sunk eight ships in the convoy totaling 50,500 tons. All torpedoes fired."

The dawn came slowly, marking the end of the "Night of the Long Knives." The other commanders were also making their reckoning—Kretschmer, Schepke, Frauenheim, Endrass, Bleichrodt, Moehle and Liebe. In two days of operating together they had achieved the staggering figure of 325,000 tons.[4] Within a few days *U 47* had returned to her base. Prien, as the

---

[4] "Night of the Long Knives"—October 8 and 19, 1940. Two convoys were involved in the attacks described above. SC 7 was attacked by seven U-boats and between the seventeenth and nineteenth of October, twenty out of the thirty-four ships were sunk. The convoy had only four surface escorts. HX 79 was attacked by five U-boats on October 19 and 20, and out of forty-nine ships, twelve were sunk. This convoy had seven surface escorts.

first U-boat captain to top the 200,000-ton mark, now became the fifth officer in the Armed Forces to receive what was then the highest decoration—the oak leaves to the Knight's Cross.

11

EARLY PROBLEMS OF ATLANTIC WARFARE

(September–December, 1940)

On September 1, 1940, Dönitz moved his headquarters from Sengwarden near Wilhelmshaven to Paris, as part of the scheme to group together all the command posts for "Operation Sea Lion"—the invasion of England. He set up his offices in one of those large, generously planned houses on the *Boulevard Suchet;* it was here that he spent what was probably the happiest time of the war—happy because the U-boats were achieving great successes while their own losses fell away to nothing. With him was his small personal staff, and every few days his U-boat captains came there to report, as they returned from patrol.

Every morning on the stroke of nine he would enter the operations room and the operational staff officer would deliver an account of the events of the night; he would report on the signals received and dispatched, the details of boats due to sail and those returning to base, and the developments of any operation currently in progress. The staff officer would be succeeded by other experts, announcing requests for escorts or submitting the latest intelligence reports, logistics, details of new boats, and so on. Occasionally the admiral would interrupt with a question as to detail and follow this up with an order. Then began the daily problem of the U-boat dispositions. What would the enemy do? Which course would he take? The main problem was always the same—what is the best way of spreading a small number of boats over the widest possible area, so as to cause the maximum damage to the enemy? There were still wide gaps in the ring round Britain and these could not be closed until there had been a substantial influx of new boats; but this could not occur before 1941.

Because of the desperate shortage of aircraft there was little information they could rely on: a handful of reports from boats at sea, an occasional intelligence report based on the interception and decryption[1] of enemy signals, a few secret agents' reports on the assembly and departure of convoys from enemy ports. There was no more urgent need than that of a regular air-reconnaissance service, and since this was not forthcoming the U-boat operations staff had to rely upon a sort of sixth sense of their own. From time to time a short incoming signal would show that their guesses had been correct. Then messengers would dash to the radio room with a batch of signals for immediate dispatch: *"U 32, 46 and 52 are to attack the convoy reported by U 48. U 48 is to maintain contact for the rest. . . ."* And then for twenty-four hours or more, the staff on shore would wait tensely for the outcome. Would the boats get there in time? What was the weather like in the Atlantic? How big was the convoy and how strong was the escort? Piece by piece they built up a picture of the operation, as brief reports came in from the attacking U-boats. At last a signal would come in which showed that the climax was approaching: "Enemy in sight, position xyz, course southeast, am attacking. . . ."

From time to time the admiral flew to the bases on the Biscay coast, to maintain contact with his men; someone who accompanied him on these trips has described a visit to Lorient. He was at the water's edge one evening, surrounded by his officers, their laughter and talk echoing out over the water. They were all awaiting the return of one of their number; they never missed such an occasion, for each of them knew what it meant to find a welcome when your boat came back from an operation.

As twilight was falling the boat came in sight, her gray paint rusted over and her colors faded. The crew were standing on deck—it was the first time for many a day that they could safely do so in broad daylight. Their beards were long and their clothes reeked of U-boat, but their spirits were high at the prospect of coming home. The U-boat slid slowly alongside; on the bridge the officer of the watch, with the confidence born of long practice, was giving orders for making fast. The cheers of greeting rang out as ropes flew through the air and were secured. There was a shout of "Finished with main engines!" and the slim young captain came quickly over the side to jump on to the landing stage.

"Beg to report, Sir, *U Thirty-eight* returned from patrol."

"Well, are you satisfied?"

---

[1] The word *decryption* is used to denote the complex cryptographic process of unraveling an encyphered enemy signal, which the enemy believed to be secure against such a process.

"Not entirely, Sir, only twenty thousand tons. We ought to have got far more."

"Muster your ship's company," said the admiral.

There was a shouting of orders, the rush of feet, then silence as he stepped on board. *"Heil, U Thirty-eight!"*

"Heil, Herr Admiral!" came the reply in unison.

He walked slowly down the line of men, each one of whom felt the searching eye upon him; then he addressed the crew. "Men! Your boat has sunk over one hundred thousand tons in only three patrols. The credit for this splendid performance goes chiefly to your gallant captain. Lieutenant Liebe, the Führer has conferred upon you the Knight's Cross and it is my pleasure to hand it to you." The broad red ribbon gleamed in the evening light as the flag lieutenant clipped it round the young officer's neck. The admiral shook his hand, then stood back and raised his hand to his cap. "Three cheers for Lieutenant Liebe!" As the cheers echoed through the harbor, Liebe stood motionless at the salute. He had a faraway look, as though still regretting the convoy that had eluded him.

In October it was finally decided to postpone Operation Sea Lion for that year, and U-boat headquarters were promptly moved to a villa requisitioned from a sardine merchant at Kernevel, which stood near the sea between Lorient and Lamorplage, in the shelter of some fine old trees. From the broad windows of the operations room there was a fine view over toward Port Louis and the fort at the entrance to the harbor.

The first year of hostilities had ushered in many changes; the war at sea grew more intense as the land victories in Denmark, Norway and France gave the U-boats valuable bases in Northern and Western Europe. Yet Dönitz made it clear to his officers that he expected even greater stresses in the future, and that the successes they had achieved so far were no more than pinpricks in the enemy's veins. Their task, he said, was to bleed the enemy white, slowly but surely; although they would soon be getting more U-boats, he warned them that the war would last a very long time.

In the quiet of his office at Kernevel, Dönitz often paced round and round the big table, absorbed in the cares which never left him, even at this time of great successes and no serious losses. The reports of returning captains emphasized the ever-growing protection that the enemy was giving to his convoys—more destroyers, more escort vessels, more star shells to lift the cover of darkness from the attacking U-boats. What of the future? Had he done all he could to safeguard his boats? He knew that Admiral von Friedeburg, the gifted head of his organization department at Kiel, had got well in hand all the problems of reinforcement and supply, of the quality and efficiency of the new boats; but he was ever alive to the possibility of new enemy A/S devices, which might force the U-boats back on the defensive. It was not essential to destroy them; all that the enemy needed was to foil their attacks by locating them in good time and forcing them under water for long enough to let the convoy get out of range.

He looked at the balance sheet for September 1, 1940, produced by Lieutenant Winter, one of his staff officers:

U-boat strength at outbreak of war	57
Boats commissioned during the first year	28
Losses during the first year	28
Strength on September 1, 1940	57
Operational boats in commission in 1939	39
Operational boats in commission in 1940	27

The reduction in operational boats in 1940 was due to more boats being on trials and shakedown. Moreover, with the prospect of many new boats commissioning in 1941, it was necessary to transfer some operational boats to the training organizations.

Thus, at the end of one year of war, the Germans had fewer boats available for operations than they had started with. On an average, only seven or eight U-boats were at sea at any one time, representing only a third or a quarter of their total strength. Yet the balance sheet for September 1, 1940, showed unmistakable overall gains. Against the loss of 46 per cent of the U-boat strength could be set the destruction of one battle-ship, an aircraft carrier, three destroyers, two submarines, five auxiliary cruisers and some 440 merchant ships totaling 2,330,000 tons.

These results had greatly exceeded all expectations. The loss of nearly half the U-boats was mainly due to two factors; the initial inexperience of captains and crews, and technical weaknesses in the boats which revealed themselves only under the stress of depth charging. On the other hand, the boats had mostly survived the ordeal of long submersion; they had not had to surface for lack of air or battery power. Nevertheless, Dönitz faced the future with considerable misgivings and exerted all the pressure he could to get the French shipyards developed and expanded; for this would not only relieve the congestion in the yards at home but would also speed up repairs and turn around between patrols. The short but highly successful patrols in the autumn of 1940 resulted in the U-boats expending all their torpedoes and then returning to base more or less simultaneously; this caused a temporary lull in the Atlantic, much to the enemy's advantage.

Moreover, since the occupation of France, the British had switched their shipping routes from the English Channel—so near to the U-boat bases—to the waters round the Rockall Bank and the North Channel. To counter this move, the U-boats were dispatched to the approaches to the North Channel, often within sight of land, and disposed in scouting lines, zigzagging to search as much of the area as possible. Their problem was still the same. By keeping close to the coast they reduced the area to be watched, but a convoy would frequently reach the safety of the North Channel before the U-boats on either wing could come up with it. If the boats moved too far out to the west, their numerical weakness made it less likely that they would locate the enemy. Without their own long-range air reconnaissance, the boats were thrown back on their own resources, and had to find their own targets. Occasionally they did so with great success, as for instance on September 20, 1940, when Prien came upon Convoy HX 72, maintaining contact until five other boats could join him; between them they sank twelve ships and damaged another within two days.[2] As already mentioned, between the seventeenth and twentieth of October, eight boats were involved in an attack on two convoys almost simultaneously and, according to British reports, sank thirty-two ships and damaged four more.

A particular problem now was the visible reinforcement of the enemy's air patrols. Since the end of the summer more and more Sunderland flying boats had been sighted, even far out to the west, and it was clear that if ever the enemy managed to extend his air patrols over the whole Atlantic, the task of the U-boats would be made much harder, especially when attacking in daylight. The secret report, drawn up each month, showing the tonnage sunk by each boat for every day spent at sea, was very illuminating. For example when, in October, the U-boats located two convoys—SC 7 and HX 79—the score worked out at 920 tons per U-boat per day; but although the radio intercept service reported four convoys at sea in November, the U-boats never found them in the stormy weather and

---

[2] Convoy HX 72, consisting of forty-seven ships, was attacked between the twentieth and twenty-second of September and lost eleven ships.

the figure for that month dropped to 430 tons per boat per day. In December, *U 101* under her second captain, Mergersen, located Convoy HX 90. Other boats, including Prien's, joined in; fourteen ships were sunk and three others damaged,[3] and the monthly figures went up to 697 tons. But the crux of the whole problem was the *finding* of the convoys; once they were located, the wolf-pack tactics proved very effective.

An average of only four to six U-boats operated off the North Channel between November, 1940, and January, 1941 —a mere two hundred to three hundred men against the whole of England! And not only against England, for they also had to battle against the everlasting storms and the cold, groping their way blindly through heavy seas which would throw the torpedoes off course and send great waves thundering down on the bridge, so that attack was beyond the range of human capacity.

12

EAGLES WITHOUT WINGS

(January–February, 1941)

Nineteen forty, the year that had seen the first great convoy actions, ended with one solitary U-boat at sea. At Christmas the offensive against England was embodied in one man— Salman, commanding *U 52*. There was a vacuum in the Atlantic; the boats which had sunk or damaged fourteen ships out of Convoy HX 90 had returned to base for lack of torpedoes, while those which remained on patrol were unable to find any targets in the prevailing fog or in the mountainous seas of the winter gales.

To add to these difficulties, the enemy convoys were taking deliberate evasive action; the ships were avoiding any point where U-boats were known or suspected to be. The enemy was almost certainly taking bearings on every radio message transmitted by the U-boats. Enemy documents captured at the fall of France showed how much value Great Britain set upon her radio-direction-finding service. For self-protection all U-boats should ideally maintain complete radio silence; but because

[3] HX 90, consisting of thirty-five ships, actually lost ten ships sunk by U-boats, one ship sunk by aircraft and one ship damaged.

there was no air reconnaissance, the U-boat Command had to depend entirely on the boats' sighting reports for operational intelligence. At one stage all U-boats west of 15 degrees west were ordered to make such reports daily; but when it was realized that the enemy could and did take regular bearings on even these short signals, the U-boat captains were ordered to use their radio only at the beginning of an operation, or when sure that their positions had already been revealed to the enemy.

All this contributed materially to the perplexities facing the Command staff. There were no precedents to fall back on, for never before had the day-to-day operations of a U-boat campaign been controlled from a headquarters on land. The men responsible for the operational planning could never know exactly the position or condition of the boats at sea—whether they were on the surface or submerged, on passage or lying in wait, about to attack the enemy or being hunted by him. There was always the risk that any orders sent out might not reach the boats at the right time, or else could not be obeyed for some unforeseeable reason. The men at headquarters had to rely entirely on the commanding officers to do the best they could on their own initiative. The only alternative would have involved a great increase in the number of routine signals, but this was impractical for the captains' greatest chances of success lay in remaining undetected. The most that the U-boat Command could do was to bring the boats into the most likely area for a successful attack; once in contact with the enemy, the U-boats at sea were entirely cut off from all tactical control by the Command on shore.

Although five months had passed since the French bases had been occupied, the U-boats were still not getting any real tactical support from the *Luftwaffe*. There had been no difficulty in practicing cooperation in peacetime between U-boats and aircraft in the Baltic; but when war came the planes just were not available. Right through the summer and autumn of 1940 the U-boat Command had never had more than four planes at its disposal. The nearest approach to regular tactical cooperation had been achieved through personal contact with Air Group 40, which managed to allocate a single Focke-Wulff 200 every day for long-range reconnaissance—one single plane for the entire U-boat offensive! "I don't know what the *Luftwaffe* men do with their aircraft," said Dönitz. "It's always 'technical defects,' 'no planes.' I call them 'eagles without wings.' Every other service has its own air reconnaissance except the U-boats."

Once again he sent the commander in chief detailed recommendations for practical cooperation between air and sea. Grand Admiral Raeder gave these ideas his full support and authorized Dönitz to convey them personally to General Jodl, head of the operations division of the Supreme Command. When the two men met on January 2, 1941, they could not foresee the numerous, often dramatic and tragic occasions on which they were to face each other in the future. The general listened carefully as the admiral outlined his need for at least twelve long-range planes to be in the air at any one time. Then, on January 7, the unexpected happened. By order of the Führer AG 40 was placed unreservedly under the operational control of the U-boat Command for reconnaissance purposes. The FW 200s flown by this group were the only four-engined German planes capable of reaching longitude 20 degrees west.

Within ten days the aircraft had commenced operations and soon they made their first sighting report; but it led to nothing. The planes came back at nightfall and took off again at dawn, but failed to renew their contact with the convoy.

Now Göring, who had been on leave when AG 40 was allocated to the Navy, came back from his hunting trip. As anticipated, he was not pleased with the subordination of his planes to a naval command. However, the Führer's order of four weeks earlier still stood. The *Reichsmarschall* promptly invited the U-boat admiral to a conference at Pontoise, near Paris, where his private train stood with steam up in a siding near a tunnel. Dönitz accepted the invitation, although he foresaw that "the fat one" would demand the return of his planes. He reached Pontoise on February 7, 1941, accompanied by Captain Godt and his flag lieutenant. The pretentiousness of the Command train did not appeal to him and he became more reserved than usual. Sure enough, the *Reichsmarschall* wanted his planes back. "Everything that flies belongs to me," he exclaimed, adding with extravagant gestures that he would not tolerate the subordination of these aircraft to any command other than his own. The admiral, relying on the authority of the Führer's directive, became even more formal. Göring at first attempted to cajole him, then tried persuasion; but the louder he shouted, the more pompous he got, the cooler became the admiral, who steadfastly maintained that the transfer was essential, without however mentioning the Führer's directive, of which Göring was well aware. The fruitless interview ended with threats from Göring. "I strongly advise you to agree," he said, "for you may regret your refusal. . . ." The atmosphere was icy as they parted, the admiral curtly declining an invitation to dine.

On the day following this meeting, fate played one of its more ironical tricks. *U 37* sighted a Gibraltar convoy, shadowed it and, in accordance with instructions, "homed" the aircraft of AG 40 on to it by emitting beacon signals. The plan was working—but in the reverse order! Five FW 200s attacked successfully on the ninth of February. On the eleventh, *U 37* also sank some ships and then shadowed the convoy for the heavy cruiser *Admiral Hipper,* which had broken through the Denmark Strait and was now raiding shipping in the Atlantic. The cruiser raced at 32 knots through the night, sighted the convoy on the twelfth and played havoc with it. It was the first occasion in history that aircraft, surface ships and U-boats had fully cooperated against shipping.

This success, however, did not prevent the *Reichsmarschall* from getting his own way with the Führer. In future, although AG 40 operated exclusively for the U-boats, it was placed under the newly appointed air officer commanding Atlantic, who took up quarters near Lorient. Fortunately the A.O.C., Lieutenant Colonel Harlinghausen, was an old Navy pilot who thoroughly understood the U-boats' requirements and lost no time in establishing a smooth and friendly relationship with the U-boat Command. But the number of aircraft was quite inadequate, never more than two FW 200s being available on any one day near the North Channel, which at that time was the principal area of activity. The great extra loads of fuel which the planes needed for these sorties made every take-off a matter of life and death. As they rolled slowly along the runways, their fuselages creaking and groaning under the weight, the pilots were on edge until at last the overburdened machines would climb painfully into the air.

Yet their courage did not go unrewarded. On February 23, a reconnaissance by an FW 200 led *U 73* on to Convoy OB 288, and although the plane failed to locate the convoy again on the twenty-fourth, *U 73*'s sighting report brought four other U-boats in contact with the enemy during a severe storm. That night the four boats broke up the convoy, sinking nine ships; only defective torpedoes—the old complaint— prevented even better results.

A few days later Lieutenant Topp, a former "canoe" commander, located Convoy OB 289 while on his first patrol in *U 552* and brought two further boats in contact. He shadowed for three days, but failed to score owing to defective torpedoes, though his two colleagues sank three ships and damaged a fourth. OB 290, the next convoy to leave the North Channel, fared no better; it steamed right across the position occupied by Prien. The famous Kretschmer in *U 99* failed to reach the convoy in time, but Prien's sighting report brought up six FW 200s which sank nine ships. Prien himself, the "First of the Sea Wolves," sank 15,600 tons and damaged three other ships.

Meanwhile back at Kernevel, Lieutenant Oehrn submitted a dispassionate report on the value of air reconnaissance. The inaccuracy of air navigation, he said, was preventing the planes from relocating a convoy on the following day. Differences of up to 70 miles had occurred between fixes as signaled by the *Luftwaffe* and those reported by the radio intercept service. Planes from AG 40 had indeed made successful attacks as a result of beacon signals and shadowing reports from U-boats; but when the U-boats had acted on the aircraft's sighting reports they had usually missed the enemy ships altogether.

Having considered this diagnosis, Dönitz came to the regretful conclusion than in future it would not pay to "home" the U-boats on to convoys without some further check on the positional data in the aircraft's sighting reports.

13

THE END OF THREE "ACES"

(February, 1941)

In February, 1941, three U-boat "aces" were among those who returned to the Atlantic after a period of rest and repairs. Schepke in *U 100* sailed from a home base by the usual route across the North Sea and round the north of Scotland; Kretschmer in *U 99* sailed from Lorient. On February 20, Prien in *U 47* also sailed from Lorient after being delayed by some minor defects.

A few days later Prien was already far out at sea reporting an enemy convoy moving west at slow speed; he had been kept under by aircraft and had lost visual touch. Five hours later after he had found the convoy again, his reports came streaming in all night and the next day. Then in the evening he signaled, "Depth-charged. Contact lost. Am continuing pursuit. 22,000 tons sunk so far." Two days later he reported a new convoy, steering northwest. Other boats, including Kretschmer's, closed in and attacked after nightfall. At 4:24 A.M. on March 7, Prien was heard reporting the convoy's position, course and speed [1]—then nothing more. When later in the day all boats were ordered to report their position, *U 47* did not answer. Matz in *U 70* reported serious damage to his conning tower; Eckermann in *U A* also signaled that he was disengaging because of damage. Kretschmer intercepted these signals before being forced to dive by destroyers; while submerged he heard the depth charges that were destroying *U 70*. Matz and most of his crew were taken prisoner. Not until late in the afternoon was the ether silent. *U 99* surfaced very cautiously and received orders to look for a ship that had been torpedoed during the night; this was the *Terje Viken*, a floating whaling factory, one of the largest cargo ships in the world. The radio intercept service had decrypted a signal reporting that she had been torpedoed amidships and was making water rapidly; but since she was still afloat, Kretschmer was ordered to finish her off. On his way he heard the base calling Prien again and again: *"U 47, report your position."* But no answer came, and as the days went by, hopes dwindled.

Kretschmer searched in vain for the *Terje Viken*, but saw only a few small boats carrying survivors and a destroyer hovering in the neighborhood, which forced him to go deep. That night he intercepted a signal from *U 110* commanded by Lemp reporting a convoy from Canada eastward bound off Iceland. Kretschmer immediately gave chase and Schepke in *U 100* also joined in the hunt; both boats attacked by night, sweeping like ravening wolves through a flock of sheep. Kretschmer fired all his torpedoes; as he disengaged he found himself over the Lousy Bank, 180 miles west-southwest of the Faroes.

Meanwhile at Kernevel, Godt and his officers were gathered round the big chart; an urgent signal was sent to all U-boats near *U 110*'s convoy to report their position, but only one or two replied. *U 99* and *U 100* were not among them.

In 1946 the British government published an official report, "The Battle of the Atlantic," in which this passage occurs: [2]

---

[1] This was OB 293, which lost two ships and had two more damaged. *U 47* and *U 70* were both destroyed by the escorts.

[2] Published by H.M.S.O. 1946, Chapter 3, page 26.

In the course of March, 1941, six U-boats were liquidated in the North Atlantic, and among them were those commanded by the three "ace" Captains. Prien's boat (*U 47*) was sunk by depth-charges from the destroyer *Wolverine* on March 8th. There were no survivors. At 3 A.M. on March 17th, Schepke's boat (*U 100*), hunted and depth-charged, was forced to the surface, to be rammed and sunk by the destroyer *Vanoc*. Schepke himself was killed, crushed by the *Vanoc's* bows between his crumpled bridge and periscope. Half-an-hour later, Kretschmer's *U 99*, which had been operating with *U 100*, suffered the same fate at the hands of the destroyer *Walker*, Kretschmer himself being a survivor.

At the time of these events the British Press came out with big headlines: "U-boats of Kretschmer and Schepke sunk, Kretschmer taken prisoner." Shortly afterward a press photograph found its way to Kernevel, showing Kretschmer striding down HMS *Walker*'s gangway. In Germany the news could not be kept secret for long and Dönitz pressed for its release, but Hitler's headquarters would not agree. It was not until the end of April that the Supreme Command of the Armed Forces announced the loss of these two U-boats, and not until three weeks later that Prien's boat was admitted lost.

Otto Kretschmer was the second U-boat captain to win the oak leaves. He had been awarded the Knight's Cross on August 4, 1940, after sinking 117,000 tons and the British destroyer *Daring*. By November 4, he had topped the 200,000-ton mark, his successes including the auxiliary cruisers *Laurentic* of 18,724 tons and the 11,000-ton *Patroclus*. At the time of his capture he was credited with the sinking of three British destroyers and a total of 300,000 tons of shipping.

Schepke, before taking over *U 100*, had already made a name for himself in a "canoe," being awarded the Knight's Cross on September 24, 1940, and the oak leaves on December 20, when the total shipping sunk by him exceeded 200,000 tons.

When these losses were confirmed, the admiral's reserve and aloofness betrayed to his closest colleagues how deeply they affected him. He himself dictated the obituary notice on Prien, which was issued as an order of the day:

The hero of Scapa Flow has made his last patrol. We of the U-boat Service proudly mourn and salute him and his men

. . . they have become for us a symbol of our hard and un-
shakable will to victory against England. In this spirit we
shall continue the fight.

14

FROM GREENLAND TO FREETOWN

(April–May, 1941)

There was no slackening in the Battle of the Atlantic. When
the convoys began to make wide detours to the north, the
U-boats followed them as far as the sixtieth parallel, continuing to sink and damage ships. Then, when a lull ensued
in these northern latitudes, the U-boats found more shipping
southwest of Rockall, whither the enemy had shifted his route
once more.

The loss of four boats in the north, including those of his
three "ace" captains, made Dönitz wonder whether the enemy
was using some new weapon, or whether these losses were
fortuitous. Commanders returning from the high latitudes
were reporting unusually strong escorts, but could not tell him
anything about any new anti-submarine measures. Following
on the wall chart what he presumed to be the new route for
the convoys, the admiral sent his boats in two pincer movements in a southwesterly direction well out into the Atlantic,
beyond 25 degrees west, where he could expect to find weaker
patrols and escort forces. He believed that the earlier losses
could be regarded as normal, but he only made up his mind
about this when the boats had been operating in their new
area up to the middle of April, during which time they located
Convoy SC 26, from which they sank or damaged fourteen
ships in one night. Then he gradually moved them back to
more easterly areas, until once again they formed patrol lines
between Iceland and Rockall, and off St. Kilda.

The full effect of the German wartime building program
now began to be felt, as new boats joined the operational flotillas. Many an officer with operational experience in the
"canoes" now found himself appointed to command one of the
new and larger U-boats. Among them was "Savvy" Krech, the
first and only possessor of a U-boat aquarium, in which every
fish bore the name of a crowned head or prime minister of

countries at war with Germany. "Wilhelmina," a handsome, tubby little goldfish, met her end during the cleaning of her bowl, "when she slipped out of the spoon into the bilges and could not be found," while "Churchill," a small but temperamental pirate fish, made three patrols before succumbing; whereupon he received suitable interment, being ceremonially sealed into an alcohol-filled glass tube which was hung under the lamp in the wardroom.

From the thousand men or so who had sailed on the early patrols, there had at last evolved the wolf packs for which the admiral had waited so impatiently; for it was not until July, 1941, that the number of operational U-boats exceeded the forces available at the outbreak of war. As the year advanced, the battleground at sea shifted from point to point over the wide Atlantic. In the early summer the focus was on the northern and eastern areas; from midsummer till autumn it moved once again to the east, and from then until November it once more covered the whole ocean east of the Pan-American Security Zone.

Now, however, when a U-boat located a convoy, the captain no longer attacked at once, but made shadowing reports to base and sent out beacon signals while waiting for the other boats to close for a concerted attack. Sometimes during these actions the contact would pass from one boat to another, as each in turn was forced under by the air or surface escorts. When one boat was compelled to break off, another would spring into the breach, and so the battle raged, conditioned on both sides by such varied factors as wind and weather, human intelligence and technical efficiency.

Britain still stood alone, while the United States maintained a so-called neutrality which was more akin to nonbelligerency, American sympathy for the cause of their British cousins being plain for all to see. The slick formula of "cash and carry" had been replaced by "lend lease," which was to play so vital a part in the war. In his fireside chats Roosevelt had spoken of the rattlesnake which must be dispatched before it could raise its head to strike, and of the pipeline that one must lend to the neighbor whose house is on fire. American ships, arms and supplies streamed toward Britain to replace her losses at Dunkirk.

Meanwhile the British shipyards were turning out more and more corvettes and frigates, specially designed for convoy-escort work—light, moderately fast and easily maneuverable vessels, equipped with the latest underwater detection gear and depth-charge throwers, and well able to ride out the Atlantic gales. For all that, nothing had yet been evolved to prevent the U-boats from pressing home their attacks. Aircraft bombs, depth charges, star shells of a new and brilliant type called "snowflakes," guns, the ram, mines, as-dic—most of these were essentially methods that had already been used in the First World War. Radar, of course, was still in its infancy and was not yet in operational use.[1]

As more of the larger U-boats became available it was possible to extend the sphere of operations. Dönitz began to send these to the west coast of Africa, in order to strike suddenly where the concentration of ships was heavy but the defenses were weak. Among the first to operate below the equator were Lieutenants Oesten and Schewe, respectively commanding *U 106* and *105*.

U 106 sailed on the twenty-sixth of February, and day after day she headed southward, passing scores of brightly lighted neutral ships, each with its national colors boldly painted on its sides; they were mostly Spanish or Portuguese and the U-boat gave them a wide berth. One day at noon, the clear blue outlines of mountains appeared over the horizon and that night the long gray shape of the U-boat slipped unobtrusively into a Spanish harbor, making fast alongside a German cargo ship which had taken refuge there when the war came.[2] Everything was ready, down to the last detail; the boat was hardly alongside before the fuel hoses were dangling above her. There were whispered greetings, the sound of moving feet and the click of metal on steel; then the hoses stiffened as the oil began to flow through them. A man came swiftly down the Jacob's ladder—a portly gentleman in a light tropical suit with yellow shoes; he was the agent of a German shipping company whose job it was to think of everything— fresh fruit and vegetables, fresh meat, eggs, bread—all collected unostentatiously. Now, over an iced beer in the hot wardroom of the U-boat, he passed on some useful information.

By dawn the U-boat was already far out at sea again. Some days later Oesten sighted his first ship, a blue funnel liner, zigzagging toward him. With some difficulty he read her name—*Memnon*. He hit her with two torpedoes and she sank in fifteen minutes. Several days then passed without any

[1] In January, 1941, the British had already begun to fit radar in A/S vessels and aircraft.

[2] The Canaries: the Spanish Government at first connived at this infringement of neutrality, but it was stopped by British diplomatic pressure in July, 1941.

further sighting; now they were near the equator, with barely a shadow cast by the conning tower. Then one day, as they crossed the line, a procession of strange figures emerged from the conning tower hatch. There were Neptune and his Court, Thetis the Beautiful—her legs somewhat hairy, but with all the right curves in the right places—and all the traditional characters to see that justice was done. A gay party this, and but for the strict watch by the lookouts, peaceful as though on a luxury cruise in some liner.

A few days later they unexpectedly met with Convoy SL 68 bound for England from Sierra Leone, in whose port of Freetown all convoys assembled. As Oesten took up his position within sight of the mastheads, a fresh trade wind from the northeast swept yellow veils of very fine dust along the surface of the water. They felt it on their skin, it gritted between their teeth, found its way into the lenses of their glasses and coated the deck and the bridge; it covered the gun and was drawn through the ventilators into the boat's interior; and it prevented an immediate attack, as Oesten remarked in his log. In time, he counted four destroyers in the escort, together with an auxiliary cruiser and the battleship *Malaya,* which had been attached to the convoy after an earlier one had been severely mauled by a German surface ship cooperating with U-boats.[3] The convoy steered westward, then turned north to pass to the east of the Cape Verde Islands; Oesten knew that *U 105* was not very far west of the Cape Verdes and accordingly he sent out short reports and beacon signals to "home" her on to the convoy, while he himself shadowed the ships as best he could in the teeth of the trade wind.

By chance, Oesten had at his disposal a superb navigational team in Captain Kamenz of the Lloyd Line and Captain Wunderlich of Hapag. Kamenz belonged to the famous auxiliary cruiser *Atlantis* and had sailed one of her prizes to Japan. He had got back to Germany via Russia and in accordance with instructions, he was being returned to the raider. When Captain Rogge next contacted the supply ship *Nordmark* in mid-Atlantic he would expect to pick up his navigating officer. Wunderlich, of the rival shipping line, was the real navigator of *U 106* and between them, these experts worked out the U-boat's position to within a pin's head. In *U 105* Schewe's navigation was equally accurate, so that

---

[3] This refers to the attack by the German heavy cruiser *Hipper* on Convoy SLS 64 on February 12, 1941, when seven ships out of the nineteen in this unescorted convoy were sunk.

despite some technical failure in radio communication between the two U-boats, they were able to keep perfect
contact with the convoy and to play it off from one to the
other in faultless team work. This operation covered a distance of 1,200 miles from Cape Verde to the Canaries and
lasted eight days and nights, beginning with the sinking of a
lone Dutchman who happened upon them. At times the two
U-boats would steam alongside each other as the captains
discussed the tactics of the next night's attack; then they
would separate in the haze to chase once more after the
convoy and its screen of destroyers and the massive *Malaya*.

The visibility was appalling. Whenever the convoy altered
course, the ships would disappear from view in a matter of
seconds. The destroyers, sweeping tirelessly in wide circles
on each flank, kept emerging unexpectedly out of the haze.
It was one long game of hide-and-seek, until at last *U 106*
swept into the middle of the ships at dusk, just as they were
outlined against the last rays of the setting sun. The huge
targets overlapped each other, so that a salvo of four torpedoes
scored four hits, but there was no time to confirm the sinkings, for the destroyers came racing up and depth charges
began to crash all around. As the noise of the destroyers' propellers grew rapidly fainter, Oesten ordered the reserve
torpedoes to be loaded; when he surfaced the convoy had
disappeared. He immediately gave chase, but on increasing to
full speed, the bows suddenly began to sink and only quick
action caught the U-boat just as she was beginning to dive
of her own accord. They soon found that a crack in the
chain locker had caused a forward tank to flood. They had
to blow the tank every twenty minutes; then as the crack
widened, every fifteen, and finally, every ten minutes.

Night after night the two U-boats kept up with the convoy,
whose commodore ordered the weirdest maneuvers turning
through 90 degrees to the east, back to the west and even
south for a spell, then back on his tracks; but all in vain, for
the two wolves continued to harry his flock. If one U-boat
were forced to dive, or held up while loading spare torpedoes,
the other would take up the chase. At first the *Malaya* had
separated from the convoy during the nights, for in the
darkness there was nothing she could do to help and indeed
she stood in just as much danger as the ships she was guard-
ing; but later the losses became so heavy that she remained
with the convoy all the time. The captain of *U 106* sighted
her, overlapped by several ships, just as he was making his
final attack. After firing the last two torpedoes he heard the

explosions but could not see what he had hit; but there followed a unique firework display. The battleship fired star shells from all her guns, large and small, which lit up the sea from one horizon to the other, and in the middle of them all burst a rocket which exploded in colored streamers in every direction. It was the signal for the convoy to disperse —the last resource to prevent further loss; the triumph of the two wolves was complete. They had sunk ten ships and damaged seven others.[4] With all torpedoes expended, they met once more south of the Canaries and then went their separate ways. *U 106* made for the supply ship *Nordmark* (Captain Grau) which for over half a year had remained in position 31 degrees west, 5 degrees north, replenishing no less than forty-five German ships of war. Here Captain Kamenz took his leave and embarked in *Nordmark*, to await the arrival of the raider *Atlantis*, while *U 106* took on fuel, food and torpedoes. This U-boat received new orders to watch the entrance to Rio de Janeiro harbor, to pick up the German Lloyd s.s. *Lech* and to escort her through the Pan-American Security Zone.

U 106 did not return to Lorient until June, having been at sea for four months. Bent and battered, pocked with rust, long streamers of green seaweed clinging to her deck and her keel, she came wearily alongside the old depot ship *Ysère*. Not until he reported to Admiral Dönitz did Oesten learn that one of his last two torpedoes had actually struck the *Malaya*. With a hole in her bows the battleship had limped slowly across the Atlantic, escorted by two destroyers, and was now in dock in New York.[5]

Looking at the balance sheet of the campaign in southern waters, there was good reason to be satisfied. After *U A* (Lieutenant Commander Cohausz) and *U 65* (Lieutenant Commander von Stockhausen) had carried out the first patrols there in 1940, there had been a pause, for the U-boats in the North Atlantic could achieve more in less time. However, the dispatch of some of the larger boats to the West African coast in February and March, 1941, had paid good dividends. They kept well out to the west while on passage

[4] Convoy SL 68 consisted of fifty-eight ships. Between the seventeenth and the nineteenth of March, 1941, seven of these were sunk between the latitudes of 14°30′N and 18°16′N. The convoy was dispersed to avoid further losses.

[5] After being hit by a torpedo from *U 106*, HMS *Malaya* proceeded under her own steam to Trinidad and then to New York, where she arrived on April 6, 1941, for repairs.

southward, remained four or five weeks in the Freetown area on patrol and then returned. They would carry fourteen torpedoes below decks and six to eight more in pressure-tight containers on the upper casing. Moreover it was found that they could greatly economize in fuel by cruising at 7 knots, setting the starboard diesel to half-speed and using the starboard electric motor as a dynamo to charge the batteries, while the port motor drew from the batteries sufficient power for slow or half-speed. Replenishing fuel, food and torpedoes from auxiliary cruisers or surface supply ships, they could remain at sea for the equivalent of two consecutive patrols, while saving some 4,000 miles journeying to and from their base. The supply ships were the *Charlotte Schliemann* and *Corrientes*, which had lain in the Canaries.

The figures of sinkings fully justified these measures. *U 38* sank eight ships, *U 103, 105* and *124* twelve each, *U 106* ten and *U 107* fourteen. *U 69,* a 500-tonner, mined the entrances to Lagos and Tacoradi and also sank six ships. In recognition of their services, Lieutenant Commanders Schütze and Liebe received the oak leaves clasp and Lieutenants Metzler, Schewe, Oesten, Hessler, Winter and Jochen Mohr all won the Knight's Cross.

As a direct result of these attacks in distant waters, the British instituted a large-scale search which ended in the destruction of the five German surface supply ships *Belchen, Egerland, Lothringen, Esso* and *Gedania*.[6] This was a heavy blow and immediate alternative methods of supplying the U-boats at sea had to be devised. It was understood that negotiations were in progress between the German Admiralty and the Vichy French Government about Dakar, but no one knew what the French would decide to do, and Dönitz felt it was safer to expect nothing from them. The only supply ships available over the next few months would be the *Kota Pinang* and the *Python,* but until they reached the South Atlantic the U-boats would not be able to refuel at sea at all; it was indeed questionable how long those two ships would survive. The destruction of five predecessors at widely separated points in the middle of the Atlantic was too striking to dismiss the possibility that the enemy had broken into the German naval codes, or that there had been a breakdown in security. In view of these supply problems, the admiral decided not to send any more boats to the south for the time

6 All these supply ships were sunk or captured in the Atlantic in the first fortnight of June, 1941.

being, and Lieutenant Hardegen in *U 123*, who was already there, was given new orders.

Meanwhile, as the number of operational boats increased, attacks on the North Atlantic convoys continued with unabated vigor. Between March and May, according to British data, the enemy lost 142 ships totaling 818,000 tons through U-boat action, which with further losses through air attack, surface ships and mines raised the total to 412 ships of nearly 1,700,000 tons.

At this time Dönitz was carefully applying the controlled-pack tactics which had begun in the autumn of 1940. As he himself said, "We must stay in one place only so long as we can assemble, maneuver and fight in that area. As soon as the enemy reinforces his defenses to the point where we can no longer form packs, there is no point in staying in those waters." He had in mind several reports of convoys escorted by eight or more destroyers, also of permanent air escort of convoys far out to the west. It was argued that, despite his irregular scattering of convoy routes over the whole North Atlantic, the enemy could not avoid concentrations of shipping at certain nodal points. One such point, the North Channel, was no longer feasible for U-boat attacks, being too strongly patrolled, but there was another off Newfoundland where the defenses were still weak.

Early in May a group of five U-boats already stationed off the south of Iceland was moved further west, where it attacked a convoy and in a long-drawn-out action sank nine ships and damaged three others. Two more boats were sent to reinforce them off Cape Farewell in South Greenland, and the whole group gradually moved to the southwest, where it was hoped to find an even greater concentration of shipping. The group located HX 126, broke through its defenses and again sank nine ships. One of the captains in this "West Group" was "Parsifal" Wohlfarth, on his first patrol in *U 556*. He had already decided it was time to return to base when he sighted another convoy and ran in to attack. He aimed two torpedoes at a tanker and set her on fire, whereupon the convoy hastily altered course and all ships launched smoke floats to cover their retreat. In the general confusion one ship steamed right across the line of his torpedo tubes and was promptly sunk. With no torpedoes and very little fuel left, Wohlfarth resumed his interrupted journey home.

At this moment he, like the rest of the "West Group," was only a few hundred miles away from the *Bismarck,* which had just broken out into the Atlantic. "Parsifal" Wohlfarth had a special and personal affection for *Bismarck,* as we shall see.

15

BISMARCK AND THE U-BOATS

(May, 1941)

On the twenty-first of May, 1941, the 40,000-ton battleship *Bismarck* and the cruiser *Prinz Eugen* sailed on a raiding expedition into the Atlantic. While the squadron was still on passage, it was located from the air and all available British forces were dispatched to intercept and destroy it. The battleships *Scharnhorst* and *Gneisenau* were already in Brest, although they had suffered some bomb damage; if they could be reinforced by *Bismarck* and *Prinz Eugen* it would mean that the Germans could put into the Atlantic a battle squadron of three brand new battleships and a heavy cruiser. In that event no one could tell what would happen to the British convoys, for even the mighty British fleet would be hard put to it to furnish adequate escorts.

Admiral Sir John Tovey, Commander in Chief of the British Home Fleet, fully aware of this danger, sent every available big ship in pursuit of *Bismarck* and *Prinz Eugen;* on the morning of May 24 a squadron composed of *Hood* and *Prince of Wales* made contact with the Germans after they had been located by *Suffolk.* After a brief exchange of fire a gigantic pillar of flame shot up between *Hood's* masts; two or three seconds later she broke in two and for a moment her bow and stern could be seen sticking vertically up out of a cloud of heavy black smoke, before she finally disappeared.

Bismarck, however, had not escaped unscathed and a broad streak of oil began to spread out in her wake as she continued her course into the Atlantic. It was not long before she altered course for St. Nazaire to effect repairs, leaving *Prinz Eugen* to act independently in the Atlantic. In the course of the day, Admiral Lütjens, flying his flag in *Bismarck,* called for a close cordon of U-boats to be stationed across his line of advance, through which he proposed to lure his pursuers. Of the six boats which accordingly took up positions some 450 miles west of St. Nazaire, two had no torpedoes and very little fuel, but it was considered that their presence might be of some help.

Neither the British nor the Germans were quite clear as to the real position. Admiral Lütjens did not know that *Suffolk* had lost radar contact with *Bismarck;* nor was he aware that for some time the British forces had steamed in the wrong direction under the illusion that *Bismarck* was making for Norway. Believing that *Suffolk* was still in radar contact, Lütjens saw no reason for maintaining radio silence, and on the twenty-fifth he made a detailed situation report. The British took D/F[1] bearings on this transmission, realized their mistake and turned their ships around. An immediate air search was ordered and on the twenty-sixth a Catalina reconnaissance plane sighted, through haze and low cloud, a dark shape ploughing through the heavy seas—the *Bismarck*.

It now became very clear to Admiral Sir John Tovey that he could not hope to overtake the German ship unless her speed could be reduced. His last hope lay in the Gibraltar squadron, consisting of the battle cruiser *Renown*, the aircraft carrier *Ark Royal* and the cruisers *Sheffield* and *Dorsetshire*, which had been hastily ordered northward; actually it was the *Ark Royal's* planes which alone were capable of attacking *Bismarck* with torpedoes and so reducing her speed that the main British fleet could catch up with her. These aircraft were the last card in the English hand.

It was blowing a gale from the northwest and the seas were running steep and high. The weather had prevented Wohlfarth in *U 556* from getting into the ordered position as second from the left wing of the line, when suddenly, on the evening of the twenty-sixth, his lookouts reported enemy warships in sight. Wohlfarth crash-dived and raised his periscope in time to see *Renown* and *Ark Royal* steaming straight toward him, their huge gray hulls plunging deep into the heavy seas. *Renown* was burying her bows and then throwing cascades of water high in the air; walls of spray were sweeping over her forward turrets smothering the whole ship in a white cloud. *Ark Royal* several times dipped until her flight deck seemed to be touching the water; Wohlfarth could see the planes on her deck with their engines running. The ships were almost on top of him now, ahead and astern. He had no need to maneuver for attack—all he had to do was press the

---

[1] D/F—an abbreviation for direction-finding bearings.

firing buttom for the forward and after tubes—but he had no more torpedoes! Such a chance would never recur—a battleship and an aircraft carrier on a straight course, without escorting destroyers, passing in front of a U-boat's torpedo tubes. And those tubes were empty! This fact was decisive in *Bismarck's* destiny. With bitterness in his heart, Wohlfarth gazed at the two huge targets wallowing in the giant waves. There was a special relationship between the *Bismarck,* the largest and latest battleship in the world, and the little 500-ton *U 556,* for *Bismarck* was the U-boat's "godchild."

Many months earlier, *Bismarck* had been exercising in the Baltic where Wohlfarth also was working up his crew in the new boat. One day the U-boat passed the battleship and Wohlfarth, who had his own sense of humor, signaled: "Personal from Captain to Captain. A fine ship you've got!" This did not seem to go down too well; the answer came back smartly and formally: "From *Commander* to Captain, report name of commanding officer." Oh Lord! thought Wohlfarth, now I've done it! His answer was: "From Captain to Captain. You try to do this!" Then he promptly dived out of sight.

Some time later he drew up a magnificent certificate of "godfatherhood," expressed in suitable terms of friendly admiration, in which *U 556* undertook the sponsorship of her big sister and pledged herself always to watch over her. Armed with this document, Wohlfarth paid a formal call on Captain Lindemann, the captain of *Bismarck.* Thus a friendship was born amid laughter between the two ships' companies and Wohlfarth, on passing *Bismarck* on his way to his first patrol, signaled: "Personal from Captain to Captain. When you follow me don't worry. I'll see that you come to no harm." But it was not to be, for now, as he watched the enemy ships disappearing in the dusk, he realized that without torpedoes he could not keep his promise. As soon as the enemy was out of sight, he surfaced and hastily reported: "Enemy sighted, one battleship, one carrier, course 115°, gridsquare BE 5382." That meant 48° north, 16°20′ west. He had tried to shadow the ships as long as the heavy seas would allow. At nine o'clock that night he intercepted a signal from *Bismarck,* in position 47° N, 14°50′W, reporting that her rudder was out of action from a torpedo hit. A few minutes later the U-boat Command came up with: "Emergency. All boats with torpedoes proceed toward *Bismarck* at full speed." But what could full speed be on a night like this? After midnight one U-boat did report momentary contact with "ships in action," but the heavy clouds and rain soon blotted out the gun flashes. During that night *Bismarck* held off the attacking destroyers with her guns; she was now 420 miles west of Brest—just outside the effective range of the *Luftwaffe*.

At about 7 A.M. on May 27, Admiral Lütjens asked for a U-boat to pick up *Bismarck's* log, and it was Wohlfarth who was ordered to close the battleship; but he did not receive the order as he had dived to avoid aircraft; when eventually he picked up the signal at ten o'clock, it was too late. *Bismarck's* last action began at 8:47 A.M. when the battleships *Rodney* and *King George V* opened fire. *Bismarck's* third salvo straddled *Rodney* without hitting and a few minutes later *Norfolk* joined in, so that *Bismarck*—an easy, almost motionless target—came under the concentrated fire of three ships. Fighting to the last, she was gradually shot to pieces. *Dorsetshire* came in close as *Bismarck's* fire began to slacken, and *Rodney* fired torpedoes but they missed. At about ten o'clock *Bismarck* ceased fire. Although still afloat, she was nothing but a wreck; her masts and funnel had gone, her upper works were crushed and riddled, her gun muzzles pointed lifelessly in every direction, and heavy black smoke poured out amidships.

Then *Rodney* fired nine broadsides at close range, the shells bursting on the target three and four at a time. *Rodney* fired her last two torpedoes, one of which hit; but *Bismarck* still floated. At ten fifteen the British C-in-C had to disengage as *King George V* was running short of fuel; as he left he ordered *Bismarck* to be torpedoed again. *Dorsetshire* fired torpedoes from both sides into the wreck, and finally, at ten forty, *Bismarck* rolled silently over on her side and went down with her flag still flying. The battle was over. Two officers and just over one hundred men were picked up by the British. U-boats combed the area for four whole days, but all they found were three men on a raft.

16

THE PROBLEMS MULTIPLY

(Spring, 1941)

Bismarck was sunk, but her supply ships were still at large in the Atlantic, and no time was lost in using them to refuel the "West Group." One U-boat after another came up to lie astern of the tankers, drawing in the oil through their long fuel lines. Claus Korth in *U 93* was one of the many captains who refueled in this way, but as he was in the middle of doing so, the tanker signaled: "Enemy destroyer in sight" and almost at the same moment the air was filled with bursting shells. In a trice Korth had disconnected the fuel lines and had begun to dive; through his periscope he could see the destroyer's shells crashing into the tanker's sides, as her crew took to the boats. The one-sided action was soon over; Korth had no chance to counterattack, for the enemy kept carefully out of his range and disappeared as soon as the tanker had sunk.

Korth surfaced and took on board the fifty survivors who, added to his own crew of forty-three, crowded together in every compartment of the U-boat. There was barely room to stand up, let alone lie down. As Korth began his return journey he ran into a convoy, but he reluctantly decided that his boat was too crowded to go to action stations, and he let the convoy go. Back in Kernevel, however, the admiral rebuked him severely. "What on earth have survivors got to do with it? You were sent out there to fight! Our biggest headache is to *find* the enemy. You find him and then you let him get away, just because you have survivors on board. You could at least have shadowed for the other boats. . . ."

"Never mind, Claus," said the flag lieutenant, as the chastened officer emerged from the admiral's office. "It's not as bad as all that. Come in here." He led the way into the operations room. "We're really up against it. Look at this—it's a new system of charting the dispositions of all the enemy's warships and merchant ships." He pointed to a number of regional charts. "Information from every source is entered here," he said, "U-boat signals, air-reconnaissance reports, messages from the intercept service and from agents, weather reports from trawlers—everything of interest sighted and reported by German or Italian U-boats or decrypted from enemy messages. It also shows what we think the enemy is likely to have picked up from our boats' sighting reports, or from his own aircraft sighting reports, or from his secret agents. All this is necessary because otherwise we can't find the enemy. You yourselves can't find him—except by chance; and we cannot run a successful campaign on mere chance."

The *Bismarck* action had shown that the enemy had a radar-location device similar to that of the Germans; and although in June and again in July, German aircraft had reported convoys giving cross bearings for the U-boats to follow, the convoy in each case had taken evasive action before the boats could reach it. It was still uncertain whether this was due to chance, or whether the enemy had managed to escape by using radar or by taking D/F bearings on German radio transmissions.

The German Admiralty now required another ten or twelve boats up north for attacks on the Allied convoys to Russia, but Dönitz protested that he could not spare even one boat from the Atlantic; he maintained that every ton of cargo or shipping destroyed in the Atlantic was potentially a ton lost to Russia. "Our job is to sink ships quicker than the enemy can replace them," he reiterated, "and to do so where it is easiest for us. To split up our forces now will reduce the sinkings. Today each boat is achieving less than in the autumn of 1940."

Another worry was the drop in U-boat construction. A shortage of copper was given as the reason for the production rate falling from twenty-five to fifteen boats every month, but Dönitz would not accept this excuse so long as any copper roofing or bronze statues of doubtful artistic value remained in Europe. The time taken for repairs was also unsatisfactory; out of every 100 days, a U-boat was spending 65 in the dockyards and only 35 at sea. The proportions should have been 40 and 60 days, or even 50-50, but at this time no fewer than 800 dockyard workers were actually being withdrawn from work on U-boats to reconstruct the *Hipper's* fuel tanks. By an error, one of Dönitz's many minutes on this subject was returned to him, with a revealing marginal comment: "We don't want to become a Navy of U-boats." That summed up the Admiralty's attitude.

Some commanders now reported that even the enemy merchant ships were carrying detecting gear. One of these commanders was Endrass *(U 46)*, who had been Prien's first lieutenant at Scapa Flow, and had since proved himself an outstanding captain. Having sighted a fine large tanker, he approached her as night began to fall. He was quite confident that he had not been observed, but even as he closed the tanker she began to move in short, sharp zigzags; just as he fired his torpedoes she turned straight toward him; it was evident that she was fitted with asdic. The two adversaries circled round each other until dawn, but then one of Endrass's diesel couplings began to give trouble and he had to abandon the chase while his engineers wrestled for fourteen hours to put the damage right.

The U-boat captains were also worried about the poor performance of their torpedoes. Lieutenant "Recke" Lehmann-Willenbrock was one of many who complained on this score. One ship, he said, required four torpedoes and also some rounds from the gun before she would sink. What was needed was an effective noncontact pistol which would explode the torpedo immediately under the target and thus cause far greater damage than a contact torpedo.

When the search for targets in the extreme western waters proved fruitless, the U-boats were brought back to more easterly areas, since it was preferable to make sure of locating the convoys even under more difficult conditions of attack, than to miss them altogether in undefended waters. Moreover there were improved prospects of cooperation with the *Luftwaffe*. On taking up his post as A.O.C. Atlantic, Lieutenant Colonel Harlinghausen, as an experienced sailor, had immediately understood what the U-boats required. The convoys sailing between Britain and Sierra Leone were going so far out to the west that the German aircraft could only shadow them for a few minutes before shortage of fuel forced them to turn back. All they had time to do was to send out beacon signals; even if they were able to make a proper sighting report, their navigational fixes frequently lacked accuracy, while their beacon-signal transmissions often did not last long enough for the U-boats to get a proper fix. Harlinghausen now proposed a new system whereby, upon sighting a convoy at the extreme limit of his plane's endurance, the pilot transmitted beacon signals to the A.O.C., who warned the U-boat Command to notify the U-boats. All this required only a few minutes. The aircraft then continued to emit beacon signals which the U-boats could pick up and, before leaving the convoy, the pilot would also signal his position.

This system soon proved its worth. With the help of the aircraft the U-boats were able to maintain contact with a convoy for as long as eight days in succession. The sinking figures rose still higher.[1]

Another source of worry at this time was that the U-boat captains' reports of sinkings were proving less reliable than in the early days. The efficiency of the A/S escorts compelled the captains to deliver their attacks swiftly and then clear out, which provided no opportunity to check the running time of their torpedoes with stop watches or to establish the size of a sinking ship through the periscope. The men on the admiral's staff who kept the secret records began to discover, for example, that the tonnage of the Gibraltar convoys, which consisted mainly of smaller ships, was often overestimated by the attacking U-boats.

One group of boats had been patrolling for three weeks to the northwest of Ireland without finding a single ship; on the other hand, reports were coming in from all quarters of strong enemy air activity. How was it that the British were suddenly able to reinforce their air patrols in the Atlantic? What conclusions should be drawn from the fact that U-boats approaching a convoy at night were very quickly attacked by destroyers deliberately detached for this purpose? The boats trying to attack the Gibraltar convoys, for example, found that the air and surface escorts had been considerably strengthened. The enemy had made much progress in the technique of denying approach to the U-boats; by day the outer screen prevented them from getting near enough to the close screen to identify the layout of the convoy as a whole, and by night the outer screen moved inward to reinforce the close screen, so forming an impenetrable cordon round the ships.

It was evident that the principal menace lay in the enemy's use of radar, and Commander Meckel, the Staff Communications Officer at U-boat headquarters, was called in to suggest possible antidotes. Meckel's first proposal was to find some way of covering the boats' hulls with a material that would absorb the radar impulses. He went on to say that a search receiver would have to be found that would register the enemy's radar transmissions; there might be some possibility of installing a search radar in the boats such as was used in destroyers and big ships, but he thought that this

---

[1] For Great Britain the summer of 1941 was perhaps the most anxious period of the whole war, for the volume of imports reaching the United Kingdom was steadily diminishing.

would have a very limited range in U-boats because of lack of height in the aerial. On being asked if it was possible that enemy aircraft were also using radar to locate surfaced boats, Meckel thought it highly improbable, as the necessary equipment would be too heavy for an aircraft to carry. He then requested and received permission to discuss these problems with the Admiralty experts in Berlin.

17

AMERICA BEGINS TO MOVE

(June—December, 1941)

On June 20, 1941, just two days before Germany went to war with Russia, there came an unexpected signal from Lieutenant Mützelburg in *U 203*, reporting that he had sighted the American battleship *Texas* in the blockade area. What did this mean? Why should an American capital ship be in an area which the Americans themselves had forbidden to their own ships? Was this a deliberate provocation? Within twenty-four hours an important signal was sent to all U-boats: "By order of the Führer all incidents with United States ships must be avoided in the coming weeks. Until further notice, attacks may not be made on battleships, cruisers and aircraft carriers unless definitely identified as hostile. Warships steaming at night without lights are not necessarily hostile."

This order meant the virtual cessation of all night attacks in the blockade area on convoy escorts or on A/S groups and destroyers sailing independently; for by night it was quite impossible to distinguish neutral from foe. The order remained in force even when, in July, President Roosevelt ordered the U.S. Navy to attack all submarines. Nor was it canceled in October, when Knox, the Secretary of the Navy, spoke unequivocally at a press conference on the sinking of German U-boats by U.S. warships.

On September 4, *U 652* (Fraatz) reported having been attacked with depth charges by U.S. destroyers 180 miles southwest of Reykjavik, and that he had fired two torpedoes in self-defense. This was known as the *Greer* incident. Hitler sanctioned the captain's action on the grounds that self-defense was permissible, but his ban on taking reprisals still stood. On the twentieth of September a U.S. escort vessel attacked a U-boat east of Greenland and some days later another U-boat sighted a patrolling aircraft with U.S. markings. On October 18 the U.S. destroyer *Kearney* attacked a U-boat, and the *Reuben James* did the same on October 31. Thus there could be no doubt whatever that the neutral United States was engaged in open hostilities against German U-boats, although war had not been declared between the two countries.

Five simultaneous search patrols were now dispatched to the less-protected areas of the Western Atlantic. The first blow was struck at the beginning of September, when the boats of the first wave encountered Convoy SC 42 close in to the coast of Greenland. Despite heavy air and surface escorts, they went straight into the attack and in an action lasting several days they sank no less than twenty ships.[1] A few days later other boats attacked a second convoy, SC 44, and after a two-day action claimed to have sunk seven ships, of which the British admitted four;[2] then the fog came down and contact was lost. Atmospheric conditions played havoc with radio communications at this point, so that only five of the boats managed to send the news of the action which was so anxiously awaited at Kernevel.

Soon after this episode the boats of the second wave located Convoy SC 48 and, despite strong opposition from the escorts, managed to sink nine ships.[3] But as October turned into November the weather steadily deteriorated; it was as hard for the U-boats to attack as it was for the convoys to keep together. In November, owing to bad weather, one convoy had 26 stragglers out of 43 ships; and the sinking figures went steadily down. Against a loss of 53 ships—over 200,000 tons—in September, the British Admiralty listed only 32 ships lost in October, 13 in November and 25 in December, 1941.

At this point orders came from the naval staff to concentrate the U-boats for the time being on Gibraltar and the Mediterranean, because of the British offensive in Libya. Dönitz realized at once that this meant abandoning the Bat-

[1] Sixteen ships totaling 68,000 tons were sunk out of this convoy of sixty-five ships on September 10 and 11, 1941.

[2] SC 44 consisted of fifty-four ships of which four were sunk on the nineteenth and twentieth of September, 1941.

[3] This occurred on the fifteenth and sixteenth of October, 1941.

tle of the North Atlantic until further notice. His first attempt to send U-boats into the Mediterranean, in November 1939, had been a failure and since then he had not had sufficient forces available to repeat it. In April and again in June, 1941, he had managed to stave off Hitler's demand for U-boats in the Mediterranean, but despite his protests, six boats were dispatched in September, which had since been operating under the control of the Navy Group South at Salamis. Six boats was not many—yet they represented 25 per cent of the total number operating in the Atlantic in September and October. And now came this new order for the immediate dispatch of six more boats to the Western Mediterranean, where they were to be based on La Spezia and Pola. The entire U-boat force was to be concentrated against Gibraltar.

Only a few weeks earlier, on the eighth of November, Dönitz had visited Berlin to expound his views on the conduct of the U-boat war. Once again he had emphasized that everything depended upon the destruction of Britain's shipping in the shortest time, and he voiced strong opposition to any plan which involved splitting the U-boat forces without comparable sinking figures being achieved. In particular he complained of the withdrawal of six U-boats for the purpose of escorting surface ships, four for reconnaissance duties in northern waters, four more in the Arctic Sea and the six already mentioned at Salamis. This policy, he pointed out, left him with only five to ten boats in the Atlantic, which was utterly inadequate. Raeder nodded sympathetically as his subordinate developed this theme; but in the end he remarked that Dönitz was not in a position to appreciate the picture of the war as a whole, and that many other factors had to be taken into consideration by the Supreme Command.

The Naval Command's new directive in December for the transfer of more U-boats to the Mediterranean meant that within a few weeks the British would be bringing their supplies into England without any hindrance at all. Despite, or perhaps because of, the numerous recommendations that Dönitz had sent to Berlin, he was evidently regarded there as a tiresome man who would let the whole of the rest of the Navy go to pieces if that would help his U-boats.

Somewhat bitterly he contrasted this attitude with that of Todt, the Minister for Construction. A year had elapsed since Hitler had received Dönitz in the Command train at Creil, a small station to the east of Paris. On that occasion Hitler speculated whether the U-boats in the Western bases ought to have better protection against air attack; his experiences in the First World War, he said, when he had seen the U-boats at Ostend, had impressed upon him the need to protect them while in harbor. Dönitz gratefully accepted this suggestion and within a few days Todt arrived in Kernevel and immediately impressed Dönitz by the speed with which he got to work. The responsibility for all naval construction still lay with the Admiralty, but by agreement with Dönitz, Todt swiftly drew up a plan for building bunkers—even though, in the case of La Pallice, this meant rebuilding half the harbor. Three days after the decision had been taken, Dönitz was rung up by Dorsch, one of Todt's assistants. "When will you get authority to proceed with the work at La Pallice? I've got twenty thousand workmen here on the Channel coast and all my equipment ready; they are only waiting for the word to move." Dönitz smiled at the recollection of it. That was the way to get things done; those were the kind of men he liked to deal with. After that experience no one would ever convince him that a U-boat required a full twenty-one months to build. Todt would build them faster, for, like the Americans, he knew the value of time.

Ah, the Americans—there it was again—that growing threat from the West.

II

THE GOLDEN AGE

1941-1943

1

PERILOUS MEETINGS

(September—December, 1941)

After an interval in the summer of 1941, some of the bigger boats once more sailed for the South Atlantic. Among these was *U 107*, Commander Hessler, who at that time held the record of 90,000 tons sunk on a single patrol. In September he came across a Sierra Leone convoy and a long pursuit followed. Some of his colleagues were as much as 1,200 miles away but managed to reach the convoy, and together they sank nine ships and damaged two others. After that nothing happened in these equatorial waters for weeks on end, until the boats were sent northward to search the waters near the Azores. Only Merten in *U 68*, Kleinschmidt in *U 111* and Müller in *U 67* remained in the south.

These three boats were ordered to rendezvous so that *U 111*, which was due to return to base, could hand over her remaining torpedoes to *U 68*, and at the same time replenish her empty fuel tanks from *U 67*. The secret meeting place was in the Bay of Tarafal, a lonely little bay on the island of St. Antao in the Cape Verdes.

The first boat to reach Tarafal was *U 68*. As she crept cautiously toward the unknown coast, a crowd of soldiers in khaki appeared out of the woods on the foreshore, piled their arms near some tents and began to bivouac. "That's odd," said Merten, "but they can't be looking for us—the Portuguese are neutral." When the men on shore sighted the U-boat they showed much excitement but no hostile intent. Shortly afterward another U-boat appeared and was identified as *U 111*. At Merten's invitation Kleinschmidt came on board *U 68* for a meal while the torpedoes were being transferred. Kleinschmidt seemed ill at ease and did not hide his eagerness to get away again as soon as possible. Merten chaffed him, but before taking his guest below, he gave his coxswain strict instructions to allow no one on board. In the middle of the meal they heard the sound of strange voices and raced on to the bridge, to find the coxswain gazing interestedly after a boat which was being rowed somewhat unskillfully back to the beach.

"They wanted to deliver a letter, Sir," said the coxswain.

"A letter?"

"Yes, Sir, there was a chap in the boat who looked just like the commissionaire outside the Ritz, covered in gold and silver with a tassel on his cap, who chattered away like a monkey and offered me a fat yellow scroll with a seal on it. But I just said 'nix, nix' and when he tried to climb on board, I showed him my tommy-gun and he was off like a flash."

"Mm—pity. I should have liked that letter for my collection. However—the order stands. Nobody allowed on board."

"Aye, aye, Sir."

Kleinschmidt had been urging the men on, and by the evening the torpedoes had been transferred. He must not stay a moment longer than was necessary, for he was due to meet *U 67* there the following day and did not want to compromise the meeting place. His presence had obviously been reported, and when he sailed again, that too would be known in a few minutes.

The anchor chain came rattling in. *U 111* went slowly

ahead, turned to make a wide sweep round the bay and headed out to sea, with *U 68* following. Darkness had fallen with tropical swiftness, but despite a faint haze Merten could see the black outline of *U 111's* conning tower ahead of him. As the two boats proceeded seaward they suddenly heard two heavy explosions on the rocky beach astern of them. Torpedoes! "Those were meant for us!" said the first lieutenant excitedly, as Merten ordered full speed ahead and began to steer a zigzag course.

The events of the night were not yet over. Soon after *U 68* and *U 111* had left, Müller arrived in *U 67*. As he was closing the shore he sighted the outline of two patrol vessels moving slowly out of the bay and this at once put him on his guard. He was considering what to do when another strange silhouette loomed directly ahead of him—an enemy submarine! Instantly he put his engines at full speed ahead and steered to ram the enemy, a *Clyde* class submarine. *U 67* took her adversary completely by surprise and her bows cut the other submarine right in two; the men on *U 67's* bridge could see her bow and stern sticking up out of the water on either side of them.[1] The collision caused heavy damage to the U-boat. Her bow caps were buckled and would not open, and the rear doors of the torpedo tubes were leaking. Müller reported these events by signal to headquarters, stating that as his bow tubes were out of action he was returning to base. Merten intercepted this signal and promptly asked and received Admiral U-boats' permission to take over Müller's surplus fuel; then, while *U 67* made her way painfully homeward, *U 68* set course for the south and Cape Town.

After days of steaming through the tropical heat, the lookouts in *U 68* sighted land dead ahead. At midnight the boat was lying off the entrance to the harbor of Ascension. Creeping noiselessly in, they saw the brightly lit barracks and heard the faint strains of dance music. They described a wide circle round the harbor, having a good look at the streets, the jetties and cranes, oil tanks and warehouses— but there was no sign of a ship. Disappointedly Merten turned away and shaped course for St. Helena. He had been

[1] HM Submarine *Clyde* had been sent to investigate at Tarafal, where she arrived on the evening of September 27, 1941. It was she who fired the torpedoes which missed *U 68* and later she attempted to ram *U 67*, but was herself *slightly* damaged aft when the U-boat rammed her. She returned to Gibraltar.

there years before in a training ship and now his memory of
that visit stood him in good stead.

Arriving off Jamestown after dark, they began their
soundless approach to the harbor. Here more guns were in
evidence than at Ascension, but nobody noticed the U-boat,
which crept nearer and nearer until the gun and searchlight emplacements seemed to be towering overhead. Strain-
ing their eyes in the darkness, they at length made out the
dim outlines of a heavily laden tanker. As they turned toward her they suddenly found themselves much closer to
their target than anticipated; quickly Merten swung his boat
to starboard and circled round the tanker. It seemed incredi-
ble that they should not be spotted, yet no sound came from
the shore defenses.

Once more the U-boat approached the silent tanker. Then
suddenly came a voice from her decks, "Submarine! Submarine!" At that very moment three torpedoes leaped from
the tubes and slammed into the tanker's side with three
mighty explosions, and the flames from the stricken ship
shot into the night air. One after another, the oil tanks
blew up; the air was filled with flaming debris, while burning oil on the water flared all round the U-boat, so that
Merten had to use high speed to get away from the danger.
Yet there was still no sign of life in Jamestown; it was seventeen minutes before the first beams of the searchlight began
to weave across the sky, and a further three minutes before
the guns on shore opened fire. By that time *U 68* was well out
to sea and heading for WallfishBay.

Kleinschmidt in *U 111* had not been so lucky. In a position some 220 miles southwest of Teneriffe he had been
located and attacked with depth charges by an A/S trawler,
which forced him to the surface. *U 111* emerged amid a
veritable hail of shells; as fast as her crew manned the guns
they were shot down. Kleinschmidt himself was killed together with seven of his men, and the rest had to abandon
the sinking boat. The trawler *Lady Shirley* returned to Gibraltar with forty-four survivors.

In November and December, 1941, a number of the larger
boats were dispatched to attack Cape Town. They included
U 124 (Lieutenant Jochen Mohr) and *U 129* (Lieutenant
Nico Clausen), which replenished from the supply ship *Python* in unfrequented waters south of the Azores before proceeding. A few days later Bauer in *U 126* did the same from
the auxiliary cruiser *Atlantis*—the famous *Ship 16* com-

manded by Captain Rogge. While the *Atlantis* was refueling, Bauer took the opportunity to have a hot bath. He was actually in his bath when the auxiliary cruiser was surprised by a British warship and sunk by gunfire.[2] *U 126* had just had time to cast off the fuel lines and crash-dive before the British shells began to burst around the raider. Bauer was among the survivors and he lost no time in getting back on board his U-boat, for the British cruiser took no risks and disappeared over the horizon as soon as the German ship had sunk. As a result of Bauer's urgent signal to headquarters, Mohr and Clausen were ordered to the spot at full speed. On the way, Mohr sighted and sank the British light cruiser *Dunedin*[3] and then resumed his race toward the survivors of the *Atlantis*. He and Clausen arrived on the scene almost simultaneously. The three U-boats embarked about one hundred men each and shaped course not without difficulty, for the *Python*. They reached the supply ship in two days and safely transferred the survivors to her.

Between the thirtieth of November and December 4, *Python* was scheduled to replenish several other U-boats; among them was Merten in *U 68*, who had sunk two ships in Wallfish Bay and who arrived at the same time as Eckermann in *U A*. Early on December 1, a lookout in *Python* reported smoke on the horizon and some minutes later a large British cruiser was seen steaming at full speed toward the German supply ship, clearly bent on her destruction. There seemed little chance of escape for *Python* unless one or both U-boats could first cripple the British ship. Merten and Eckermann disconnected their fuel lines and moved to the attack. Merten was the first to dive but as he did so, his U-boat stood on her head and plunged toward the bottom like a stone. Having just completed taking on fuel stores, Merten had no time to adjust his trim for the new load. By the time he had regained trim the enemy ship was out of his range but still heading toward *Python*. Eckermann had no better luck; he fired three torpedoes, but they all missed. *Python's* fate was sealed.[4]

As the two U-boats approached the little huddle of boats and rafts which marked the scene of her end, an almost insoluble problem presented itself, for the survivors in-

[2] *Atlantis* was sunk by HMS *Devonshire* on November 22, 1941, in position 4°12′S, 18°42′W.

[3] HMS *Dunedin* was on patrol in the South Atlantic on November 24, 1941, when she was sunk by *U 124* with heavy loss of life.

[4] *Python* scuttled herself on the approach of HMS *Dorsetshire* on December 1, 1941, in the South Atlantic.

cluded the crew of *Atlantis* as well. The survival of all these men depended upon two U-boats, a handful of lifeboats and one small motorboat. The plan evolved by Merten and Captain Rogge was to divide the survivors into three parties. One was accommodated below decks in the two U-boats; a second party was placed on rafts on the U-boats' decks, and the third remained in the boats which were towed astern of the U-boats. This plan offered the best chance of survival in the event of a surprise attack. If the U-boats suddenly had to dive, it would be a simple matter to cast off the tow lines, while the rafts would automatically float off the decks as the U-boats submerged.

Then began the long, long trek, starting in about 30 degrees southern latitude under a fierce tropical sun, and ending safely in Western France. On December 6, the two U-boats met those of Mohr and Clausen, and the survivors were divided up among the four boats. Three hundred miles from their starting point they met four Italian submarines, *Torelli, Finzi, Tazzoli* and *Calvi*, each of which took a share of the survivors. With the congestion thus relieved, all boats were now able to move faster. On Christmas Eve, 1941, *U 68* and *U A* raced each other on the last lap to St. Nazaire, while the other U-boats reached the base safely before the year was out. Thus ended the greatest rescue operation of the war, covering over five thousand miles.[5]

This was not the first time that Italian submarines had cooperated with their German allies. When Italy came into the war, she had offered to send forty boats to the Atlantic, an offer that was gratefully accepted, for any reinforcements were welcome at that time. The first three Italian boats reached Bordeaux in September, 1940, and Italian commanding officers began to sail as guests of their German colleagues in order to learn about conditions and German methods in the Atlantic. At a conference between Dönitz and the Italian Admiral Parona at the end of that month, it was agreed that the over-all control of operations in the Atlantic should remain in German hands, while the Italians should operate independently within the framework of the general scheme. Parona proposed a capable young officer, Lieutenant Sestini, as liaison officer with the German Command, and in return asked for an experienced senior U-boat commander who spoke Italian, to teach the Italians the

5 "A rescue for which the enemy must be given full credit" is the comment in the official (British) *History of the War at Sea*, Vol. 1, p. 546.

German methods. Parona readily admitted that the Germans knew a great deal more about this type of warfare than the Italians. Dönitz selected Commander Rösing to go to Bordeaux. "Your job is not an easy one," he warned Rösing as he said good-by. "You will need tact and understanding. As things are, the Italians must learn from us, and naturally their national pride will not take easily to that. Let them feel that they have discovered their own shortcomings, but not that you are bringing these to their notice."

Although the liaison between the two commands on shore developed swiftly and smoothly, the practical cooperation at sea did not come up to expectations, for the system of training and background of the two navies were too divergent. Unexpected difficulties arose in radio communications; there were wide differences between the positions at sea as estimated by each side, so that the German U-boats failed to reach convoys reported by the Italians. A series of failures resulted.

In the early summer of 1941, as new boats gradually became available to the Germans, the Italians were given a separate operational area where they could work quite independently. But despite all efforts to cooperate it was evidently hopeless to match up the unequal partners. Nevertheless, the Italian submarine commanders did their best to prove themselves worthy, and their efforts did meet with some success. In the period from September, 1940, to July, 1943, about 30 Italian boats sank an aggregate of 105 identified ships of 588,553 tons and damaged another 14 of 117,646 tons and one destroyer; confirmation was lacking as to their claims to have sunk an additional 22 ships of 151,000 tons. Ten Italian boats returned to the Mediterranean at different times; of the remaining 22, 16 were lost on patrol in the Atlantic, 5 were taken over by the Germans when Italy collapsed in 1943 and one sailed to Durban and surrendered to the British. The most successful Italian boats were:

Da Vinci—which sank 18 ships of 125,633 tons and damaged one of 7,167 tons,
Tazzoli—19 ships of 93,397 tons sunk, one of 5,222 tons damaged, two of 10,000 and one of 5,000 tons unconfirmed,
Cappellini—six ships of 31,653 tons sunk, one of 5,231 tons damaged,
Barberigo—six ships of 34,464 tons sunk, two of 12,123 tons damaged and one unconfirmed destroyer;
Morosini, Finzi, Calvi and *Archimede* each sank five ships.

On her best patrol, *Da Vinci* was commanded by Lieutenant Gianfranco Gazzana. This boat was lost off Cape Finisterre in May, 1943, after Gazzana had been awarded the Knight's Cross for sinking 97,000 tons. This decoration was also awarded to Lieutenant Carlo Fecia di Cossato of *Tazzoli* for sinking eleven ships.

2

THE GIBRALTAR MOUSETRAP

(Winter, 1941)

The extraordinary similarity between the circumstances leading to the action off Tarafal and the sinking of *Atlantis* and *Python* did not go unnoticed at U-boat headquarters. Tarafal was an isolated island; it had never been used before by U-boats. No U-boat had sent any signals by radio in its neighborhood, and each one had gone there under conditions of the greatest secrecy. Yet they had found a British submarine there! And how had the British cruiser managed to arrive at exactly the right moment and at the right spot to destroy *Atlantis* as she was refueling *U 126?* The question applied with equal force to the loss of *Python* a week later.

The possibility of treason arose, and not for the first time; for as early as the spring of 1941 the enemy had evidently had foreknowledge of U-boat dispositions in the Atlantic. Steps were then taken to reduce to an absolute minimum the number of people in the know. The boats' dispositions were no longer passed to "Group West" Command in Paris or the air officer commanding Atlantic, or to the German liaison officer with the Italian U-boats at Bordeaux. A special new cypher was evolved for the use of the U-boats only, and from September, 1941, onward, all references to grid-square positions in signals had to be doubly encyphered as an extra precaution against British decryption.

But then came the incident of *U 570,* the full details of which were not known to the Germans until much later. This boat was in the act of surfacing some eighty miles south of Iceland when she was sighted and dive-bombed by a British aircraft. The captain was on his first patrol in command and, losing his nerve, he waved his own white shirt in surrender.

On the following day—the lapse of time showed that the boat was still seaworthy—*U 570* was captured by the enemy.[1] It was not known whether the U-boat's confidential documents had been destroyed in time or whether they had been captured along with the boat. In the latter case the enemy would now be in full possession of the vital cyphers, which would explain the mysterious appearance of hostile ships at Tarafal and again at the rendezvous points of *Atlantis* and *Python*.

Rear Admiral Maerten, Director of Naval Communications, carried out the most systematic investigations which failed however to reveal any breach of cypher security or other cause of leakage. Meanwhile the first lieutenant of *U 570* was known to have escaped from the prisoner-of-war camp in England in an endeavor to reach the U-boat and sink her alongside the jetty. He had been recaptured, and a second valiant effort to retrieve the situation had cost him his life.

The second and third groups of boats ordered to the Mediterranean had got through, but at heavy cost. One of the four boats in the second group had been sunk and, out of the twenty-four in the third group three had been lost, while five others had to turn back to base after being damaged by air attack. Despite these heavy losses the inactivity of the Italian Navy compelled the German Admiralty to call for a further six U-boats to be sent to the Mediterranean. The intention was to station ten of them in the Eastern Mediterranean, leaving fifteen on either side of the Strait of Gibraltar. This was more than Dönitz could provide, even if he detailed all the operational boats then in the Biscay bases and those still due to arrive from home ports. From personal experience of the dangers of the strait during the First World War, he was averse to risking the venture. The lull in the Atlantic had enabled the British to reinforce their A/S defenses in the strait, and Gibraltar was now crammed with destroyers, frigates, corvettes and every other sort of patrol vessel. Aircraft were now patrolling night and day, and in bright moonlight were proving a serious menace to the U-boats. The third group therefore had a much poorer chance of getting through than the first two. They had to work their way into the strait in short rushes, hugging the coastline, surfacing only at night so as to make the best speed under cover of darkness, and navigating for the rest of the way submerged until well clear of these concentrated patrols. The endurance of their batteries

[1] In August, 1941, *U 570* surrendered to an aircraft of Coastal Command and was towed to Iceland, later to be commissioned as HM Submarine *Graph*.

was not sufficient for a submerged passage right through the danger zone.

Gibraltar was like a mousetrap. Any boat trying to return from the Mediterranean to the Atlantic bases would have to struggle against the strong easterly currents. Once in, therefore, they must stay in.

Yet the U-boats' activities in the Mediterranean were not without results. On November 13, Guggenberger in *U 81* and Reschke in *U 205* located the Gibraltar squadron consisting of *Ark Royal*, another carrier and the battleship *Malaya* with cruisers and destroyers. Guggenberger sank *Ark Royal*,[2] one of the latest British carriers, and one which could carry seventy aircraft; *Malaya* limped back to Gibraltar badly damaged.

When attacking at dusk, U-boat captains always had to race the oncoming darkness. If they kept at too great a distance they would lose sight of the convoy; but if they came in close too soon, they ran the risk of being pounced on by the air escort or the ships of the close screen. One of the most experienced U-boat commanders, Lieutenant Suhren, now made an important discovery. During an attack on a convoy lasting five days, he was located and driven off by destroyers no less than four times in the hours of darkness. This convinced him that the British destroyers were equipped with some sort of device similar to the radar gear carried in German capital ships; but he also discovered that this apparatus seemed to have a "blind spot" at ranges under 2,000 yards. He described how, by deliberately keeping within 1,200 yards on the quarter of a destroyer sweeping ahead of the convoy, he had remained undetected long enough to fire several torpedoes successfully. He persevered with these tactics until a defect in one of his torpedoes threw it off course and it sank the destroyer by chance.

This new and worrying development came at a difficult time. It was only a week since Berlin had rejected Dönitz's suggestion to reduce the number of boats around Gibraltar, where many were being lost without any compensating results. True, in the Mediterranean von Thiesenhausen in *U 331* had sunk the battleship *Barham*,[3] but that was not near Gibraltar. News now came in of another convoy assembling at Gibraltar which appeared to have an unusually strong escort. First reports from the watching U-boats indicated that the convoy

---

[2] HMS *Ark Royal* was torpedoed on November 13, 1941, and sank early the next day twenty-five miles from Gibraltar, to which she was being towed. Only one man lost his life.

[3] HMS *Barham* was sunk on November 25 with heavy loss of life.

consisted of thirty-two ships with eighteen escorts. Eighteen
—that was far more than they had ever known. On the second day out, the FW 200s flew over and confirmed that among
the escorts was an aircraft carrier; that was new too.

On the third day Baumann in *U 131* was sighted by enemy
aircraft twenty miles ahead of the convoy and was then attacked by five escort ships. They forced the U-boat to the surface, whereupon her gunners shot down an aircraft, but the
rain of shells from the ships was overwhelming and the boat,
badly holed, sank beneath their feet. On the fourth day Heyda
in *U 434* suffered the same fate; while shadowing the convoy
he was located by two destroyers and sunk after an hour's
chase.

As night fell the remaining U-boats closed in for the attack.
Gengelbach in *U 574* saw a destroyer in his sights and fired;
the enemy ship blew up, but at the same moment the U-boat
was located by another destroyer, *Stork,* which steered to ram
her and opened fire. Gengelbach turned sharply away and
tried to keep inside the destroyer's wider turning circle, but
after ten minutes of this hide-and-seek the destroyer bore
down upon him and finished him off with ten depth charges.
Soon afterward one of the merchant ships was struck by a
torpedo—but she was the only victim after four days of attack!
On the fifth day the enemy shot down two FW 200s. As night
fell Lieutenant Bigalk succeeded in sinking the escort carrier
Audacity [4] (a converted merchant ship) and also another merchant ship. But as the ships steamed steadily northward the
thunder of the depth charges continued, accounting for one
of the best and most experienced commanders, Endrass in
U 567, who had won the oak leaves to the Iron Cross. After
nine days of bitter fighting, the last three U-boats disengaged
from the convoy on December 23 as fresh destroyers and aircraft arrived from England to reinforce the escort.

Dispassionately Dönitz reckoned up the cost—five U-boats
lost, including Endrass. That was the highest loss to date in
any single convoy operation. How many times had he warned
the Admiralty in Berlin against this very danger? On the thirtieth of December, 1941, the latter at last approved Dönitz's
urgent request to withdraw the U-boats from the Gibraltar
area.

[4] HMS *Audacity* was sunk about five hundred miles west of Finisterre on December 21, 1941. Only two merchant ships were lost out
of the convoy, which was the first ever to receive carrier escort.

3

WAR WITH AMERICA

(December, 1941–June, 1942)

The Japanese attack on Pearl Harbor came as a complete surprise to the German Admiralty—not less so to the flag officer, U-boats, at Kernevel. Only a few days previously Godt, returning from a visit to Berlin, had reported to Dönitz on what he had learned from the German naval staff. Despite the clear evidence of all-out help being given to Britain by the United States, the Supreme Command's policy was to treat America as 100 per cent neutral; nothing was to be done—least of all by the U-boats—to heighten the tension between America and Germany.

Then came Pearl Harbor. Dönitz realized that the outbreak of war in the Pacific would soon have repercussions on the U-boat war in the Atlantic. Although the boats' task was still that of sinking enemy shipping, the emphasis had shifted. Where previously the objective had been to starve England to death, it was now a matter of sinking ships faster than the Allies could build them. To achieve this they would have to improve substantially upon the figure of 250,000 tons a month sunk in 1941.

In the first six months of 1941 there had been an average of eighteen boats at sea; in the second six months the number was thirty-three. They could reckon on twenty new boats joining the Command in each month of 1942. If they could count on their own losses remaining so low, the chances of locating targets should improve with the growing numbers of U-boats. Lack of experience among escort ships in the hitherto untouched waters of the Western Atlantic should be in Germany's favor, particularly at the nodal points of the shipping routes. Dönitz's main problem was still the same—how to dispose his U-boats in the most rewarding manner, how to discover the enemy's weakest spots where the greatest damage might be inflicted with the least risk to his own forces. The obvious place to begin such a campaign was off the coast of America itself; he was aided in this decision by the knowledge that in March, 1942, he would begin to receive the first

U-tankers, which would enable even the smaller boats to operate in distant waters.

Fresh operational orders were issued to the commanders.
A surprise raid was to be launched simultaneously off several
American ports and only targets of over 10,000 tons were to
be attacked. They were not to begin operations until they
received the code word *Paukenschlag*.[1] They were to load supplies suitable for all climates, both hot and cold—tropical gear
and warm clothing—since their operational areas might be
anywhere between the extreme north and the extreme south
of the North American continent.

The U-boats sailed in heavy wintry weather. As they battled
their way across the Atlantic, they picked up a stream of messages from ships in distress, which had been battered by the
storms, but the boats ignored them in favor of the bigger game
that lay ahead. At length came the signal: *"Paukenschlag* to
take effect January 13."

On January 12 Hardegen in *U 123* was not far away from
his allotted area at the approaches to New York when smoke
was sighted. *U 123* headed at full speed toward her victim,
whose masts, funnel and superstructure gradually appeared
above the skyline.

"That's a fine big ship, Sir," said the first lieutenant, "we
can't let her go, can we?"

Hardegen hesitated for a moment. 'D' Day for *Paukenschlag*
was the thirteenth; really he ought to wait until tomorrow—
but a 10,000-tonner . . . ! Would it be possible to sink her
quietly so that the news would not be made public for a few
days? What would the admiral do in his place? He would
probably attack. That decided the matter.

After one hit in the engine room the British freighter *Cyclöps*
of 9,076 tons lay stopped. The crew manned the gun and
doubtless she also used her radio, but at the second torpedo
hit, her bows reared up and she slid at a steep angle to the
bottom.

As the new moon rose *U 123* reached her position off New
York. She had not long to wait before her lookout picked up
the sound of an approaching motor ship. *U 123* turned toward
the target and seconds later her torpedoes hit, sending a column of flame and black smoke skyward. The U-boat's radio-
man reported that the ship's distress signal revealed that she
was the tanker *Norness* and was under the impression that
she had struck a mine.

[1] *Paukenschlag*: literally, a beat on the kettle drum.

"A mine!" said Hardegen contemptuously. "Nobody seems to be expecting any German U-boats around here." He waited for a while; then, as the tanker still did not sink, he fired again and this time her stern sank quickly, while at least 90 feet of her bows remained out of the water. It was evident that her stern was resting on the bottom, for the water was shallow at that point.

Paukenschlag had begun.

The next day *U 123* intercepted an American radio broadcast concerning "the wreck of an unknown tanker south of Long Island." An *unknown* tanker? That meant that the survivors had not yet reached shore and that the Americans would still be unaware of the presence of a U-boat. Hardegen ordered permanent watch to be kept on the radio broadcasts, including the 600-meter wave band, for that was their best possible source of information.

Twenty-four hours later they intercepted another 10,000-ton tanker outward-bound. As their torpedoes caught her amidships, the flames turned the darkness into day. The next day they learned from the German radio at Buenos Aires that thirty-eight survivors had been rescued from the *Norness;*[2] and on the following day came the news of the sinking of their second ship. The secret was out at last!

The Americans sprang into action. Destroyers foamed up and down the coast and the air was full of planes; but the U-boat lay quietly on the bottom and only surfaced as night fell. After she had sunk a third ship, she moved further south toward Cape Hatteras. This was obviously the right spot for her—the sea fairly swarmed with ships. *U 123* crept in toward the Cape, hugging the coast, until she reached the spot where, within the next few months, some four hundred ships of all shapes and sizes were to fall victim to German U-boats.

Her first target here was a 4,000-ton ship, heavily laden, which came into view fully lighted. Hardegen's first torpedo missed and with a curse he swung his boat around to follow and fire again. As he was passing the light buoy marking the northeastern end of the Wimble Shoal, he sighted three more ships coming toward him, but he decided to leave them for the moment in favor of his original target. At 450 yards he fired and thirty seconds later his torpedo exploded abaft the ship's funnel. Her stern sank until it was touching the bottom, while her bows stuck out high in the air. Hardegen swung round again and raced after the other ships. Again he got

2 Motor tanker *Norness,* 9,577 tons, torpedoed and sunk in 40°28′N, 70°50′W, on January 14, 1942.

into position and fired, and again a column of flame towered
into the air as his torpedoes hit. He had only two torpedoes
left now; he came back to the lightship and almost immediately sighted five ships in a row, fully lighted. Five ships
—and only two torpedoes. There was only one thing for it—
to attack with gunfire. He sent for his gunnery officer, who
listened skeptically to his commanding officer's proposals.

"Attack while running up astern of them?" he repeated
doubtfully. "Can't be done, Sir. For one thing they'd be bound
to see us before we had fired the first shot, and then we'd get
it in the neck."

"Nonsense! In the first place they probably aren't keeping
proper watch, and secondly they don't know what a U-boat's
conning tower looks like. Guns are not in my line, but I've got
a hunch it will work. . . . Stand by for gun action!" he called
down the hatch.

Hardegen turned back to von Schroeter, his gunnery officer.
"The bolder you are, the more likely your bluff will work.
If we score hits with our first rounds, the enemy will lose his
head. We must make use of those first few moments of con-
fusion." Leaning over the rail he yelled, "Hold tight on deck!"
With spray breaking over them, the gun's crew held on grimly.
"Range two hundred yards . . . half ahead both . . . ten rounds
. . . open fire!"

As the cordite fumes swept back over the bridge, they could
hear the crash of their shells exploding on the target. A tiny
spark of flame appeared on the tanker's deck, which quickly
grew to a conflagration and then came the detonation as her
tanks blew up. Meanwhile the after lookouts were reporting
that the other ships had doused their lights and were turning
away. The gunners ceased fire and the U-boat swung round
in pursuit of a 6,000-tonner. Just as she reached full speed,
the port diesel stopped with a broken cooling-water pump.
Although the starboard diesel was run at full speed, the 6,000-
tonner got away. There was now but little darkness left and
Hardegen had to decide quickly how best to use his last two
torpedoes.

They had long since left the burning tanker astern but suddenly they picked up her signals again. "Tanker *Malay* on fire
after being shelled by U-boat. Please inform nearest naval
command. Fire under control. Am making for Norfolk."
"*Malay* is eight thousand, two hundred and seven tons," added
the U-boat radio operator.

"Good God, I'd no idea she was so big," exclaimed Hardegen, "we'll give her our last torpedo. Chief, when will you have that engine ready?" . . . "Can't say yet, Sir."

U 123 went hobbling along on one engine. Suddenly a towering shape hove out of the darkness. Luck was still with them. All the captain had to do was to turn and fire. The torpedo hit abaft the funnel; the ship broke in two and sank in five fathoms of water. Her bow and stern reared above the surface, the two masts slanting toward each other. From her distress signals they learned her name and that she was a 5,000-tonner. "Tell the captain," said the U-boat's radio operator, who was keeping the score, "that *U 123* has now sunk more than two hundred thousand tons."

One hundred thousand tons of which, thought Hardegen, as he peered into the darkness for the *Malay*, while under my command! Even as he sighted her, the tanker saw him and turned sharply away; but she could not remain on that course as the water was shoaling fast. As she altered course once more, Hardegen fired and hit her fair and square in the engine room. The *Malay* sank swiftly.[3] Below decks in the U-boat the waiting hands heard the welcome order, "Right full rudder, set course for home!"

The operational zone off the coast of America was soon extended. Operation *Paukenschlag* had covered the waters from the mouth of the St. Lawrence to Cape Hatteras; the next group of large boats proceeded to Trinidad and Aruba, while the second wave of medium-sized boats was given freedom of action westward of Newfoundland. The planners at headquarters were beginning to realize that these medium-sized boats had a much longer range than had been thought. The use to which they had been put in the past had given them no opportunity to demonstrate their economy of fuel while on a long passage. By the beginning of March these relatively small boats were operating off New York; a fortnight later they were off Cape Hatteras.

There was still no evidence that the Americans were switching over to wartime conditions. After two months of war their ships were still sailing independently. Their captains stopped close to torpedoed ships and asked for information over the loud hailer; should a ship be hit but remain capable of steaming, the captain never bothered to steer a zigzag course or vary his speed so as to impede the U-boat in dealing the coup de grace. And they had no idea of security; they chattered

[3] Tanker *Malay* was attacked on January 19, 1942.

about everything under the sun over the 600-meter wave band —and as if that were not enough, the coastal defense stations sent out over the air a regular program of information, giving details of rescue work in progress, of where and when aircraft would be patrolling and the schedules of A/S vessels. The outward-bound U-boats would tune in to this wave length while still in mid-Atlantic. The information was of enormous help in their operations, as every ship gave her position and they were thus able to form a very accurate picture of the traffic at sea, even to the extent of calculating the ratio of tankers to ordinary merchant ships that they could expect to find. For several weeks the Americans relied for protection upon a few weakly armed patrol vessels, whose crews were as lacking in confidence as they were in experience; consequently several U-boats were able to escape after being surprised on the surface because the enemy broke off the action too soon.

The destroyers patrolling the sea routes came and went with such clockwork regularity that the U-boats could have set their watches by them. Hence in these waters in 1942 the German commanders were bolder than ever they were in 1939 off the British coasts; they even attacked ships with gunfire while within sight of the shore. Never before or since has the gun played so big a part in U-boat operations. Although there was more activity in the air than on the sea, particularly off Halifax, New York and Cape Hatteras, the planes at that time did not interfere unduly with the U-boats, for the air crews lacked the experience of their British counterparts who were making life very difficult for U-boat men in the Eastern Atlantic.

However, the successful prosecution of this campaign suddenly received a setback from a totally unexpected quarter. Just as Dönitz was planning to send two groups of boats newly arrived from the training bases into the Atlantic, the German Admiralty announced that Norway was in danger. The Führer himself was deeply worried about a possible Allied invasion of Norway, which he regarded as the "decisive area of the whole war." He ordered the defenses of this northern bastion to be reinforced by surface ships and U-boats, and even demanded that *all* the U-boats should be disposed in the Norwegian area, in order to act as reconnaissance forces against a hostile invasion. His reading of intelligence reports had convinced him that the Allies still possessed sufficient ships to effect such a landing, and the Naval Command agreed with him.

Dönitz was beside himself at the futility of this order, which

(photograph by Commander Saunders)

Grand Admiral Dönitz

(Acme)

The Reich war flag flying for the first time from the prows of new German U-boats.

Berliners cheering Commander Guenther Prien, Captain of the German U-boat which sank the British battleship *Royal Oak*, as he rides on his way to be received by Hitler.

(Acme)

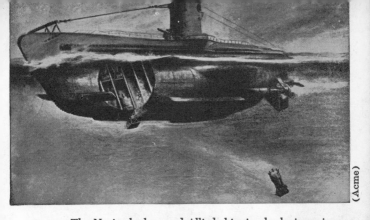

(Acme)

The Nazi subs harassed Allied shipping by laying mines as well as by direct torpedoing. This German drawing shows how the mines are planted from slotted chambers in the bottom of the U-boat. Below, a German drawing of a depth-charge attack on a U-boat.

(Acme)

The nerve center of the U-boat Arm—Dönitz and his staff in the control room at Headquarters.

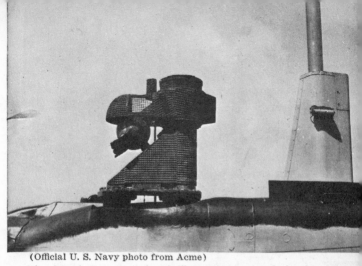

The famed German "schnörkel" resting on the deck of a Nazi U-boat. When released, the "schnörkel" leaves deck and floats to surface, connected to the submarine by flexible air hoses.

The bombproof U-boat bunkers at Trondheim, Norway. The U-boat on the left is Type VII, that on the right is Type IX.

U-boats nearing completion in a Hamburg building yard at the time of the surrender.

ont was sunk, and at the end of February they found
oy ONS 67. And now, for the first time, came news of
orpedo nets being used. Two tankers in one convoy were
to be carrying them and a U-boat reported a strange-
ing vessel—a sort of cable layer—on the Newfoundland
k, on which a torpedo hit appeared to have no effect what-
r. It was only after the war that it became known that the
tish had equipped some seven hundred ships with this de-
e, of which fifteen had been saved from destruction includ-
a troop transport which had unwittingly carried a live tor-
do in its nets for thirty-six hours before it was discovered on
aching harbor.

Opinions at the German Admiralty began to change again
s they slowly came to realize the importance of doing the
tmost damage to the enemy's fuel supplies. From Grand
Admiral Raeder himself came a personal order: the new campaign against fuel supplies was to be begun not with the sinking of fuel-carrying ships but with the direct destruction of
fuel plants on shore by gunfire.

Hartenstein in *U 156* was the first man to go for the fuel
tanks at Aruba, but disaster overtook him almost before he
had begun. The premature explosion of the first round from
his gun wounded two ratings and wrecked the gun muzzle.
Working at top speed, he managed to make the gun serviceable again after some hours by sawing away the damaged part
of the muzzle, but in the meantime the alarm had been given
at Aruba and the operation had to be abandoned, although
Hartenstein later sank two ships with his sawed-off gun.

U 161 was sent to Port of Spain, Trinidad. Achilles, her
captain, knew the place well from peacetime and he used this
knowledge to insinuate himself right into the harbor, where
after dark he sank a tanker and a freighter before making a
safe exit. He repeated the experiment a week later at Port
Castries on the island of St. Lucia. While he was earning for
himself the nickname of "The Trinidad Well Borer," his comrades were busy destroying a whole row of feeder tankers carrying oil straight from the wells to the storage tanks on the
islands.

At the same time—it was the third week of February—
Captain Poske in *U 504* was opening the season off the har-
bors of Florida, such as Charleston, Savannah, Jacksonville,
Jupiter and the luxury resorts of Palm Beach and Miami.
U-boats had never been seen there before. The shipping routes
were crowded with traffic as in peacetime and all the shore

U-boat on Arctic patrol.

The *U-333* returns
home damaged aft-
er an Atlantic pa-
trol.

(Imperial War Museum Photograph)

A British Coastal Command Sunderland attacks a U-boat with machine guns and depth charges. Shortly afterward U-boat sank.

A U. S. Navy boarding party on the *U505* after it had been blasted to the surface by depth charges from the destroyer escort Chatelain (in left background) and strafed by planes from the escort carrier USS *Guadalcanal*.

(U. S. Navy photo from Acme)

conflicted utterly with his own conception; bu
him the arrival at this moment of the first repo
in the American waters caused the Führer's
twenty-second of January to be suspended. Th
U-boats off Norway, however, remained effectiv
and at the beginning of February the Admiralty
following dispositions: Eight boats to keep watch
bounded by Iceland, the Faroes and Scotland;
northern waters; and two each standing by in
Tromsö, Trondheim and Bergen.

This involved a total of twenty boats, which left
spare for the Atlantic. Despite all his protests D
forced to comply, but as he had anticipated, the res
poor in the extreme. Owing to an unexpected redu
new boats arriving from the training bases at the end
ruary, he had to move six boats from the Biscay bases
North, including Degen's *U 701*, Thurmann's *U 55*
Mannstein in *U 753* and Hinsch in *U 569*. All were
rienced commanders who could ill be spared from the A
can campaign—and what did they achieve? One small freig
and three patrol ships sunk off Seidisfjord.

Berlin maintained that the U-boats could only give mate
support to the German land campaign by maintaining
offensive against the Allied Arctic convoys running to Arc
angel and Murmansk, and to this end ordered four of th
boats then operating off the Hebrides to be placed at the dis
posal of flag officer, northern waters. When Dönitz pointed
out that these boats were not suitable, the Admiralty merely
postponed the transfer until adequately equipped boats from
the training bases should be available; at the end of March
twenty boats in northern waters were removed from Dönitz's
immediate control.

The admiral continued to press home his point that the
main objective was to sink ships quicker than the Allies could
build them. The greater part of the new shipping construction,
he pointed out, was being completed in America; therefore
attacks must be concentrated on the United States and particularly on American fuel supply lines. Every ship sunk in
those waters would mean one less for the supply of munitions
to Russia as well as to England, and would thus strengthen
the German defense of France and Norway.

U-boat activities off the American coast were continued
with such forces as were available. Only on two occasions did
the boats encounter a convoy; at the end of January they
located a fast transport convoy in which the British destroyer

lights were burning. The following laconic entries are from Poske's log:

21.2. Reached operational area. Fired double salvo at tanker steering south in ballast. Hit fore and aft. Ship sank by the stern. Next evening chased a merchant ship but lost her in a rain squall. Half an hour later sank a four-masted ship in night attack. Ship turned turtle. Steered south for Jupiter. Attacked large tanker. Tremendous explosion and ship at once burst into flames. She was carrying 12,000 tons of petrol. Picked up destroyer noises in bright moonlight; sighted enemy and dived. Was attacked with depth charges and pursued for three hours, but although enemy passed overhead several times he did not attack again, and finally cleared off. A little later made submerged daylight attack on a 7000-ton petrol tanker which blew up. Three days later attacked a Norwegian ship but all three torpedoes missed. Serious damage sustained on deck from heavy seas which impeded action. Set course for home at slow speed. Sank a ship making for Bombay carrying deck cargo of motorcars. Ship blown to bits. . . .

With the return of Bauer in *U 126* from the Windward Isles there was a temporary lull in the Caribbean. All the U-boats had fired their stock of torpedoes at the same time, and no reliefs were available to take their place. It was not until the U-tankers, the so-called "milch cows," began to commission in April that a permanent force could be maintained in the very rewarding waters of the Caribbean.

It had been calculated that twenty new boats would be commissioned in each month of 1942, but the severe winter and icing up of the Baltic had delayed the commissioning of forty-five of them. Between January and March only thirteen new boats joined; between April and June only ten. After deducting twelve lost at sea and those which were detached for service in the northern waters and the Mediterranean, there was an accretion of only thirty new boats instead of eighty.

Every available boat was dispatched to the American front. They were few enough in numbers—an average six or eight at any one time—but their commanders were old hands who had gained their experience in the hard school of British anti-submarine defenses. Lieutenant Topp was one of them in *U 552*—an "ace" against convoys; there was Mützelburg in *U 203* and Lassen in *U 160*, each of whom destroyed five or six ships; Hardegen was there again in *U 123* and sank eleven ships while Jochen Mohr's score in *U 124* was nine on one patrol; he further distinguished himself by reporting this suc-

cess by signal in a couplet addressed to the admiral, which
caught on throughout the U-boat Service:

> The new-moon night is black as ink.
> Off Hatteras the tankers sink.
> While sadly Roosevelt counts the score—
> Some fifty thousand tons—by
>
> MOHR

Under this rain of hammer blows the Americans slowly began to reorganize their defenses and the U-boat captains were
quick to notice the change. Ships no longer sailed as and when
they chose but at different times and at varying distances from
the coast—sometimes singly, sometimes in groups. Aircraft
began to attack the U-boats by night, driving them away from
the coast during the periods of moonlight. But very soon
Schuch in *U 105* discovered another nodal point for shipping
three hundred miles east of Cape Hatteras and once more the
Sea Wolves gathered to attack.

Hardegen's second American patrol in *U 123* had begun
auspiciously. He had scarcely reached his patrol area on
March 22 when he sank the 7,000-ton tanker *Muscogee* from
Wilmington. The next day he sighted another one but—and
this was a new experience in the days of *Paukenschlag*—the
ship was zigzagging and moreover she carried guns. Hardegen
counted two 10.5s aft, two 8.8s [4] amidships and several light
A.A. weapons on the bridge; but he was not the man to be
put off by such a display of strength. He bore down on his
unsuspecting enemy under cover of a rainstorm and fired.
One torpedo stuck in the tube while the roar of its propellers
echoed through the boat, but at last it slithered out and Hardegen breathed again. The range had been 900 yards when
he fired and in the meantime he had come considerably closer
to his heavily armed target. A bright flame shooting up from
the forepart of the ship showed that one torpedo at any rate
had got home. The crew were running for their lives; at any
moment further explosions might tear the ship apart. Nobody
in the doomed vessel thought of opening fire.

"Gun-action stations! Fire six rounds into her engine room,
two in the afterholds!" A ball of white fire soared into the sky
as the first shot hit; five and a half hours later the ship, still
burning, sank beneath a gigantic cloud of smoke.

The same evening the U-boat sighted a single steamship of
about 3,000 tons, steering a straight and peaceful course,

[4] Probably two five-inch, and two three-inch guns.

occasionally letting off quantities of black smoke. Not content to rely upon his own judgment, Hardegen summoned both his navigating officer and his midshipman to the bridge; none of them could see anything suspicious about the ship and Hardegen eventually decided to attack on the surface. At a range of about 650 yards a single torpedo hit the target well forward, sending up a towering column of black water; the ship stopped and fire broke out on board. She radioed: *"Caroline* torpedoed—burning—not bad—position xyz." She began to list slightly; one lifeboat dropped into the water, another was still hanging in the davits. "Not bad?" thought Hardegen. "We'll see about that."

U 123 swung round the ship's stern in a close circle so as to attack with gunfire from the other side. Hardegen sat on the bridge rail and watched; the *Caroline's* second boat was being manned. "Let the men get away from the ship," said Hardegen as he saw them climbing into the boat, "don't want to shoot them up as well." Suddenly the *Caroline* showed two red lights and looked as though she were making slight way ahead. It was not clear whether she still had way on or whether she had begun to move again under her own engines, but in either case the range suddenly shortened down to a few hundred yards. Rather suspiciously Hardegen ordered half-speed ahead on his engines and turned to starboard. *Caroline* turned too! Could it be a coincidence? Hardegen increased speed and again turned to starboard; *Caroline* turned again; her speed increased and suddenly she came to life. Trapdoors collapsed, tarpaulins were whisked away and then came the flash of guns firing and the stammer of her machine guns! Black clouds of smoke plumed upward as the U-boat's diesels roared into full speed. Shells from *Caroline's* two large guns burst astern and then to one side, while colored tracer from her machine guns whistled overhead and then began to strike the conning tower. The midshipman gave a groan and collapsed and at the same moment there was a loud explosion below decks.

"Clear the bridge! Close watertight doors!" Only the captain and first lieutenant remained on the bridge to face the storm of shells. The wounded midshipman lay close to the conning-tower hatch, his right leg badly smashed. As the ratings slithered down the ladder the coxswain tried to bind him up. There were more heavy explosions and menacing splashes; then Hardegen saw some large black object sailing through the air toward him and it dawned upon him that *Caroline* was carrying depth-charge throwers. She was a Q-ship and he had been fooled by her like any amateur! He could not dive so long as the midshipman lay helpless on the bridge, and for all he knew the boat might no longer be watertight. He lost his balance and fell as the first lieutenant dragged him under cover.

The black pall of smoke from his own diesels lay between him and the *Caroline*, obscuring her from sight. How often had they cursed when the diesels had hidden a target; this time it was to be their salvation. The range increased and *Caroline* ceased fire; Hardegen fell rather than climbed down the ladder. They laid the midshipman in the wardroom and cut off his blood-soaked trousers, while the navigator made a tourniquet out of his own belt. The midshipman was conscious, his face gray, his eyes enormous and dark, his lips tight shut. He made no sound. They had put a towel over his legs and this Hardegen carefully lifted to look at the terribly torn flesh. He saw at once that it was hopeless and having given him an injection of morphine and made him as comfortable as he could, turned away to the control room and took the boat down to periscope depth. As soon as she had leveled off he turned toward the *Caroline*, which was lying stopped apparently awaiting a fresh attack. Her bows had not sunk any deeper and the fire had been put out; she was floating as though her holds were full of empty barrels. The "panic party" appeared to have returned on board; her boats were back in their davits.

Calmly and carefully Hardegen brought *U 123* into firing position, taking aim deliberately until *Caroline's* engine room was directly in his sights. Twenty-four seconds later a column of water shot up beside the ship's funnel and she lurched forward and down until her bows were under water as far as the bridge, and her screw and rudder lifted high out of the water. Hardegen watched through the periscope as the crew once again ran to the boats and lowered them into the water. At half past five he surfaced well out of range and lay watching the *Caroline*. Her boats were no longer in sight. A few minutes before six she suddenly lifted her bows; three heavy explosions echoed through the U-boat—then she was gone.[5]

Late that night the midshipman's face grew suddenly smaller; he stretched himself slightly—and died, peacefully and without a struggle. The coxswain fetched a new hammock from the store; as the first hint of dawn stood in the eastern sky the U-boat was stopped. In the stillness of the morning Hardegen's

[5] Tanker *Caroline* sunk by U-boat on March 27, 1942, in approximate position 36°N, 70°W.

voice was heard intoning the Lord's Prayer; then, at a barely perceptible signal from him, the dead officer's body slid gently into the sea to his last resting place, while all hands stood at the salute.

On April 14 the Americans scored their first success. Greger in *U 85* fell a victim to a depth-charge attack by the U.S. destroyer *Roper* east of Cape Hatteras. The American defenses, though still very weak, were gradually improving as a regular coastal patrol service was built up with destroyers, coast-guard vessels and small patrol craft, which also provided local escort for the merchant ships. Nor was this the only zone where the U-boats suffered losses in the early months of 1942. On February 6, while returning from patrol, Siegfried Rollmann in *U 82* reported a small and apparently weakly escorted convoy west of the Bay of Biscay; he was ordered to maintain contact, but after a few signals *U 82* went silent and failed to answer. On March, 26, *U 587*, also returning from patrol, reported a small and weakly defended convoy in the same area. In accordance with instructions Commander Borcherdt shadowed it, but after a few hours his reports also ceased. On the fifteenth of April a new commander, Lerchen, on his first patrol from Kiel in *U 252* sighted a convoy in the same area which could not be related to any of the known shipping movement identified by U-boat Command, A.O.C. Atlantic or the Admiralty. He at once received orders to move with the utmost caution and to attack only at night under most favorable conditions—but shortly afterward *U 252* ceased to answer signals.

To this problem of unexplained losses was added yet another. In March a captain returned from patrol with the disturbing report that, while steaming on the surface in the Bay of Biscay at night, he had suddenly observed a searchlight a few hundred yards astern of him, directly in his wake. This was something quite new; they had already experienced night air patrols off Gibraltar and more recently off Trinidad when the moon was high, but this was the first they had heard of planes equipped with searchlights. Dönitz promptly dispatched a staff officer, Lieutenant Meckel, to Berlin to get a firm answer to the question: Can an aircraft detect a U-boat so accurately at night that it can fly straight toward her? The experts at the Admiralty thought that this was highly improbable.

"Highly improbable is not good enough," said Dönitz's emissary. "What the admiral wants to know is not whether it is probable but whether it is technically feasible." "We cannot tell you for certain," was the reply, "but from our own technical knowledge we would say not."

All these new experiences, together with the vast size of the new area of operations, made it essential for the U-boat Command to be kept as fully informed as possible on all details. The previous policy was accordingly reversed and all boats were now ordered to make detailed signals reporting everything that happened at sea. U-boat captains were ordered to run the risk of the enemy taking bearings on their transmissions, for the information that they could and did send was vitally important to the planning of operations.

Operation *Paukenschlag* had ushered in the Second Golden Age for the U-boats, which lasted for three full months before the enemy's countermeasures in the waters between Nantucket and Cape Hatteras became really effective. In March, 1942, the first U-tanker—*U 459* under Commander von Wilamowitz-Möllendorf—made its appearance. These Type XIV "milch cows" were slow, clumsy boats of nearly 1,700 tons, able to carry 700 tons of fuel, of which the greater part was available for refueling other U-boats. They had no torpedo tubes and were armed only with two 3.7-cm. guns and one 2-cm. A.A. gun. They were not built to fight but were intended purely as supply ships. Their tanks held sufficient to give 50 tons of fuel to twelve medium-sized boats, enabling them to operate in the furthest corners of the Caribbean, or 90 tons to five of the larger boats operating as far away as Cape Town. They carried a store of spare parts as well as a doctor and a number of technicians to replace torpedo ratings, radiomen or electronics technicians when necessary. The U-tankers were generally regarded as a gift from heaven and they and their commanders were all extremely popular; von Wilamowitz-Möllendorf had commanded a U-boat in the Great War and was one of the very few officers to do the same in the Second World War. Between 80 per cent and 90 per cent of the boats in the Caribbean came to refuel from von Wilamowitz-Möllendorf and the other U-tankers commanded by Schorn, Stiebler, Vowe and Wolfbauer; there can be no doubt that without them the Caribbean campaign would have lost much of its sting.

In April there was a sudden lull in the traffic in the south, coinciding with the period of full moon. It was not until May 9 that a convoy was sighted, heavily escorted and keeping close in to the shore, which made conditions for attack much more difficult. But, while Suhren in *U 564* and Cremer in *U 333* managed to sink a dozen ships in all, the fourteen other commanders spread out along five hundred miles of coastal waters barely achieved as much among them. American ships were now sailing in regular convoys, closely escorted by destroyers and patrol vessels under strong air cover. The escorts had profited by experience and were attacking more accurately. Three boats—one third of the forces between Halifax and Hatteras—fell victim to them; *U 215* under Hoeckner, Heinicke's *U 576* which was lost with her entire crew and "the gallant Degen," as Dönitz had called him, who was taken prisoner with some of the crew of *U 701*.

To avert further disasters all boats were ordered to withdraw from the immediate vicinity of Cape Hatteras. For half a year the Sea Wolves had been harrying these waters, where the last resting place of several hundred ships was shown on the operations-room chart by thickly bunched gold pins; and for the first time in six months peace reigned once more round Cape Hatteras while the U-boats drove deeper into the Caribbean, where attack conditions were still favorable. As an immediate result, six ships were sunk by each of nine U-boats operating between the Bahamas and the Windward Passage, in the Gulf of Mexico, in the area south of Cuba as far as the Yucatan Narrows, off Curaçao, Aruba, Trinidad and the coast of Guiana. The enemy was taken completely by surprise here, for the attacking boats found no sign of regular air patrols nor any system of sailing ships in convoy.

These successes encouraged Dönitz to press once more for the release of the boats operating in the Far North, at least during the summer months, so that they could reinforce the Atlantic operations. But the German Admiralty rejected his argument that every ship sunk in the west was one less for the enemy's Russian front; and even went so far as to maintain that the Arctic U-boats were doing a vital job of shadowing for the *Luftwaffe* planes operating against the Arctic convoys. Dönitz came near to despair. German naval statisticians had calculated that not less than 700,000 tons must be sunk per month, merely to keep level with the enemy's new construction; only when that figure was exceeded would his shipping reserves begin to shrink. Yet the Admiralty was proposing to ignore the rich harvest that could be garnered in the west and to keep twenty boats "in cold storage" in the Arctic.

In the middle of May, Marshal Pétain's administration

learned that there was a possibility of an American attack on Martinique; the waters off Fort de France were being continuously patrolled by light U.S. warships and flying boats. The Vichy Government could not rely upon the French warships and merchant ships in harbor and suspected that they were preparing to break out and join forces with the enemy.

Hartenstein in *U 156* and Zahn in *U 69* received orders to keep watch on the threatened French colony and to attack and sink any American warships or French ships attempting to break out. *U 156* arrived off Fort de France in a period of full moon, which was so bright that there were hardly any hours of darkness at all; Hartenstein was forced to remain submerged throughout the day and night, except for the minimum of four hours in which he could recharge batteries. The men groaned and sweated as the temperature in the boat became unbearable. After seven days of this—120 hours submerged—Hartenstein had to signal to headquarters that he had reached the limit of endurance, and he was forthwith given another operational area.

This signal caused much concern to Dönitz. (He was no longer at Kernevel; since the British raid on St. Nazaire earlier in the year, a direct order had come from Hitler to withdraw U-boat headquarters to Paris and he had set up his command post in the *Avenue Maréchal Maunoury*). Hartenstein was one of his best officers and it would take a lot before he would complain about the limits of endurance; but great heat was not the only thing they had to contend with in these waters. Almost at the same time as Hartenstein's signal was received, came news of the failure of three boats bound for the Brazilian coast to attack a convoy in West African waters. They were just not capable of shadowing it under the constant pressure of sea and air patrols. Things had indeed changed since the exploits of *U 105* and *U 106* in the same waters a year earlier!

Witte in *U 159* had been on patrol off the coast of Venezuela and was due to start for home after expending all torpedoes and most of the gun ammunition. His 3.7-cm. gun was out of action and the condition of the few remaining rounds of 2-cm. was doubtful, ever since the U-boat had been heavily depth-charged during a deep dive.

Two days after they had turned for home they sighted a large tanker just as dusk was falling, and Witte decided to surface and try to set her on fire with his remaining ammunition. The third shot landed right on the bridge and all the next rounds hit, but very few of them exploded; they had all been affected by the depth charging. The tanker did not return the fire. They heard her signaling: *"E. J. Sadler* [6] shelled by submarine" and giving her position; immediately afterward her first boat swung out. The ship lost way and broached to as the lifeboat moved away from her. Her gun was unmanned; three other boats followed the first into the water. "Set the bridge on fire," Witte ordered. As the gun roared again, the shells began to take effect; splinters flew into the air, steel plates buckled, fire broke out and the bridge soon disappeared in a sheet of flame. The U-boat's gun went on firing until the last round had been used. Then they waited for the ship to sink—one hour, two hours—but the fire still burned, while the ship showed no sign of going under. Time was passing—it would soon be dawn—so Witte decided to send the dinghy over with a demolition party. Consumed with impatience he waited anxiously until the first lieutenant returned, bearing under his arm a memento of his visit— some whisky and gin from the ship's pantry. Then four dull explosions rumbled through the tanker and she began to settle, stern first. Slowly and majestically her bows lifted above the waves until her hull was standing vertically out of the water; then quietly and still slowly she sank beneath the waves.

The history of this period of operations in the Caribbean and Mexican Gulf is full of similar actions, in which daring gun actions, bluff and surprise contributed to the sinking of even bigger and better-armed adversaries than the *E. J. Sadler*. Toward the end of June there was evidence for the first time of a gradual reduction in shipping in the Caribbean, while air patrols increased; and at length came reports of the first small convoys off Trinidad, off the Greater Antilles and Key West, and finally, off Yucatan Strait. Only in the Gulf of Mexico were ships continuing to sail alone and unprotected; in accordance with the principle of going after the ships where they were easiest to get, a group of U-boats was sent there, while at the same time boats were withdrawn gradually from the other positions in the Caribbean, always excepting the fruitful field of Trinidad. This was not because the A/S defenses off the American coast had grown too strong, but because with the end of independent sailings and the introduction of convoys it was no longer worth while to send boats

[6] The *E. J. Sadler,* a tanker of 9,639 tons, was sunk by gunfire from this U-boat on June 22, 1942, in 15°36'N 67°52'W.

so far out. So the Sea Wolves gradually returned to the Atlantic.

The Second Golden Age—the campaign in American waters—was over.

4

THE RADAR THREAT

(June-November, 1942)

During those adventurous early months of 1942 in the "Golden West," the U-boats had sunk—by Allied computation—495 ships of more than 2½ million tons, including 142 tankers; but by the beginning of the summer the wolf packs were ranging back to their old hunting grounds along the convoy routes between England and America.

Dönitz had never regarded this phase off the American seaboard as anything more than a lucky break which sooner or later must come to an end; and with that in mind he had ordered his boats to attack any England-bound convoys they might locate on their way across the Atlantic. Reports from the radio intercept service indicated that the enemy was no longer spreading his convoys all over the North Atlantic but was sailing them along the great circle between Newfoundland and the North Channel, which made it easier to locate them. Yet it was not clear whether this policy had been adopted because of the cessation of convoy attacks in the previous November, or because of shortage of shipping or loss of ships in American waters; whatever the cause, the fact remained, and at the beginning of May, 1942, eight U-boats sailed to carry out a two-pronged search along the Great Circle.

Before they had reached their operational area, one of them—Hinsch in *U 569*—sighted a southwest-bound convoy and shadowed it until five other boats could join him. Then the wolf pack fell upon the flock and seven ships were sunk in the first night; the U-boats lost contact at dawn but sighted a straggler who led them back to the convoy. Again they lost contact through bad weather, so headquarters ordered them to head west at high speed and form a line across the enemy's route. Meanwhile the intercept service had identified another convoy, eastbound this time, which was some three hundred miles west of the U-boats. The group was ordered to steam slowly toward the first convoy, so as to be in a position to attack first it and then the second. This operation was a failure; *U 406* did not keep proper station, and the convoy slipped through the gap thus made. As soon as they realized this, all boats turned westward to search for the convoys, but visibility was against them and at length they all concentrated on *U 116,* a big mine-laying U-boat acting as a tanker. They had barely completed refueling before headquarters formed them once again into a search group heading northeast. On the very first night they sighted a convoy in brilliant moonlight, but the weather remained so consistently bad that it was eight days before any attack could be made—and then only two boats managed to get near enough. The enemy lost five ships and a destroyer.

Since several of the boats still had a full complement of torpedoes, they were told to remain in the area. Their attempted attack on an American-bound convoy a few days later was driven off by the strong escorts, many of the U-boats reporting serious damage. The boats were ordered to break off the engagement and return to base at their most economical speed.

While these operations were in progress in the North Atlantic, another group of five boats—later reinforced by four more—was sent against a convoy reported by agents to be leaving Gibraltar.[1] Owing to a navigational error the boats missed the convoy on their first attempt, but contact was finally made and five ships were sunk by *U 552.* Her captain, Erich Topp, winner of the swords to his Knight's Cross, was later sent to teach young U-boat officers how to attack heavily defended convoys at the Tactical Training School at Gotenhafen. No other U-boat was able to break through the escorting screen. Once again Dönitz ordered the boats to disengage, and in the following weeks he instituted a most searching analysis of all these operations and circulated it to all operational and training flotillas; his forecast proved correct—the U-boat's main battleground would move steadily away from the American coast and back to the Atlantic.

The conditions under which convoys could be successfully attacked had not changed much since the early days; the opportunities were still there. At the moment, however, the

---

[1] German agents in the Bay of Algeciras had no difficulty in observing the assembly and departure of convoys at Gibraltar.

average tonnage sunk by each boat in a day was not one
tenth of the figure for 1940. Yet the number of new boats
becoming available was mounting steadily and this would
help in the race between sinkings and new-construction shipping. From May, 1942, onward, thirty new boats manned
by fully trained crews were reaching the operational bases
every month. As a flotilla commander said after the war, "It
must not be forgotten that by the side of Dönitz at that time
stood the greatest organizing genius that the Navy has ever
produced—Admiral von Friedeburg. It was he who created
the 'endless belt' system for new boats and for their crews.
The personnel for the bases at home and in occupied territory, the men for the schools and the training establishments,
and for everything else, were conjured up by him out of
thin air."

Dönitz was ever preoccupied with the problem of radar
location. Several months had passed since his communications expert, Meckel, had gone to Berlin in search of an
antidote. The admiral was convinced that the enemy was
up to something and that the menace of that "something"
was greater than ever; but detailed information was lacking.

On June 17, 1942, in the middle of a convoy operation
he called up Jochen Mohr on the "scrambler" radiotelephone
—the latest development in radio communications—to ask
if Mohr had had any personal experience of radar-location
devices in enemy surface ships. Mohr at once described an
action on the previous day, when on two occasions he had
been forced to dive by destroyers which came toward him
from well below the horizon, dropping small depth charges
over him when he dived. Nevertheless, said Mohr, he believed that their movements were nothing more than normal bold sweeps, because the destroyers never steamed
straight at him, nor did they turn to follow when he took
evasive action. What neither Mohr nor Dönitz knew at this
juncture was that the destroyers did indeed have radar, but
were purposely not steering straight at their targets so as not
to betray the fact.[2]

The difficulty of establishing whether or not the enemy
was using radar increased when the Germans discovered that
the enemy could very speedily identify the wave length on
which the U-boats were sending beacon signals to "home"

---

[2] Although the destroyers did have radar, they did not always go
straight for the U-boat because the radar contact faded at close range,
and not for the reason suggested by the author.

other boats on to a convoy. On two separate occasions escort vessels suddenly appeared from below the horizon to attack Kuppisch in *U 94* while he was emitting such beacon signals. Had the enemy taken D/F bearings on his transmissions, or had he been located by radar? It was all very mysterious.

Conditions in the Bay of Biscay began to deteriorate sharply; the whole area was now patrolled by many more fast aircraft by night as well as by day. The passage through the storm-swept bay, which, in 1940, the crews had regarded as merely the prelude to a pleasant period of shore leave, now became a nightmare stretch of highly dangerous water. Aircraft swept in to attack out of the sun or the clouds so swiftly that the boats no longer had time to dive deep; and bombs falling round a diving boat 150 feet down could easily prove lethal.

Then there was the problem of aircraft equipped with searchlights. Time after time came reports of U-boats being surprised on the surface at night by aircraft which swept down upon them out of the clouds.[3] Boats were being lost on the last stretch of their homeward run. Von Rosenstiel in *U 502* was lost in this way as he was returning from a successful patrol in American waters; Hoffmann was lost in *U 165* on his way from Kiel to France; Rehwinkel was sunk in *U 578* on his way out from La Pallice and so was Horn in *U 705* and Bigalk in *U 751*.

Meckel explained to the admiral his belief that the aircraft were in fact using radar. It was known that radar was ineffective below a certain minimum range, and it was to overcome this "blind spot" that, having got as near as he could, a pilot would then switch on his searchlight, thus making the final approach by eye. Dönitz decided to send for Rear Admiral Stummel, the Director of Naval Communications. The latter agreed with Meckel's theory. "I am now convinced," he said, "that our U-boats are being located by airborne radar. The existence of such equipment in enemy aircraft has already been reported by our shore-based radar search receivers, particularly those on the channel coast." There was silence in the room as the three men pondered over this ominous diagnosis; then Dönitz asked whether there was any antidote.

---

[3] "Leigh Lights" for aircraft had been developed in the Coastal Command in 1941 and were being extensively used in combination with ASV (Air to Surface Vessel radar) by British aircraft at this time.

There were two antidotes, said Stummel—an active radar set or a passive radar interception set. He referred to them by their initials in German—FuMO and FuMB. The FuMO would indicate the range and bearing of the enemy, but its disadvantage for use by U-boats was that the radar impulses traveled much further than the maximum practicable range of an echo from a target.

"Please explain that," asked Dönitz. Stummel hesitated for a moment as he sought the clearest method of explanation. Then, "Let us suppose that a beam is transmitted from Point A with sufficient strength to enable its reflection from Point B to be measured. I can then obtain the bearing and distance from Point B. Reception from anywhere beyond Point B is unreliable because the echo is too weak; but the energy which is not reflected back from Point B travels beyond it at least as far again. Thus an enemy with an ordinary receiver at a point *beyond* B is capable of getting a bearing on my own radar transmission and can locate me while I am still unaware of his presence." Stummel went on to explain that the existing type of FuMO could be installed in U-boats but would need a special aerial, and even then would not provide complete security. It would take time to design and install the equipment. "But we need something immediately," said Dönitz impatiently.

"The alternative," went on Stummel unperturbed, "is the radar interception device or search receiver, the FuMB. With this, the situation is reversed; the U-boat can detect the enemy's radar impulses sooner than the enemy can locate the U-boat. What is more, we could supply the FuMB more quickly, because we already possess such a device in the *Metox,* which was originally developed by the French for a different purpose; the only thing lacking is an aerial but that is easy to rectify. The disadvantage of this detector device is that it will give only a very rough idea of the enemy's bearing and no indication whatever of his range."

Two days later the decision was taken that all U-boats were to be equipped as a matter of the utmost priority with radar search receivers, while the radar location set proper was to be developed for U-boats later on. Admiral Stummel was also asked to investigate the possibility of using an anti-radar "camouflage" which would absorb or deflect the enemy's radar impulses. The need was urgent, for in June alone three U-boats had been attacked by aircraft in the Bay of Biscay and so badly damaged that they had had to return to base without being able to submerge. Moreover, despite the efforts of the A.O.C. Atlantic to comply with Dönitz's urgent request, the *Luftwaffe* was unable to provide aircraft with sufficient range to give the damaged U-boats fighter protection.

At the beginning of July Dönitz obtained permission from the Admiralty to fly to East Prussia on a personal visit to Göring; it seemed the only way of getting the planes he needed so badly. The two men had last met in that train at Pontoise, when Göring had won the day. The *Luftwaffe* chief's manner and bearing on that occasion had been utterly repugnant, but Dönitz was ready to swallow his aversion if only he could get the planes.

Göring and his staff received the admiral and heard his story; then Göring's Chief of Staff, Colonel-General Jeschonnek, spoke. "I can allocate twenty-four Ju eighty-eight type C six to the A.O.C. Atlantic for your purposes," he said, "but I cannot send more or better planes as none are available." "You see," said Göring with a smile, "we do what we can." The parting between the two men was very cool.

A few weeks after the conference with Stummel in Paris, the first *Metox* radar search receivers began to arrive at the U-boat bases. The first hastily improvised aerials were installed on the boats' bridges—"Biscay crosses," they called them—plain wooden frames bound with wire and set on a shaft connected with the receiving set below deck by a cable running through the conning-tower hatch. The "Biscay cross" had to be revolved by hand and before diving it had to be dismantled and carried below; a rating was specially stationed in the conning tower to rush the "cross" below as soon as the *Metox* gave out a steady note. There would be a shout of, "Radar tone is steady!" followed by the order "Down cross! Crash-dive!" in quick succession. And it worked! The Biscay nightmare faded steadily before the crew's rising morale as they learned how to pick up the radar tones and then dive deep before the enemy aircraft could swoop down on them. Later *Metox's* equipment had an improved waterproof aerial which could be safely left on the bridge when diving. Further modifications included an automatic wave meter and a "magic eye" on the receiver. The only disadvantage of this device was the psychological effect on the crew. Previously only the captain had known when danger was near, but now everyone in the boat could hear the sudden change from a varying tone to a steady whistle, which got on everyone's nerves; several captains used to switch the receiver off as soon as they located a convoy.

Soon after the *Metox* had been installed, two boats registered reception of radar transmission from destroyers on very high frequency. This could explain why in the summer several boats had been suddenly attacked by gunfire at night or in fog. But was the enemy's radar adequate in itself to locate a target blindly in fog, or was he using some additional unidentified device such as infrared or ultraviolet waves for fire control, or an ionization indicator which would reveal the presence of diesel exhaust gases? Nothing seemed impossible.

Dönitz kept up a ruthless pressure on the experts in Berlin. The slightest reference to this new weapon in any incoming signal was analyzed and dissected and compared with similar reports; and every new theory was at once passed on to Berlin. The suspicion that the enemy possessed a new and vitally important invention hung like a cloud above their heads. Nevertheless the boats continued to attack—and with no small success. As a British official writer put it:

> The battle did indeed stagnate for a while but the initiative still lay with the enemy. His energy and resourcefulness in finding new remedies were immense and we learned from experience how ably and imaginatively he could exploit the steady increase in his forces, despite an increase in the number of U-boats destroyed. From August onwards the U-boats were coming off the launching-ways faster than we could sink them. The enemy had some 80 boats at sea and although the coasts of North America offered few prospects of success, he was able to fight a ten-day battle off Trinidad at the same time as he was launching a slightly less heavy attack in the Windward Passage southeast of Cuba. Through these waters came the ships carrying bauxite from South America for the American armament factories, and other war supplies for the Middle East. . . . Other groups of U-boats were operating in the Mediterranean and the Arctic, still others off Freetown, while some probed for weak spots in our defenses as far as the Cape of Good Hope. However the main German forces were concentrated in the North Atlantic employing their well-known "wolf-pack" tactics against convoys. During this month U-boats sank 108 Allied ships of more than 500,000 tons. Attacks were sustained by day and night; in one operation lasting four days a convoy lost eleven ships, yet in the whole of August only four U-boats were destroyed.[4]

[4] From *The Battle of the Atlantic*, published by HM Stationary Office.

The Battle of the Atlantic became ever more intense. In 1941 the enemy planes' radius of action did not exceed five hundred miles; there was still an extensive gap in the middle of the North Atlantic—the "Devil's Gorge"—where the attacking U-boats were out of range of land-based aircraft. But by the summer of 1942 planes based on England, Northern Ireland, Iceland and Newfoundland were ranging eight hundred miles into the Atlantic—the gap was narrowing. In September more than one operation had to be broken off (as had happened once before in July) because the air escorts were too strong to allow the U-boats to approach the convoy. The *Metox* was of course nothing more than a weapon of defense; it could not be expected to improve the U-boat's chances of attacking successfully. The effective range of the enemy's radar was increasing all the time, and with every new improvement his ships and aircraft were able to attack a U-boat more accurately and more quickly than before; to "attack" in this sense did not necessarily involve the destruction of the boat—it was sufficient to force it to remain submerged until the convoy was out of range. Such tactics rendered the classic attack by night on the surface almost inoperable.

The autumn of 1942 ushered in many new ideas. First there was the Pi 2, the long-awaited magnetic pistol for torpedoes, which detonated the warhead immediately beneath the target's keel and broke its back. Then came the G7a-FAT and the G7e-FAT torpedo—a murderous new weapon, almost a robot, which after running a straight course for a set distance, described a series of deep or shallow loops to cover the water over which the convoy would pass. And there was more to come, the experts promised; soon they would be producing the "destroyer killer"—an acoustic torpedo. The standard torpedo offered little danger to a destroyer because of her relative high speed and shallow draft. It was realized that in future the U-boats would have to eliminate the convoy escorts before they could come at the merchant ships themselves; this new weapon, guided by engine or propeller noises, would seek out its own target. In this connection Meckel had even proposed the manufacture of a rocket projectile with a powerful warhead for use against destroyers, "such as is now being developed at Peenemünde . . ."

Dönitz, watching the first demonstrations of the FAT torpedoes at Gotenhafen with Admirals von Friedeburg,

Ciliax and Backenköhler,[5] was deeply impressed. The first experimental torpedoes were fitted with luminous dummy warheads, so that the practice target ships of a "convoy" could see them under water and report each "hit" by firing a Very light. Soon the sky was filled with Very lights, as the torpedoes found their mark. Dönitz returned to Paris full of hope; the FAT torpedoes should be available in large number by October. They could not be delivered too quickly, for the current models were far from satisfactory; between January and July over eight hundred torpedoes had been needed to sink four hundred ships. A new and improved pistol was of the first importance.

Weapons of defense were as important as weapons of offense. Among the requirements for new developments forwarded from the U-boat Command to the Admiralty at this time were a combined radar search and radar detection receiver with a revolving antenna; two 3.7-cm. A.A. guns[6] and a twin MG 151 gun for every U-boat, of the type used in the *Luftwaffe;* a second platform to hold a multiple-barrel 2-cm. gun [6] and some superheavy machine guns; U-boats as anti-aircraft traps, which would draw the fire of attacking planes and shoot them down; and more Ju 88s and the new He 177s to patrol the Bay of Biscay. The latter were the four-engined double-prop planes with a radius of 1,400 miles.

On the whole the situation had improved considerably since July. From 504,000 tons in that month the sinking figures had risen to 650,000 tons in August and to about the same in September. U-boat losses had dropped from 15 per cent in July to 9.5 per cent in August and 6 per cent in September—and this despite the enemy's reinforced escort forces and his use of air to surface vessel radar. Since the beginning of the year the electric motors and other vital parts of all U-boats had been fitted with special rubber mountings, which greatly reduced the damaging effect of depth-charge explosions. Another new device, the "Bold," introduced in the spring, had already proved effective. It consisted of a container with a chemical substance; several of them could be discharged at intervals from the submerged U-boat while the latter was being tracked by the asdics of the hunting destroyers. When one came in contact

[5] At this time Admiral Otto Ciliax was head of the Torpedo Inspection Department. Admiral Otto Backenköhler was the Director of Naval Armament Production.
[6] Equivalent to U.S. 40 and 20mm machine guns.

with the sea water the chemical substance formed a large mass of bubbles which remained capable of reflecting the asdic impulses for some fifteen minutes before disintegrating. The enemy would get bearings on the bubbles and attack them, while the U-boat would escape in another direction. In short, the "Bold" was an asdic decoy.

In the late summer and autumn of 1942, the Battle of the Atlantic reached a new peak of ferocity. The ability of the staff officers on shore and the endurance of the men at sea surpassed all previous efforts. It took three to four days for the boats, using their *Metox*, to get clear of the bay and a day or two longer to reach their patrol areas; after that they came under the direct control of the U-boat Command, which promptly assigned them to one or other of the search groups already in position, lying as close in to the coast as the enemy's air patrols would allow and watching the routes which the outward-bound convoys would take. The boats themselves were keeping closer together than before; the intervals between them were not more than fifteen to twenty miles, where previously they had stayed as much as thirty miles apart. They would remain submerged for days at a time, so as to avoid detection; absolute radio silence was imposed, and when they were ordered to change position they did so as unobtrusively as possible. Nearly all their patrol positions were sited to the north or south of Ireland where the westbound convoys were sure to pass; these were routed either direct across the Atlantic to Halifax or by Iceland, Greenland and Newfoundland, while the ships destined for Bermuda left the Irish Channel on a southwesterly course via the Azores. It mattered little that the westbound ships carried less valuable cargoes than those steering east, for the U-boats' objective remained the same—the destruction of as much shipping as possible.

While the men at sea ate and slept amid the ceaseless humming of the electric motors, in Paris the staff officers were sorting and analyzing reports from secret agents, decrypted enemy signals and any other intelligence that came in, in an unceasing effort to identify all the necessary data about the sailing of convoys. Their task was rendered somewhat easier by the enemy's own tactics. He no longer spread his convoys over the length and breadth of the Atlantic as he had done in 1941; now he was sailing them along a narrow channel and often by the shortest route. Dönitz knew that he was running a neck-and-neck race against time; he had to sustain the level of sinkings so as to keep the initial advantage he had won. Time was everything; that became his motto and he drove himself without thought of rest or recreation. His only relaxation was an occasional visit to the Cathedral of Notre Dame: Bach's music, played on the great organ with clarity and power, could soothe him.

And the successes continued. On October 16 eleven ships were destroyed out of a convoy of forty [7] against the loss of one U-boat sunk and another badly damaged. Between October 24 and the sixth of November, Convoy SC 107 [8] was engaged in a bitterly contested action with a group of U-boats code-named "Violet." After the war the enemy admitted that in October, 1942, they lost ninety-three ships of more than 600,000 tons, including five large and fast liners which had been sailed independently as their high speed had been regarded as sufficient safeguard. The U-boat losses were low by comparison, and the crews were more likely at this time to fail through fatigue from so many attacks, than through enemy countermeasures.

5

NEW IDEAS FOR OLD

(Autumn, 1942)

The extraordinary run of success that the Sea Wolves were enjoying did not blind them or the admiral to the menace of developments in the enemy's radar. The German experts had been only partially successful in their search for a covering for the U-boats' hulls which would absorb ASV impulses; to all intents and purposes a U-boat on the surface at night was still "visible" to the enemy. It was becoming clear that there was already a need for a new type of genuine underwater warship—one that could live and fight more or less permanently submerged. With these thoughts in mind Dönitz summoned a conference in Paris in the autumn of 1942, to which he invited Schürer and Bröcking, the two U-boat designers, and Professor Walter, the inventor of the

[7] On October 13 and 14, eight ships were lost out of forty-seven in Convoy SC 104; and two out of the forty in Convoy ON 137 on October 18 and 19.

[8] British records show that Convoy SC 107 (thirty-nine ships) lost fifteen of its number between the second and fourth of November, 1942.

system of propulsion that bore his name. Having failed in his previous attempts to institute regular planning conferences at the Admiralty, Dönitz had decided that the best way to achieve his objective was to get the designers themselves to come to him.

The admiral opened the meeting by explaining the vital need for U-boats that could move as fast and as far submerged as the existing ones could move on the surface; whereupon Professor Walter pointed out that the first U-boat to be fitted with his turbines had reached a speed of 23 knots submerged, compared with the eight or nine knots of the standard boats. "I can only regret," Walter went on, "that we are not further advanced. Had I received full and timely encouragement from our Admiralty, I should now be at least a year ahead, so that the first trial boats could have been in service this autumn, instead of at the end of 1943."

Dönitz then called for alternative suggestions that would cover the period until Walter-type boats would be ready. Thedsen, the senior U-boat engineer officer, proposed building bigger boats with larger batteries, provided always that the heavier displacement did not negate the extra energy. Schürer pointed out that this would require much more steel, which in turn would mean fewer U-boats, but Bröcking promised to look into the problem at once. The admiral reminded them, however, that larger batteries would take longer to charge, which would involve spending more time on the surface.

Professor Walter was outlining an idea on his scribbling pad. "To overcome this," he said, "we ought to build a sort of air pipe with a float-operated valve at the top, which opens and shuts automatically to keep out the water. While at periscope depth the diesels could draw their air and exhaust their gases through this tube, and the batteries could be charged at the same time. That would surely help your boats in the Atlantic. They could charge batteries submerged; for an object as small as the valve head of a snort tube would be invisible at night and difficult to locate by day. Moreover the batteries themselves could be made larger, which would give you higher speeds submerged, greater endurance and better chances of attack and—when necessary—escape."

This was the birth of the *Schnorchel*, which before the end of the war became standard equipment for all U-boats.[1]

[1] The first to use the SNORT principle were the Dutch, one of whose submarines, so fitted, was found at Amsterdam by the Germans at the invasion of Holland in 1940.

As a result of that Paris conference, Hitler, already briefed by Captain von Puttkamer about Dönitz's anxiety, decided to summon a meeting on future U-boat plans. The admiral got ready to fly to Berlin on the appointed date in September, when the meeting was suddenly postponed for four days. When eventually Dönitz entered the Reich Chancellery he found Grand Admiral Raeder already surrounded by a host of technical experts who were laying before Hitler innumerable drawings and tables in explanation of Raeder's plans for the U-boats. Dönitz, standing apart from the rest, listened to all this, his silence and remoteness seeming to express his dissatisfaction with the form of the presentation, particularly with the inadequate emphasis on the Walter U-boats. When he was eventually called upon to speak, he warned Hitler that soon the U-boats, which still did most of their attacking while on the surface, would have to give up these tactics because of the air menace. But if they kept under water they would achieve far smaller results, and the effect on the war would be most serious. It was vital, he said, to introduce new types of boats with the utmost priority.

Hitler listened attentively, put a few questions to Raeder and then to Dönitz, and relapsed into a long silence. "Thank you, Admiral Dönitz," he said at length, "but I can hardly believe that the whole Atlantic and every single convoy could be effectively covered by air patrols. The distances are too great." He stood up, dismissed first Raeder, then Dönitz, and turned away to other matters. The conference was over.

Flying back to Paris, Dönitz felt deeply disappointed at the lack of support or sympathy in high quarters. Sitting as usual alongside his pilot, he reflected on the recent developments in his relations with his commander in chief. Raeder had always impressed him as being clever, if somewhat cold. The contacts between the two men had always been more formal than was usual between a superior officer and his subordinate.

As the Junkers thundered over the Ruhr, ploughed fields alternated with smoking chimneys and lofty slag heaps. The towns seemed to grow toward each other, the thickly populated districts looking like one huge city linked by a maze of shining railway lines. The smoke from a myriad of chimneys hung in the air like a thick brown blanket. Mercifully there was little evidence of bomb damage; the landscape lay intact and peaceful beneath him. But how long would it remain so?

The admiral thought of the first heavy air raid on the center of Lübeck in the previous March. Places which could not possibly be considered as strategically important had been wantonly and uselessly destroyed. There were no factories in the heart of that island city; the target chosen for destruction was one of the finest examples of a medieval town; the churches of St. Mary and St. Peter and the Cathedral of Henry the Lion had gone up in flames. His own pilot had flown over the burning city next day and had seen the five lofty spires blazing like giant torches, symbols of an age that stopped at nothing, held nothing sacred and stood condemned by its own outbreak of inhuman hatred. Everybody knew that the *Luftwaffe* was unable to prevent such attacks or to make adequate reply to them; the fat *Reichsmarschall* had overreached himself with his boastful claims.

The Junkers was now roaring over the Vosges; the pilot had gone very high. The thick blanket of cloud beneath parted occasionally to reveal wooded hills and deep valleys with villages, church spires and little winding streams. Occasionally a short, sharp squall would hit the aircraft, forcing it to climb into calmer air, and the sea of clouds would spread out beneath like an unending feather mattress.

In his cramped seat Dönitz ruminated over the grand admiral's apparent indifference toward the U-boat Service. As a member of Admiral Hipper's staff at the Battle of Jutland, Raeder was of course a "big ship man," and it certainly was not his fault, but rather his personal tragedy, that the outbreak of war had found his fleet only half built, with none of the heavy ships ready for service. He never really seemed to understand that the only effective units with which to strike at the enemy were the U-boats—the classic weapon of the weaker naval power. Dönitz had continually to ask for more than Raeder, viewing the Navy's needs as a whole, was prepared to concede; for the grand admiral had very strong views on the scope and limitations of naval expansion, and nothing would induce him to change those views. Ever since 1941 this fundamental disagreement had been the cause of a steady deterioration in their personal relations. Being so utterly different in character, they blended just about as well as oil and water, and it was only the strict code of discipline between senior and subordinate that enabled them to work together at all.

Despite their differences of opinion, Dönitz had hoped that the mounting successes of his U-boats in 1942 would bring about an improvement in their relations; instead of that they got steadily worse. Now, in the autumn of the third year of war, with not more than about twenty boats at sea at a time, the monthly tonnage of ships sunk was rising steadily toward the million mark. Think what could have been done with the one hundred boats that had been asked for in peacetime! Once again—as in the First World War—the enemy had been given the chance to build up his defenses; the great opportunity had passed, and with it the chance of victory. Germany's only hope now was to fight the war to a standstill, so that both sides would agree to a compromise peace. To achieve even this would require an all-out effort; there was no room for personal recriminations.

Into the admiral's field of vision came a dark spot, which grew rapidly larger until it looked like a bollard on a jetty— the top of the Eiffel Tower rising above the clouds. Thank God, home again, the admiral thought involuntarily, as the plane slid down through the cotton-wool clouds and circled to make a landing. It really was like coming home, every time he returned to Paris. This was his headquarters, here was the circle of men who, like him, thought only of how to help the U-boats on to victory; here was the atmosphere of hard work, of faith and devotion to the cause, where he could keep in constant touch with those far out at sea who were bearing the brunt of the battle.

If Dönitz hoped that his plea would speed up the building of better and faster U-boats, he was soon to learn otherwise. His proposals evoked in the commander in chief a totally unexpected reaction, in the form of a brief written order. By this new directive the flag officer, U-boats was henceforward forbidden to handle technical problems, confining himself solely to operational matters. The order bore the personal signature of the grand admiral, with its huge initial R followed by precisely formed smaller letters.

Dönitz sent for Godt and slid the paper across the desk to him. "What do you make of that?" Captain Godt read it through carefully, then went red. "The grand admiral seems to have misunderstood your motives, Sir," he said at last.

"The order is inoperable," said Dönitz angrily. "I cannot obey it because it won't work. Every single day I have to deal with all sorts of technical questions about repairs, training, alterations, trials. How can I know when a boat is ready for sea if I can't communicate with the dockyard?" He picked up the telephone.

"Admiral here. Get me Admiral Schulte-Mönting [2] in Berlin." There was silence for a moment, then a voice at the other end of the line. "Schulte-Mönting? Dönitz here." The

[2] Chief of Staff to the Commander in Chief.

admiral's voice was once more under control. "I have today received a personal directive from the commander in chief." He picked up the paper, smoothed it out impatiently on the desk and read it aloud, adding, "Please inform the grand admiral that I cannot obey this order. At the very least I must keep control of everything that goes on in the dockyards and armament depots." He hung up. "Well, Godt," he said, "if I were in Raeder's place I would probably sack the flag officer, U-boats for this; but we'll see what happens."

But nothing further was heard from Berlin, and several weeks went by while Dönitz carried on as usual. Then, late in the autumn, in the middle of a very difficult operation involving the Atlantic boats off Gibraltar, something happened which seemed bound at last to bring matters to a head between him and his commander in chief. Once again a directive arrived from Raeder.

"I have decided to reorganize the U-boat Service, as it is now too big to be controlled by one man. Details of the new scheme are on the enclosed plan, which is to be put into effect without any basic alteration. However, if flag officer, U-boats has any recommendations or improvements as to detail, he may submit suggestions accordingly."

In this new organization the flag officer, U-boats was to retain control only of operations in the Atlantic. Training and shakedown of boats at home bases would come under the orders of the admiral commanding the Baltic at Kiel. Dönitz read no further; he was boiling with rage. This plan, if carried out, would mean the dismemberment of the U-boat Service, the self-immolation of the one and only instrument left with which the Navy could hope to bring about a peace on reasonable terms. Guse, the Admiral Commanding the Baltic, knew nothing about U-boats; it was vitally important that the whole of the service should remain under one experienced commander; its efficiency depended upon such unity. It depended upon the close coordination between the men under training and those on active operations, whereby the best and most experienced operational officers could be constantly exchanged between the battle zone and the training bases. Every new development at sea was passed by signal almost daily to the training centers, where it could be properly evaluated. Operational bases and home bases were like two limbs of the same body; the organization had grown from small beginnings and had expanded with the needs of the moment. It had produced training conditions as near as possible to the real thing, had proved itself in action and had reduced the incidence of loss. Now this link was to be snapped—right in the middle of success which in itself justified the existing organization. Furthermore this drastic change, which cut right across Dönitz's responsibilities, was to be effected without even asking his advice. He was not prepared to accept this and wrote a letter to the Chief of Staff to the Grand Admiral, in which he set out the disadvantages and inevitable consequences of the new proposals, adding that, should the grand admiral stand by his decision, he would immediately ask to be relieved of his command.

Meanwhile Godt, who had been shown this letter, feared that neither admiral would retreat, which would inevitably force Dönitz to resign. On his own initiative Godt therefore visited Captain von Puttkamer, the Führer's naval adjutant, to warn him of the critical positions so that, if necessary, Hitler could intervene.

But the crisis was avoided. The chief of staff handed the letter to Raeder. The grand admiral read it, and the new directive was suspended.

6

FROM THE ARCTIC TO THE BLACK SEA

The fact that the Atlantic was the scene of the most crucial part of the U-boat war tends to make us forget that in other waters, too, the U-boats faced heavy odds.

Once they had been removed from Dönitz's operational control, the twenty U-boats of the Northern Waters Flotilla were lost to the Battle of the Atlantic. Wearing the distinctive mark of a polar bear, these boats sailed from their bases at Bergen and Trondheim, Narvik and Kirkenes, to wage a hard and thankless war against the enemy's convoys to Russia. Their hunting ground was the Far North—the Arctic Sea between Spitzbergen and the North Cape, Novaya Semlya and the southern edge of the pack ice, in a wilderness of desolation, where summer was perpetual daylight and winter one long night. Here Nature allied herself to the enemy, with raging storms, ice, fog and snowdrifts. The light—or the lack of it—was always against them. In the summer they could never attack by night, in the winter they could not attack by day. Their objectives were the convoys carrying American lend lease supplies to the northernmost parts of Russia, to Murmansk and Archangel, where the tail end of the Gulf Stream ensures ice-free access to the ports.

They cooperated with the *Luftwaffe* just as their comrades in the Mediterranean were doing; they shadowed convoys for the planes and were distant witnesses of many an air attack, when the echoes of the bursting bombs would thud against their hulls. Their crews spent months and years in the Arctic wastes or in some isolated anchorage enclosed by bleak rocks and snow; home leave was all too rare—and what a contrast it provided as the men traveled through the green and pleasant landscape of their native land! When the war ended, some of these men had spent upward of four years in the frozen North.

In the autumn of 1942, six "canoes" were transferred from Gotenhafen to Kiel, where they went into dock and were paid off; but not to be broken up as scrap, as anyone might have thought on seeing their batteries, engines and motors being removed and their conning towers dismantled. On the contrary, they were being prepared for the most improbable journey—right across Europe.

First the empty hulls were loaded onto barges and towed through the Kiel Canal and up the river Elbe to Dresden; thence they were taken by road to Ingolstadt on the Danube, where once again barges were used to carry them down to Galatz in Rumania. Here at a temporary base, they were reassembled and continued under their own power to the seaport of Constanza, where they were to form the Black Sea Flotilla. This little flotilla with five hundred men and six "canoes" under the command of Lieutenant Rosenbaum, was given the task of harrying the Russian coastal shipping routes.

The first patrol of the flotilla was made by Lieutenant Schmidt-Weichert in *U 9* in January, 1943. It was a very different type of warfare from that being waged in other waters. Here were no great convoy battles as in the Atlantic; none of the struggles against the endless nights or unending daylight of the Far North; no hide-and-seek with the ever-present aircraft and destroyers of the Mediterranean. The "canoes" spent most of their patrol time lying on the sea bed listening, rising to periscope depth only when the thrashing of propellers announced the approach of one of the small convoys, which usually consisted of a couple of freighters sailing between Batum and Novorossisk under heavy air and surface escort. This type of warfare was monotonous in its regularity, and successes were few and far between; it was more than a year, covering twenty patrols, before Lieutenant Fleige in *U 18* could earn his Knight's Cross.

When the base at Constanza was eventually abandoned in the face of the Russian advance, the three boats in harbor were scuttled by Lieutenant Petersen, who had succeeded to the command of the flotilla when Rosenbaum was killed in an air accident in May. On September 10, 1944, the three others scuttled themselves at sea off the Turkish coast, since any idea of a break-through by way of the Dardanelles was out of the question. The crews were interned by the Turks and the "Black Sea Flotilla" ceased to exist—and with it the last of the "canoes."

7

THE LUCK OF THE DRAW

(October–November, 1942)

The concentration of large numbers of ships in British and American ports in October, 1942, had not escaped the notice of German Naval Intelligence. The air was full of rumors; the long-expected opening of a second front by the enemy might come at any moment. When the blow fell, in the early hours of November 8, 1942, at Casablanca, Oran and Algiers, it was evident that the Allies had completely deceived their adversaries.

The Germans were indeed expecting an attack on Africa, but they thought it would be aimed at Dakar on the coast of Senegal. A number of "wolf packs" had been assembled off the Azores, with which it was hoped to attack the invasion fleet while it was still on passage; but the enemy avoided Dakar and, entering the Mediterranean, landed on the coast of Morocco. In doing this, they had one of the most fortunate strokes of luck in the whole war. The inadequacy of German air patrols had enabled them to transport their entire expeditionary force in seven major convoys of some eight hundred ships clear across the Atlantic, unseen and unheralded. The Germans had assumed that the assembly of numerous ships at Gibraltar merely foreshadowed the passage of an exceptionally large convoy to Malta, and they had disposed their U-boats accordingly.

But then the giant convoy, with its powerful escort, suddenly split up as it turned to starboard toward the African coast, and the first waves of assault craft stormed through the surf to the beaches. It was only when the Allies' real intentions became clear that the greater part of the U-boats on patrol in the Atlantic were hastily summoned to the Gibraltar area, to attack the second wave of supply ships, while those in the Mediterranean were rushed to the assault area. It was immediately clear that the fate of Italy and of the German positions in the Mediterranean would depend upon the outcome of Operation Torch, the code name of the Allied assault. The U-boats did what they could to light their own torches; but a U-boat is not a maid of all work. They could harry the enemy, score individual successes here and there; with luck and daring, tie down defensive forces and create a measure of confusion—such as Henke did in *U 515*, when he sank the liner *Ceramic*, loaded with troops. It is one thing to harry an invasion, but quite another to prevent it. Although Kals in *U 130* and Henke achieved some success against supply ships, they had done so off the Atlantic coast of Morocco; the waters of Gibraltar, on the other hand, were more dangerous than ever for the larger boats. On November 26 the admiral received permission from the Admiralty to move them back again into the open ocean, where they were designated the "Westwall Group."

The early resumption of their normal function against Atlantic shipping was fully justified by results. Although the enemy now had shore-based aircraft which could fly as far as eight hundred miles out, in August 1942 the Wolves destroyed 108 ships aggregating over half a million tons, and in September their score was 98 ships of 485,000 tons, as revealed by British statistics.

In September, as we now know, the British for the first time sailed an auxiliary aircraft carrier equipped with the old swordfish planes as escort to a convoy, and in the same month the new escort groups began to work as hunter-killers in cooperation with aircraft, achieving their first successes against U-boats. Nevertheless, 93 ships totaling more than 600,000 tons were sunk in October, and the Germans claimed about one million tons sunk in November, against the British admission of 117 ships of 700,000 tons.

Even these figures recalled the critical days of 1917, and Mr. Churchill found it necessary to set up a committee to coordinate all Allied anti-U-boat measures, the first session of which was attended by Admiral Sir Dudley Pound, Chief of the Naval Staff, and Air Marshal Sir Charles Portal, Chief of the Air Staff—indications that the anti-U-boat war was receiving top priority. Fifteen ships had been lost out of a single Atlantic convoy during three stormy November nights. The drop in losses to sixty-one ships of 336,000 tons for December was poor consolation to the enemy; for in the last days of 1942 twenty U-boats had sunk fourteen ships in a battle with a Newfoundland convoy which continued for four nights. The weather in this fourth winter of the war was, if anything, worse than the year before; 116 days of gale out of 140! The British, with their sense of seamanship, realized that the decline in their losses at this period was due more to the prevalence of bad weather than to improvements in their A/S measures.[1] Allied losses in 1942 were serious enough, although less than the figures published in Germany. According to these, the U-boats had sunk 6¼ million tons of Allied shipping in that year—nearly three times as much as in 1941. Yet the U-boat losses had by no means risen in equal proportion. The steady reinforcement of British A/S forces was most noticeable in the Bay of Biscay and the waters to the north of the British Isles. The enemy kept special anti-U-boat groups stationed permanently here, while the skies swarmed with aircraft. Air patrols in the Atlantic, too, were now flying so far out that there was only a narrow stretch of ocean left in which the boats could move unhampered on the surface; and even this gap was reduced as soon as the enemy brought his auxiliary carriers in as direct escorts for the convoys.

The main problem had changed from the year before; it was no longer a question of finding the convoys but of fighting a way through to them, despite a nonstop screen of aircraft and surface ships which accompanied the convoys from the moment they left port to the moment they arrived at

[1] See Appendix 2. Graph of the Battle of the Atlantic.

their destination. What could a U-boat captain do when he was forced under by an aircraft which then signaled the convoy to make a detour? As soon as the boat submerged, the pilot would drop bags of colored dye to enable the A/S ships to locate the spot where she had last dived.

But for the enemy there was bad news too from the South Atlantic. In October, 1942, a group of six U-boats made a surprise appearance off Cape Town, and the hunting and killing that ensued recalled the "Golden Age." Merten in *U 68* sank nine ships of 61,600 tons, Emmermann in *U 172* sank eight ships of 59,800 tons, Witte came back via the Brazilian coast in *U 159* to sink ten ships of 55,900 tons, Poske in *U 504* sank six of 36,500 tons, Gysae in *U 177* eight of 49,300 tons, Lüth in *U 181* twelve small ships of 38,400 tons, while Ibbeken in *U 178* sank six ships of 47,100 tons and damaged a 6,000-tonner. Sobe, commanding *U 179* —one of the first "U-cruisers"—sank one ship and then fell a victim to two destroyers.

Cremer in *U 333* was off Freetown at this time, hoping to force his way into the harbor to attack some transports which were known to be there. He was already inside the fifty-fathom line when he was surprised by the British corvette *Crocus*, which came storming toward him out of the darkness. Even as Cremer sprang to the bridge, *Crocus* opened fire and a rain of metal whistled past the captain's ears. The stricken ratings of the bridge watch collapsed in a groaning heap about him as he ordered, "Lifebelts on! Stand by to abandon ship!" But within seconds the corvette's stem crashed into and over the U-boat's stern, forcing it under water for a few moments. However, the U-boat continued to move at full speed under full helm, her hull apparently undamaged and still buoyant. Her propellers continued to turn —and she answered the helm.

On the bridge only Cremer was still standing, though severely wounded with a bullet in his left arm and splinters all over his body. Covered with blood, he continued to pass orders to the helmsman and the engine room, altering course violently to upset the enemy's aim; but this gained him only a few moments' respite before the shells began crashing round him again. Realizing that his only chance was to dive, he deliberately reduced speed and did a "wounded duck" trick to lure the enemy to try to ram him again. As the corvette rushed toward him he ordered full speed on his engines.

Taken by surprise, *Crocus* raced past his stern before she could turn. Now was his chance!

"Crash-dive!" He never knew how he got down the conning-tower ladder, or managed to close the hatch. Falling half-conscious into the control room, which was full of water, he fainted and only came to at the sound of depth charges exploding round the boat, which was resting on the bottom. The first lieutenant and six men were dead, the captain and second officer badly wounded; the U-boat was in the hands of the third officer—a mere youngster—and the coxswain.

"Blow your tanks!" said Cremer, "we must get away from here before daylight." The U-boat came slowly to the surface and coxswain and third officer sprang to the bridge. *Crocus* lay some way off, probing the water with her searchlight, evidently looking for survivors. Carefully the U-boat's bow was brought round and she crept away into the night; it was a long time before they dared start up the diesels, while the corvette continued to search in the distance, firing star shells.

While temporary repairs were made, seven of their comrades were committed to the deep as the chief engineer recited the Lord's Prayer. *U 333* reported to admiral, U-boats, and received orders to rendezvous with Wilamowitz in *U 459* to embark a doctor and replace casualties. They steamed steadily northward, moving at periscope depth by day because the stern tubes leaked too badly if they went any deeper. For four long days they just managed to sustain the life of their captain and second officer. Cremer was dying from loss of blood, but just as the crisis came, a doctor reached him from *U 459*, remaining at his side until *U 333* reached La Rochelle; here he was taken to the hospital, where he eventually recovered.

Yet the story of how "Ali" Cremer escaped from the gunfire, the depth charges and ramming by HMS *Crocus* off Freetown is only one of the hazardous adventures that befell the U-boats in those waters.

While operating against a convoy in fog near the Azores, another U-boat was surprised on the surface by a destroyer and rammed. The situation seemed hopeless; as the enemy ship swept down upon them, the U-boat captain ordered, "Lifebelts on—stand by to abandon ship!" The order was promptly executed by a petty officer and a rating on the bridge who, when the destroyer's sharp stem cut into the

U-boat's stern, jumped overboard without waiting for further orders, believing the U-boat to be doomed. As the men came to the surface and looked about them, they saw their boat going down steeply with a gaping hole in her stern. At the same time the destroyer was crawling painfully away with a heavy list and badly damaged bows, her half-exposed screws splashing the water wildly beneath her stern; within a few seconds she had disappeared in the fog.

The two survivors started to swim in the rough sea, which plucked them hither and thither. Crazy things happened sometimes; perhaps the corvette would turn back. But the fog was thickening and there was nothing to be seen but waves and more waves.

The rating lost his nerve, shouting and yelling for help. The petty officer, who was made of sterner stuff, managed to calm his comrade and for a time they trod water in silence. "It's hopeless," said the rating, "we'll drown sooner or later anyway—why not now?" . . . "It's not cold," said the petty officer, "I can stand it and I'm not going to drown before I have to." They swam a little further; the wind was rising, dissolving the fog into tiny raindrops that splashed softly around them. Suddenly a gap in the fog revealed a dark object drifting in their direction—a raft. With difficulty they swam toward it and clambered over the barnacle-covered side. It had evidently belonged to some sunken ship and must have been drifting for a long time half-submerged; but it bore their weight. As dusk fell, the seas rose higher and higher, tossing them to and fro, while the sharp-edged barnacles tore at their clothes, their hands and knees. They were weak with hunger and desperately weary; twice the raft overturned, and each time the petty officer managed to drag his apathetic companion back to it. The third time, however, the attempt failed and the petty officer was alone.

With the first hint of dawn, the wind freshened again. The solitary survivor could see nothing but huge waves with foaming crests. Before he was properly aware of it, the raft was torn from under him; when next he rose on a wave crest he could see that it had drifted thirty yards away. He knew he could never reach it again and so he waited patiently for the end.

But what in heaven's name was this? Barely a stone's throw away the seas parted—and a U-boat came to the surface! The unique, the utterly improbable thing had happened. In all the vast spaces of the Atlantic, a U-boat had chosen to surface

precisely where one man was about to drown. The captain
came on to the bridge and took his first careful look round
the horizon; he was on the point of ordering the diesels to
start when he heard faint cries and saw a man bobbing about
on the waves. Within a minute he had turned the boat and
picked him up.

The captain made a routine signal to admiral, U-boats, and
there the story seemed to end. But that same evening the
rescued man's U-boat was heard reporting by radio that it
had lost two men after being rammed, but had crash-dived
and managed to escape. Headquarters then ordered a meeting
point for the two boats, and the survivor, restored to his own
boat, soon recovered from his ordeal and sailed happily
home with his comrades.

This strange tale of chance evoked much speculation at the
U-boat bases. It was suggested, with all respect, that God Al-
mighty must have had a special reason for intervening, having
gone to the trouble of picking this man out of the vast Atlantic, only to set him back on his little U-boat.

8

DÖNITZ SUCCEEDS RAEDER

(December, 1942–February, 1943)

By the end of 1942 the tide was already turning at Stalingrad and in North Africa; but the U-boat successes against
enemy shipping were continuing. Unshaken in spirit, the
crews entered the fourth year of war confident that they
could contend with the growing countermeasures. They were
not told the official figures of German losses, but were well
aware of the heavy risks they ran, and on each return to harbor they could not fail to notice the gaps among their comrades. Very few of those who had sailed forth in 1939 were
still with them.

The true losses were always known to Dönitz, and in
August, 1942, he was ordered to send them to the Führer's
headquarters:

U-boat Losses up to August 24, 1942

1. Materiel

Number of operational U-boats commissioned since
the war began 304

Number of operational U-boats lost since the war
began 105

Average monthly loss 2.9

Average monthly loss as a percentage of opera-
tional boats at sea 4.9%

2. Personnel

	Officers	C.P.Os.	P.O.s.	Ratings	Total
Killed	185	184	515	1075	1959
Captured	112	113	323	600	1148
Missing	63	58	192	382	696
Total	360	356	1030	2057	3803

This was equivalent to a loss of 38 per cent of operational
personnel every year.

The men of the U-boats could look back with pride on their
achievements in many waters, from the Caribbean to West
Africa, from the Arctic to the South Atlantic. As 1942 drew
to a close, however, they did not guess that a naval action was
about to precipitate a crisis in the high command of the German Navy, which would directly involve their own leader.

On December 22, Hitler listened with his usual care to
Grand Admiral Raeder's report on the Mediterranean situation. When Raeder drew his attention to the serious shortage
of steel for naval construction, the Führer was sympathetic
and explained in detail the reasons which prevented him from
making a larger allocation; having consulted Speer, he saw
no immediate prospect of helping the Navy but he hoped for
better news in the future. There was every evidence of good-
will in his manner. Although he liked to have direct control
over everything, Hitler had seldom interfered in naval affairs,
for he had a deep respect for Raeder's intelligence and fore-
sight. Having been brought up far from the sea, Hitler had no
understanding for that element, which he seemed to mis-
trust. "On land I am a hero, at sea a coward," he had once
said.

Yet, frank and straightforward as were the relations between the Head of the State and his naval chief, this state
of affairs did not survive the end of the year. A joint attack

by U-boats and surface ships had been planned to take place over the New Year against a PC convoy bound for Murmansk, similar to the attack on PQ 17 in the previous summer. Owing to the darkness of the Arctic winter, the *Luftwaffe* could not participate, but Operation Rainbow—as it was called—held some prospect of success. The U-boats located the convoy and the heavy cruiser *Admiral Hipper* with the pocket battleship *Lützow* and six destroyers made contact with it on the morning of December 31.

At this stage the convoy was escorted only by five destroyers, two corvettes and a trawler, but by launching a series of attacks out of the mist against the superior German forces, the destroyers managed to keep the German ships at bay long enough to allow the cruisers *Sheffield* and *Jamaica* to reach the scene. These two ships had separated from the convoy three days earlier, owing to bad weather, and were twenty-five miles to the north when the action began. Conforming to the strict injunction to avoid any engagement with an equal or superior enemy, the German admiral broke off the action, though not before the British destroyer *Achates* had been sunk and most of the others more or less badly damaged, while *Hipper* sustained considerable damage and one German destroyer was lost. The convoy reached its destination without loss, for the U-boats also failed to attack it.

Operation Rainbow was a failure—a victory for the enemy —since its main purpose, the destruction of the convoy, had not been accomplished. The shortage of warships had forced the German Naval Command to put the safety of their fleet above all other considerations.

This failure evidently gave Hitler the impression that the Navy too was now suffering reverses, to add to the woeful reports from Stalingrad and North Africa. His reaction to the news was more violent than was justified by the facts. In the course of the forenoon the newly appointed Admiralty Liaison Officer at Supreme Headquarters, Vice-Admiral Krancke, had already informed him of the impending action, and by midday had reported that the action was over. According to a U-boat report that had just come in, "a red glow was all that could be seen in the Arctic twilight," and from this inadequate report it was concluded that the action had been successful. Hopes ran high as the day wore on, but no further news came in. The ships, still at sea, were maintaining radio silence so as not to reveal their position. Hitler waited with growing impatience; a naval victory at the turn of the year would compensate him for the gloomy news from Stalingrad.

The first definite news arrived late in the evening, when Reuter announced that an Allied convoy had escaped unharmed after being attacked by German forces in the Arctic, and that one German destroyer had been sunk and another damaged. Wracked by uncertainty and exasperated by the continuing silence of the German squadron, Hitler directed Raeder to tell his ships to report. The grand admiral refused; radio silence must be maintained at all costs. So Hitler had to wait all through the night; not until New Year's Day did *Hipper* drop anchor in her Norwegian base.

But now there was further trouble. A teleprinter line broke down somewhere between Trondheim and Hitler's headquarters, with the result that the action report failed to arrive in time for the midday conference. Hitler was beside himself. "It is scandalous!" he screamed, "that twenty-four hours after the action the supreme commander should still be without any news, whereas the British last night announced their success to the whole world." White with anger, he ordered Admiral Krancke to send a signal to the battle squadron to report without fail. Then he was heard using most uncomplimentary language about the uselessness of the big ships, and the incapacity and lack of initiative of senior naval officers. Admiral Krancke had to abandon all attempts at explanation.

The report of the action, scrappy and hastily compiled, eventually arrived during the afternoon. At the evening conference Hitler broke out with renewed denunciations. He reminded his audience that only quite recently he had had to resolve an argument on priorities between Göring, Kesselring and Raeder over the use of sea transport in the Mediterranean. Interservice rivalry in such matters ought to have been eliminated, but now it seemed to be breaking out again like a barely healed wound. He was sick of the bickering at headquarters and of reverses at the front; as for the Navy, he would have these useless big ships *decommissioned* and scrapped! It was uneconomical to use capital ships to achieve what bombers could do at far less cost! The steel from the big ships would be very useful for the Four-Year Plan!

That night he dictated the plan for scrapping the ships, to be inserted in the official War Diary as his irrevocable decision. Grand Admiral Raeder was told to report immediately at headquarters. Raeder, however, calmly asked to be excused until he could fully acquaint himself of the position; he was well aware that Hitler had worked himself up into a meaningless and quite unnecessary rage, which could not have been allayed by certain injudicious remarks of Admiral

Krancke. It would be wise to give the Führer time to cool off.
When eventually he reported to Hitler's headquarters on the
sixth of January, he was unaware that Göring had used the
incident to point out how a valuable *Luftwaffe* squadron was
being contained in Norway for the sole purpose of protecting
the inactive ships.

The commander in chief summarized the subsequent interview at *Wolfsschanze*—Hitler's headquarters near Rastenburg
—in the following words:

> The Führer spoke for an hour and a half on the role of the
> Prussian and German navies since their inception. The Ger-
> man Navy had originally been planned on the pattern of the
> British Navy, but had proved of no importance in the wars of
> 1864, 1866 and 1870. . . . In the First World War the U-boats
> had been the vital branch of the Navy and they must be
> regarded as equally important in this one. In the last war the
> High Seas Fleet had achieved nothing worth mentioning. It was
> the fashion to put the blame on the Kaiser, but this attitude
> was unjustified. The true reason was that the Navy had lacked
> able men, ready to fight with or without the Kaiser's support.
> . . . The revolution and the scuttling of the fleet in Scapa Flow
> had added nothing to the Navy's reputation. The Navy had
> taken care never to attack unless its forces equaled those of the
> enemy. The Army did not operate on this principle. As a
> soldier, the Führer expected his ships, once joined in battle,
> to fight it out to the end. The present critical situation re-
> quired that all available fighting strength be thrown into the
> battle, and he could not allow these big ships to lie idly at
> anchor for months on end. . . . Up to now, the small ships had
> borne the brunt of the fighting. Whenever the capital ships
> went to sea they had to be escorted by the small ships. It was
> not the big ships that protected the small ones, but the other
> way round. . . . The big guns from the larger ships should be
> set up ashore for coastal defense. Mounted at points where
> large-scale assaults might be expected, these naval guns could
> effectively prevent such landings. . . . It should not be re-
> garded as a degradation if the Führer decided to scrap the
> big ships. . . .
>
> The Navy should examine the following questions: where
> could the ships' guns be most usefully installed on land? In
> what order should the ships be paid off? To what extent could
> the U-boat program be expanded and expedited if the capital
> ships were withdrawn from service? The commander in chief
> of the Navy was to produce a memorandum on these points.
> It would be of the greatest value and the Führer would ex-
> amine it very carefully. . . .

Raeder was cut to the quick by Hitler's crude denunciation

of his life's work. He was not prepared to argue the rights and wrongs of the case. He did not bother—nor had he been given the least opportunity—to point out the mistakes and misrepresentations contained in that ninety-minute tirade. When the Führer finally ceased speaking, Raeder demanded a private interview, whereupon Field Marshal Keitel and the two stenographers withdrew. The door had barely closed when Raeder began, choosing his words deliberately.

"Since you have made it abundantly clear in your speech, *mein Führer*, that you do not agree with the way I am running the Navy, I beg to be allowed to resign, for I cannot fulfill my task unless I enjoy your confidence. I would like to add that I am nearly sixty-seven, and since my health is not of the best, my replacement by a younger and stronger man would be advisable and logical. . . ."

Before Raeder had finished, Hitler made an appeasing gesture. *"Herr Grossadmiral,"* he said precipitately, "I never intended to condemn the entire Navy, but only to criticize the big ships. The age of my collaborators has no significance for me, as I have often shown. Your resignation at this moment would only mean that I myself would have to shoulder yet another heavy burden." There was a pause; the grand admiral knew only too well what was implied—the heavy battles in progress at Stalingrad, where defeat might come at any moment, and the serious situation in the Mediterranean. Since Hitler remained silent, Raeder resumed, "All the same, after the way you have spoken to me in the presence of witnesses, I can no longer remain in office, for my authority has been impugned and will be more so, if the fleet is paid off. January thirtieth is the tenth anniversary of your seizure of power; it would be a suitable date to take my leave of you. Such an arrangement will look quite natural and would obviate any public suspicion of differences between us." Hitler had a fixed look, his lips tight-pressed. After a pause he raised his head and said, "Very well. I agree. Send me the names of two officers whom you consider fit to succeed you."

Thus it came about that, to his complete surprise, Admiral Dönitz in Paris received a long-distance call from the grand admiral. This was only the second time since the outbreak of war that the two men had communicated over the telephone. But if the call was unexpected, the words that followed were even more so, as the grand admiral, after intimating his intention to resign, said, "I intend to recommend Admiral Carls[1]

[1] At that time *Generaladmiral* Rolf Carls was Flag Officer Commanding, Navy Group North, with headquarters at Kiel.

and you, Dönitz. Please let me know within twenty-four hours whether you feel physically able to succeed me." The line crackled and went dead. Mechanically, Dönitz put the receiver back on its hook.

Offered the choice of Admirals Carls and Dönitz, Hitler chose the latter who on the thirtieth of January, 1943, was promoted to grand admiral and placed in charge of the entire Navy. In the meantime Raeder, who had been created inspector general of the Navy, drew up a carefully worded memorandum of five thousand words. It was his final plea to Hitler.

"The decommissioning of the fleet," he wrote, "would mean conceding an effortless victory to the enemy. It would bring joy to the enemy's heart and deep disappointment to our Allies—particularly the Japanese. It would be regarded as a sign of our weakness and of our failure to appreciate the overwhelming influence of naval warfare on the outcome of the war." Hitler received this memorandum on January 15; within two days Admiral Krancke telephoned the Admiralty that Hitler was as determined as ever to pay off the fleet, and the following directive was issued on the twenty-sixth of January:

1. All building or conversion work on the big ships is to cease immediately.
2. Except where required for training, all battleships, pocket battleships, heavy and light cruisers are to be decommissioned.
3. All naval personnel, workmen, etc., who become available as a result of these measures, are to be employed immediately in the construction and repair of U-boats.

A secret covering note added that "in view of its political and psychological significance, this order is to be restricted to the smallest possible number of officers." Despite this, the news spread like wildfire through the Navy; and everywhere, except in the U-boat Service, the rumor was, "That's Dönitz —the new broom sweeping clean—everything for the U-boats!" A picture that currently decorated many wardrooms, showing nothing but a billowing blue seascape, provoked the newest joke of the new era. "D'you know what that is? The German Naval Review of 1950." . . . "Why?" . . . "Nothing but U-boats—all submerged!"

On January 31 Grand Admiral Raeder took leave of the Navy which he had led for fifteen years, in good times and in bad, and to which he had given his life's work. He knew that his new title of inspector general was a sinecure, created only to preserve a semblance of good relations between Hitler and himself. Retiring to his home at Dahlem, he became a mere observer of events; only on rare occasions thereafter did he seek an audience of the Führer.

On the eighth of February Grand Admiral Dönitz—in office only a week—made a critical report to Hitler on the general position of the war at sea. The first point for discussion was the U-boat campaign. At the time of the transfer from Paris to the Hotel am Steinplatz in Berlin, the U-boat Command had been made aware that the enemy convoys, surprisingly well-informed about U-boat dispositions in the Atlantic, were taking very effective evasive action. .

"How is that possible?" asked Hitler.

"Either through treason—and as far as that is concerned, all possible precautions have been taken," answered Dönitz, "or else through air patrols which locate our forces without our seeing them. The complete lack of air reconnaissance is the weakest factor in our naval strategy, and to compensate for it we must send more U-boats to sea. That involves speeding up repairs and hurrying on the construction of new boats. I am therefore forced to request the exemption from military service of all workmen engaged in building or repairing U-boats, and the retention of all personnel needed for the ships that serve them."

"Can we do that, Speer?" asked Hitler.

"As it is obviously essential, we must do it," answered the minister for armaments, "but only if no extra personnel are called for to replace losses in the Navy."

Hitler agreed to issue the necessary directive as soon as he had discussed the issue with Field Marshal Keitel. "Rest assured, Admiral," he added, "that I will do all I can to help the Navy. What else have you?"

In view of the recent crisis, the moment seemed inappropriate to champion the future of the big ships—that could always be done later. So Dönitz proceeded to lay before Hitler the schedule for the progressive paying off of these units. Hitler glanced through the paper and returned it. "I have no comments to make, *Herr Grossadmiral*," he said. "You already know my views on the value of the big ships; please give me your own at a later date." Dönitz bowed, his face expressionless. Later that evening he flew back to Berlin.

On the following morning Vice Admiral Krancke read out a summary of Dönitz's views to Hitler: "As the future of the big ships was not further discussed last night, I am instructed to report that the commander in chief considers it his duty to send the capital ships to sea whenever the chances of success seem favorable. Once at sea, the admiral commanding the squadron will have complete tactical freedom to fight as he thinks best, without directions from any superior authority. Under these circumstances, however, there will always be the risk of losses."

Having listened without comment, Hitler replied that he fully concurred with these views. Thus the first step toward the retention of the big ships had been taken. Three weeks later, on February 26, 1943, Dönitz, paying his second visit to the Führer, reopened the question. Although the views of the two men were sharply divided, the unexpected happened. Hitler partially withdrew his order for the decommissioning and scrapping of the ships.

The question was never raised again, and thereafter Dönitz retained a free hand in matters affecting the employment of the big ships. He had won the day, and the fleet was saved.

III

THE DECLINE

1943-1945

1

TOWARD THE CLIMAX

(February–May, 1943)

Early in 1943 both U-boats and convoys were encountering some of the worst weather of the war; ships were falling out of line with hulls, rudders or engines damaged by the fury of the waves, while their escorts strained every nerve to keep them in convoy. According to British statistics for January, thirty-seven ships of 200,000 tons were lost in the Atlantic, the Mediterranean and off the coast of Brazil; these included eight out of nine ships in a tanker convoy, which were sunk in a seven-day battle with U-boats between Trinidad and the Canaries.

At headquarters, Admiral Godt and his staff were anxiously

tracking some convoys in the North Atlantic. Through decryption of Allied radio signals they had been able, despite the bad weather, to move groups of U-boats into the anticipated path of the convoys, for they knew pretty accurately the number of ships in each, their sailing date, speed, course and destination. Yet instead of getting the expected shadowing reports from the U-boats, they received fresh intercepts which showed that the convoys had made bold alterations of course —not once but several times. These evasions made it clear that the enemy was remarkably well informed of the U-boat dispositions.

Once again the specter of treachery within their ranks raised its ugly head, but proof was lacking. It was evident that now more than ever before, the solution to the problem of finding the convoy lay in constant long-range air reconnaissance. As long as he remained ignorant of the true reasons for these new developments, all that Dönitz could do was to space out his boats as widely as possible, in the hope of deceiving the enemy as to his real intentions; and at the same time give his commanders a better chance of happening upon a convoy. Once again he approached Göring for help, but the *Reichsmarschall* could give him little hope. He mentioned the BV 222, which would not be coming off the assembly lines until October, 1943; and the plans for the Me 264 which, he said, would be able to bomb America; but when Dönitz pointed to the urgent need for fighter protection over the Bay of Biscay and for unremitting *Luftwaffe* attacks on British Coastal-Command bases, Göring could only make vague promises which, from past experience, Dönitz knew were worthless. He returned empty-handed to Berlin, to wrestle once again with all the daily problems of enemy carrier-borne aircraft, air patrols over the Bay of Biscay, and the new and more powerful enemy depth charges. He was not at this time aware of the secret decision taken by the Allies at Casablanca in January to give top priority to the anti-U-boat campaign. This decision was eloquent of the fact that, until they had overcome this particular menace, the Allies could not hope for final victory. At that time there was no significant indication that it would be overcome.

In the stormy days of February there were further violent battles between the wolf packs and the North Atlantic convoys. On one particular stormy night Münnich in *U 187*, a newly commissioned boat only three weeks out from Kiel, made contact with a convoy that had been widely dispersed by bad weather; sixty-four ships and twelve escorts were scattered over some fifty square miles of sea. Despite the most adverse conditions, Münnich clung on the fringes of the convoy for forty-eight hours, sending out beacon signals which eventually brought twenty other boats upon the scene. It was a classical example of the lessons taught by the two veteran commanders, Topp and Suhren, at the Tactical Training School at Gotenhafen, where they did their best to reproduce in the Baltic the conditions that would be encountered in the Atlantic. Nine ships were destroyed that night, but three U-boats—*U 187* among them—failed to report the next morning.[1]

The losses in February as admitted by the British amounted to sixty-three ships of some 360,000 tons—small figures compared with the previous November, but higher than the January figures by 160,000 tons. In March, however, the U-boats attained the peak of their successes with over one million tons of Allied shipping believed sunk.

Figures available after the war show that Allied losses were in fact much smaller than this. Apart from the tendency —common to all belligerents in the heat of battle—to exaggerate their own successes, it must be realized that as, in the course of the war, the Allied A/S measures became more effective, so the U-boat captains found it increasingly difficult to observe the actual result of their attacks, particularly when several boats were simultaneously attacking a convoy. Once the attack had been delivered, the chief concern of the U-boat was to evade the dangerous pursuit by destroyer escorts. Usually the only indication of a successful attack was the sound of the detonating torpedo. Sometimes two or more U-boat captains claimed hitting what later proved to be the same vessel, each believing that his own torpedoes had found their mark. Dönitz was aware of these factors, and the sinking figures issued by him made some allowance—not always adequate—for exaggerated claims. He resisted pressure from the Propaganda Ministry to issue higher figures, for he compared the U-boat Command to a "sound business concern, which must always adhere to true statistics."

Between March 10 and 13 a group with the code name *Neuland*, acting on information from decryption, located and attacked Convoys SC 121 and HX 228, sinking a number of ships. As the U-boats were still well stocked with fuel and torpedoes they were then divided into two groups, *Stürmer* and *Dränger*, for the intercept service had reported a third convoy,

[1] According to British records this was SC 118, consisting of sixty-one ships plus nine A/S escorts, from which nine ships were sunk between February 5 and 8, 1943.

HX 229, eastbound in mid-Atlantic on the evening of the thirteenth. *Dränger* was ordered to attack it, while *Stürmer* and a third group, *Raubgraf,* were ordered to search for SC 122, which had also been identified by the intercept service. On the morning of the fifteenth one of the *Raubgraf* boats reported that she was in contact with a convoy at the same moment as a decrypted enemy signal reached the U-boat Command. A completely new situation now arose as it became clear that the Halifax convoy which the *Dränger* group had been ordered to attack was not in fact eastbound, but had been diverted toward the east coast of Newfoundland to avoid the danger area. *Dränger* was therefore ordered to join forces with *Raubgraf* and *Stürmer*—making some forty boats in all —and attack SC 122. By midday the first *Raubgraf* boats reported making contact, and by that evening eight boats had come up with the convoy, among them three highly experienced commanders.

But now their troubles began. The moon would be full within three days; already it was hanging like a brilliant lantern in the sky. The British convoy commodore and the U-boat commanders alike cursed its brightness. The ships in silhouette made a clear-cut target, but the same moonlight compelled the Germans to hold their distance from the convoy and to fire torpedoes at greater ranges. Nevertheless they resolutely exploited every chance—and when March 17 dawned, SC 122 had lost fourteen ships of 90,000 tons, while six others had been seriously damaged. During the day other boats from *Stürmer* and *Dränger* came up and twelve more ships were destroyed. Within the next few days nearly thirty boats were swarming round the convoy and each night a few more ships were sunk. On the night of the eighteenth, headquarters received a report that yet another convoy was sailing barely 120 miles away from SC 122. The boats were ordered to operate against this one too. However by the evening of the following day, all U-boats except one had lost contact with the convoys and were searching vainly around in rising seas. Eventually the single shadower managed to home the others onto the convoy and finally some twenty-four U-boats were once more snarling at its heels. After two days of heavy fighting against the enemy's ubiquitous air and surface escorts, the U-boats received orders to break off the action; the moon was now so bright that further attacks would be unwise.

The U-boat Command's reports on this three-day action ends with the words: "In all, 32 ships of 186,000 tons and one destroyer were sunk,[2] and hits were scored on nine other ships. This is the greatest success ever achieved in a convoy battle and is all the more creditable in that nearly half the U-boats involved scored at least one hit."

By the end of March, fifteen U-boats had been lost compared with nineteen in February; this represented 13.4 per cent of the forces at sea, which was rather higher than the figure considered as unavoidable in this period of the war. In the same month six large U-cruisers began to operate for the first time near Madagascar in the Indian Ocean, from a base provided by the Japanese at Penang. A group of Type IXc boats was due to follow them at the end of the monsoon period. It was also in this month that the long-awaited anti-destroyer torpedo, the G7, became available. It was used with good effect in the action against SC 121 and HX 228.

After reaching a peak provisionally estimated at about one million tons in March,[3] enemy losses dropped in April to fifty-six ships of 328,000 tons. In that month disturbing reports came in from the boats at sea that their radar-search receivers frequently failed to warn them of the approach of enemy aircraft. Did the *Metox* have a "blind spot"? Was the enemy using frequencies beyond the scope of the instrument? Dönitz summoned the leading brains of industry and science and told them bluntly that the U-boat war would be lost, unless an antidote were found to the enemy's radar. As a result, a scientific research committee was set up under the chairmanship of Professor Küpfmüller. Meanwhile every effort was being made to complete the new A.A. guns for the U-boats—20 mm. twin-barreled and four-barreled guns, 3.7 cm. twins, and super-heavy machine guns—to protect them from the deadly menace of the air. By the end of June they could expect to get the powerful new incendiary high-explosive ammunition, known as "hexogen shells." Then there was the *Aphrodite*, a balloon carrying sheets of tinfoil which could be released at night to drift above the sea and thus confuse the

[2] SC lost eight ships of 47,000 tons out of fifty-one between March 17 and 19; HX 229 lost thirteen ships of 93,500 tons out of forty between March 16 and 19. The total sinkings by U-boats in the Atlantic between March 13 and 19, 1943 were, according to British records, twenty-five ships of 168,000 tons, which included four ships lost between March 13 and 17 out of Convoy UGS 6 (a southern convoy from the U.S. to the Mediterranean).

[3] The *official* German estimate for March, 1943, was about 780,000 tons sunk, but the actual figure was nearer 500,000, which indeed was serious enough. Aggregate Allied shipping losses in the same month from *all* causes in *all* theatres of war were 693,000 tons.

enemy radar; and the *Thetis* buoy—another radar decoy—which, it was hoped, would also prove very useful in the Bay of Biscay. Meanwhile at the Design Department at Blankenburg in the Harz Mountains the designers were working in the closest cooperation with experienced U-boat commanders on the plans for the fast new types, XXI and XXIII.

It was true that these boats, which were expected to herald a fundamental change in submarine warfare, would not be ready until the end of 1944; but the knowledge that they were being built and the prospect that the Sea Wolves would again become undetectable from the air and difficult to locate when submerged, was tremendously important in mitigating the strain and the feeling of helplessness against an ever-present danger. That strain was very real and weighed upon every man, according to his duties, not least upon those who bore the responsibility for sending the U-boats against convoys that were becoming almost impossible to reach. Was it fair to expect commanders and crews to go to sea when so little was known about the enemy's devices?

At the Atlantic bases the flotilla commanders—all experienced in submarine-combat conditions—were expected to advise the U-boat captains in all tactical matters. But what were they to say? Was it right to tell them to stay on the surface and fight it out against the enemy aircraft, or should they be advised to dive? What was a flotilla commander to say, as he waved good-by to his departing boats—"Good luck and good hunting"? That valediction had almost lost its meaning.

The heaviest strain fell upon the captains and their crews —the strain of doubts that would not be stilled, the silent voices that whispered uncertainty in the lone watches of the night. They *had* to go on—they had to show a fearless front and set an example to their comrades. Pride it was that urged them on—and maybe a secret shame at the thought of being afraid; but they also had a sense of honor to inspire them, and their own resolution to sustain them.

Then came May, 1943—and calamity. Although in that month Britain lost fifty ships of 265,000 tons, this was barely a quarter of the March figures; but infinitely more serious was the inescapable fact that thirty-eight U-boats had been lost—an appalling price to pay. The thunderbolt—so long and so fearfully awaited—had fallen at last. The figure of thirty-eight represented more than thirty per cent of the boats at sea and was well above the average monthly delivery of new ones. It meant that more than two thousand highly trained officers and men were lost to Germany—many of them never to return. Worst of all, there was no clear-cut explanation for the disaster, no certainty as to why one boat after another had failed to answer signals from headquarters.

While the men at the flotilla bases had no precise details of these losses, a disaster of this magnitude could hardly remain secret for long, and ugly rumors began to spread from base to base. At the conferences which Captain Rösing, as Senior Officer of U-boats in the West, called from time to time at Angers, no attempt was made to hide the truth. Here the flotilla commanders met—the winners of the Knight's Cross and of the oak leaves of the earlier years; there were "Peddl" Winter and "Recke" Lehmann-Willenbrock of the First and Ninth Flotillas from Brest, Kals and Kuhnke of the Second and Tenth at Lorient, Sohler and Emmermann of the Seventh and Sixth at La Baule, Zapp of the Third at La Rochelle and Scholz of the Twelfth at Bordeaux. They came to exchange opinions and experiences, to share each other's burdens, to ask each other, "How many have you lost? . . . And you?" Such men were accustomed to clear thinking and quick decisions, but now they were no wiser than the staff in Berlin.

U-boat headquarters in the Hotel am Steinplatz was the scene of endless debate and speculation. Should the U-boats be sailed in groups through the Bay of Biscay, forming their own defensive A.A. barrage? The new A.A. guns would not be ready for another two to four months. Would it be wiser to withdraw all boats from the North Atlantic until then? No, it was impossible, for only 110 berths were available in the U-boat bunkers and any boat left out unprotected would soon be bombed to bits. They had already seen the damage that the enemy's "carpet bombing" could do to the towns of St. Nazaire and Lorient—although the U-boats in the bunkers were safe enough.[4] The cessation of attacks on the convoys would liberate enemy aircraft to strike at the towns and cities of Germany as they had struck at the U-boat bases; in twenty minutes they could knock a whole town flat. The U-boat war *must* go on—if not in the Atlantic, then elsewhere; it was not the campaign that was lost but only one battle in that campaign.

In the last days of May all boats that were low in fuel were very secretly ordered to withdraw to the area southwest of the

---

[4] No U-boat was ever destroyed by the bombing of the French bases, although a considerable force was from time to time allocated to this task, and some heavy losses were sustained among the bombers, and among the French population in the target area.

Azores to refuel. But even here they were not safe, for aircraft from the carrier U.S.S. *Bogue* (CVE) took heavy toll of them. The enemy's aircraft seemed to be everywhere at once. The strain of these days showed plainly on the faces of the young captains as they stepped ashore after weeks of being hunted, and Dönitz was prompted to ask them whether they were still prepared to go to sea under present circumstances with the older types of boats. Their answer was always "Yes, *Herr Grossadmiral!*" There was nothing wrong with their morale or with that of their men; it was only that nowadays they had so little chance of attacking. Every time they surfaced to charge batteries they did so with their hearts in their mouths, while the old method of coming up and then hauling ahead of a convoy on the surface was no longer feasible. "Give us more A.A. guns," was their constant plea, "so that at least we can defend ourselves."

On May 31, 1943, Dönitz flew to the Berghof to report to Hitler. He made no attempt to conceal the gravity of the crisis; for one thing, the enemy was flying as many sorties for convoy protection between Iceland and the Faroes in one day, as he had formerly flown in a week, while escort carriers were providing air cover right across the Atlantic. But the decisive factor was that the enemy was using a new radar device in his aircraft which enabled him to locate the U-boats without betraying his own position, particularly in low cloud and bad visibility. As a result more U-boats were being sunk by air attack in the transit areas than were being destroyed by surface escorts. It was significant that 65 per cent of the U-boat losses had occurred while on passage, or while awaiting an opportunity to attack in the operational area. Only 35 per cent were sustained in actual convoy battles.

Dönitz then gave the Führer the figures which have already been mentioned, and warned him that losses at that rate could not be endured indefinitely. His face grew stern as he went on, "I have therefore decided to abandon the North Atlantic and have sent the boats to the area west of the Azores in the hope of finding less enemy air activity there. I am also sending the new boats, as they become available, out to more distant waters, where the air patrols are probably not so well equipped with radar. However, I intend to resume the attacks on North Atlantic convoys with the next new moon, provided the boats have received their new anti-aircraft armament in time."

He went on to outline his immediate requirements. First

on the list was an effective radar search receiver capable of registering the frequencies being used by attacking aircraft. Secondly there might be some way of upsetting or dispersing the enemy's radar transmissions. Thirdly he needed a radar location set for use against aircraft; the trouble was that in a U-boat the search-sector would probably be too small—about as wide as a searchlight beam—and it would take too long to search the whole sky. Some sort of antiradar covering for conning towers was also needed, Dönitz went on, while as regards armament the demand was for more 20mm. twin machine guns and the acoustic torpedo for use against destroyers. Dönitz glanced at his notes before proceeding to his last point.

It is absolutely essential to provide concentrated fighter cover over the transit area in the Bay of Biscay," he began. The Ju 88s were liable to be shot down unless they flew in formation, so he urged that Me 410s be sent to the bay. "I doubt if that aircraft is suitable for the task, Admiral," answered Hitler, "but I will find out." After a moment he went on, "Even if we did have long-range bombers, I would have to consider whether they should be assigned to the war at sea or for attacks on Britain." The grand admiral interjected that it was a pity no steps had been taken before the war to build aircraft that could operate over the sea. Hitler warmly agreed with him, adding, "But in those days nobody said anything about it to me!" . . . "It would not be too late even now," said Dönitz slowly, "to create a naval air arm." As Hitler indicated full agreement with this, the grand admiral went on, "In that case we shall have to begin immediately with the basic training of the air crews in conjunction with the U-boat Training School, so that the men of each service learn to speak the same language and use the same methods."

Again Hitler nodded, then he rose suddenly and began to pace the room with his hands behind his back. Dönitz continued. "Despite all our difficulties, I am convinced that we must carry on even if results are not so spectacular as before."

"There can be no question of abandoning the U-boat war," Hitler broke in abruptly, "the Atlantic is my forward line and if I have to fight defensively, I would rather do so there than along the coasts of Europe. Even if the U-boats do not achieve great successes, they commit the enemy to such huge defensive resources that I would not voluntarily make him a present of them."

Encouraged by this support Dönitz came to his final point: the expansion of the building program. He had, he said, discussed with Speer the possibility of raising U-boat production from thirty to forty per month. Speer had said it could be done and all that was needed now was Hitler's signature to a draft directive which Dönitz had brought with him. The Führer bent over the paper and signed it without further ado; shortly afterward the admiral took his leave.

That same day Dönitz paid another visit to Speer. He had at length resolved to put into effect a plan which he had been considering for some time: he would place the entire responsibility for the naval construction program in Speer's hands; he trusted the young minister and he saw no advantage in keeping the Navy's war economy separate from that of the Army or the *Luftwaffe*. He was never to regret his decision.

2

STRUGGLE FOR SURVIVAL

(June, 1943–February, 1944)

The direct result of the threat from the air and the losses sustained during May was an order, issued on June 1, that U-boats would in future sail in company through the Bay of Biscay so as to provide mutual protection from air attack. Outward-bound boats were to travel in groups of five, but on the homeward run they might proceed in twos or threes. This order was not too popular among the crews, but they knew that something had to be done, and at the beginning at any rate the new tactic was successful, the boats keeping up a hail of fire at their attackers while steering a zigzag course at top speed.

The failure of several planes to return from the bay soon caused the British pilots to adopt new tactics. They kept outside the range of the U-boats' guns, radioed for reinforcements and when these arrived, attacked with bombs and guns from several directions at once. Such engagements were short but fought to a bitter finish. Frequently they resulted in casualties among the men behind the U-boat guns, and sometimes in the loss of the boat.

On one occasion the A.O.C. Atlantic sent his entire force

of twenty-three Ju 88s to the defense of the bomb-damaged *U 563*. They shot down four enemy planes but the U-boat was lost. Soon afterward *U 564* was severely damaged off Cape Ortegal; Maus in *U 185* raced to her assistance but the attempt to tow the damaged boat back to base failed, and all he could do was rescue the survivors and hand them over to two destroyers, *Z 24* and *Z 25*, which had come out from Royan. Within two months Maus was again rescuing survivors —this time from Höltring's *U 604*—and within another fortnight he himself fell a victim to planes from the American carrier *Core*.

Manseck in *U 758* was luckier; his was one of the first boats to be equipped with the new four-barreled 20 millimeter guns. On the evening of June 8, he was shadowing a convoy; his log contains a good description of the first time these guns were fired in anger:

1918. Dive-bombed by single-engined carrier plane, Lysander type, which attacked from starboard. I opened fire and scored several hits as it ran in. The plane turned away and jettisoned four 200-lb. bombs which fell 200 yards away on my starboard quarter, then dropped a smoke float near me and returned to its carrier. I steered at full speed southwest. The damaged aircraft was relieved by two more, a Lysander and a Martlet, which cruised round me at a distance of 4000-5000 yards at 9000 feet without attacking. They opened fire from time to time but did not score a hit.
1945. Another Martlet dived on me, firing its guns. I scored several hits. The plane turned sharply astern of me and dropped four bombs, which fell about 25 yards astern. Black smoke streamed from the plane, which crashed after going into a shallow dive. With my guns I was able to keep the bombers at a distance of 3000-4000 yards.
2000. Two Mustang-type fighters made a low-level attack with gunfire. Several hits observed on both machines. One plane flew back to the carrier and was replaced by others. My 2-cm. automatic guns were damaged by direct hits. Both mountings were shot up, eleven men at the guns and the lookouts were slightly wounded. I decided to dive. . . .

Manseck's report was typical of this period. The aircraft attacked like hornets, singly and in groups, dropping bombs and firing their guns at the conning tower, where men were packed tightly together with scarcely any protection. Inevitably guns were damaged and men were wounded or killed. As a result, orders were given for doctors to be embarked until such time as trained hospitalmen became available to replace them.

In the first days of June two groups of boats with the code

names of *Trutz* and *Geier* were ordered to the Azores area to attack convoys sailing between the United States and Gibraltar, but this carefully planned operation failed. High-flying aircraft sighted the U-boats and diverted the convoys away from them. Not a single ship was sighted, let alone sunk; but two U-boats were destroyed during the operation and three more were lost on the way home. It was useless to continue such tactics; after Operation *Trutz*, the wolf-pack system was abandoned in the waters south and west of the Azores.

Nor were these the only setbacks. Thirteen boats sailed from German and Norwegian ports in the first ten days of June; two were destroyed by the strong Iceland air patrols, two were lost on operations, and two others only just managed to reach Biscay ports after being heavily bombed. The valuable U-tanker fleet was also suffering heavy losses. By the end of May U-tankers of Types XIV and X had refueled and replenished nearly four hundred U-boats in the waters south and north of the Azores, losing only one of their number in the process. But by June 12, only one out of the four tankers in this area was left, and some of the larger boats had to be sent out as auxiliary tankers; they supplied oil through their fire-fighting hoses to the boats destined to operate off Rio or Florida or in the Gulf of Guinea. The tanker losses persisted, and by August only three of the twelve original "milch cows" remained. The overall situation, however, improved slightly by the end of June. Only sixteen boats had been lost, 18½ per cent of the boats at sea as against more than 30 per cent in May.[1]

On June 15 the grand admiral paid another visit to Hitler —this time to plead for more men for the Navy. Not so long ago he had been compelled to ask for 90,000 additional dockyard workers; now he needed men to man the boats which would be commissioning in the following year. Since 1942 the Army had taken priority in manpower allocations, so that the quota of 30,000 men assigned to the Navy barely replaced normal losses. The Navy's manpower problems had been aggravated by the increased number of ships in commission. the expansion of the Coastal Defense Service and the Naval Anti-Aircraft Service, and by the requirements of the establishments in the Mediterranean. The recent decision to increase the monthly output of U-boats from thirty to forty

---

[1] U-boat losses in the Bay of Biscay fell as soon as they gave up sailing in groups on the surface. The U-boats were naturally safer against air attack when submerged, but their passage time was thereby greatly increased.

further complicated matters. Hitler listened somewhat impatiently to this recital of figures.

"I haven't got the men," he said in his harsh voice. "Our anti-aircraft defenses and our night fighters must be built up to protect our towns, and we badly need reinforcements on the Eastern front. Then where can I find them?"

"In that case," said Dönitz, "I must draw your attention to the consequences if we abandon the campaign. At present we are losing U-boats faster than we can replace them. Should the enemy throw all his resources into the attack on Europe, our coastal supply lines will also be imperiled. But if we cease to attack the Allied communications at sea, the war is as good as lost. As regards our own officers, we have reached the limit. Already the officer-cadets of 1939 are being put in command of U-boats."

In the oppressive silence that followed, Hitler sat hunched in his chair, staring gloomily in front of him. "There can be no question of abandoning the U-boat war," he said suddenly. "Somehow or other we will find those men for you. Let me have a note of the numbers and the dates when you need them, and I'll see that the necessary steps are taken."

But the grand admiral had not yet finished. "The expansion of the U-boat building program and the increased construction of mine sweepers, motor torpedo boats and so on necessitate more steel and more workers in the building yards. Unfortunately we are finding that, far from getting the extra men we need, the latest comb-out of civilians for the forces has actually taken men away from us." Hitler turned to Keitel. "Field Marshal, you will please take the necessary steps. The new naval building program must go through at all costs." He assured Dönitz that he would himself speak to Minister Speer and let the admiral know the result immediately.

While at the highest level all necessary measures were being taken to implement the new conception of total underwater warfare with new types of U-boats, the Sea Wolves continued to fight with such means as were available. By the end of June it was already clear that the system of sailing boats in groups on the surface was not having the hoped-for success. The British were throwing in such huge numbers of planes, including four-engined aircraft, that hardly a single U-boat could traverse the Bay of Biscay undetected.

There was for example the *Monsoon* group of eleven boats which left the Biscay ports at the end of June for the Indian Ocean, with orders to refuel on passage from a U-tanker off the island of St. Paul. The group was made up of Type IXc "sea cows" and U-cruisers of Type IXD2. Five of the eleven were lost, as well as the tanker, *U 462* (Vowe) and the auxiliary tanker, *U 487* (Metz). This meant that two of the *Monsoon* boats had to empty their tanks into the rest and return to base.

The bay was swarming with English, American, Canadian and Australian planes—Sunderlands, Liberators, Catalinas, Halifaxes, Wellingtons—all armored and bristling with bombs and guns. On locating a group of U-boats, they gathered like vultures, flying round in circles until enough of them had assembled. Then they attacked simultaneously from all sides so as to confuse the U-boat gunners, at the same time summoning the hunter-killer groups of destroyers, frigates and corvettes. These then took up the pursuit and all too often succeeded in sinking those U-boats which had managed to evade the planes.

These hunter-killer groups had evolved a new system of attack. They no longer overran the U-boat as soon as it was located by sound gear. Now they were operating in pairs; the hunter would maintain the sonar contact while signaling to the killer the U-boat's position. The killer would then make the approach—unheard by the men in the U-boat, which by then might be 600 feet below the surface. At a signal from the hunter, the killer would drop his deadly load; and all too often the attack would result in an oil slick appearing on the surface, followed by a bubble of air carrying wreckage up with it—a German uniform jacket, or perhaps a carton of food—as proof of a successful attack.

In July fate struck at Wilamowitz, the *doyen* of the tanker commanders. On being attacked by a Wellington he returned the fire to such good purpose that the attacking plane crashed —right on the deck of *U 459*, crushing the A.A. guns and setting the U-boat on fire. When at last they got the flames under control, the U-boat crew pulled from the wreckage of the plane the rear gunner who had miraculously escaped the fate of his comrades. But as they heaved the wreckage over the side they made another discovery; two depth charges were jammed in the wooden gratings of the upper deck. Very carefully they pried them loose. This was not the first time that depth charges had fallen right onto a U-boat, and they knew exactly how to deal with the situation; the U-boat had to work up to full speed before the deadly canisters were tipped over the stern, so as to get as far away from them as possible before they exploded. On this occasion, however, one of the depth charges went off prematurely, damaging the stern so badly that the boat could no longer dive. Wilamowitz and his crew knew what that meant in the Bay of Biscay; the captain ordered the rubber dinghies to be launched and instructed his crew to abandon ship. As they paddled away, close-packed in the tiny craft, the English airman among them, the gallant captain on the bridge waved to them once, then went below unhurriedly to open the vents and flooding valves. He went down with his ship. The survivors were soon picked up by British destroyers.

According to British statistics, forty-five ships of 244,000 tons were sunk by U-boats that July, but German losses mounted again to thirty-three, despite the fact that from the beginning of the month no U-boat had been allowed to sail unless equipped with the new four-barreled A.A. guns. It was thus evident that the reinforced A.A. armament was not sufficient to guarantee a safe passage through the bay, where seven boats were lost in the first three weeks of July alone, while three others had to return home seriously damaged. One of these last was *U 441*, which was navigated back to base by the ship's doctor, Pfaffinger, after her captain, von Hartmann, and twelve others had been wounded and ten killed in a fierce action with Beaufighters. Fortunately for *U 441*, Pfaffinger was a veteran yachtsman.

In the third week of July the Battle of the Bay reached a climax when ten out of seventeen boats which had sailed since the twentieth failed to return. However, it is always darkest before the dawn; on July 8, the grand admiral reported to Hitler at the Berghof that the plans for the Type XXI had been completed and that work on the new boats would be put in hand at once. The planned maximum speed submerged of these boats was 19 knots; in other words, they would be able to travel under water faster than many A/S vessels could move on the surface. This meant that the enemy's whole technique of anti-submarine warfare would be thrown out of gear—and their convoy system as well, for the Germans reckoned that the majority of ships of the types then used in convoys could never be made to steam at more than 10 knots. Very little modification had been required in the design of the engines and motors for the new boats, but certain ideas had been borrowed from the design of the Walter-boat's hull, which was specially adapted for high underwater speeds.

Hitler listened eagerly to Dönitz's report, plying him with

a whole row of technical questions; this was one of many occasions when the Führer astounded his audience with his wide grasp of technical subjects. He wanted to know the radius of action of the new boats, their maximum speed above and below the surface, their system of loading the spare torpedoes in the tubes, their armament, defensive armor and radar equipment, and many other things.

Events followed rapidly in the succeeding weeks. The Allies landed in Sicily—not in Sardinia or Greece, as had been expected. The Italian Navy was proving unreliable and its morale was falling daily while its ships lay inactive in harbor. The Italian Naval Command no longer enjoyed the confidence of the younger officers, in particular of the Italian submarine commanders. If the Italians could not be kept up to the mark, it might be necessary to seize and overpower them, to prevent their defection to the enemy.

On July 31, the grand admiral was warned by telephone from the Führer's headquarters that there was clear evidence of Badoglio's government playing a double game. A senior staff officer at the Admiralty was being dispatched to Rome with detailed instructions for the German Naval Command there. Later that day the grand admiral was summoned to the Führer's headquarters. After the morning conference on August 2, while lunching alone with Hitler, he steered the conversation round to Hamburg, which had suffered very heavy air raids for several days on end. No one had been able to estimate the full damage, and Dönitz was concerned as to the effect of any repetition of such events on the war economy. Hitler spoke reassuringly. "Despite the heavy attacks on the Ruhr," he said, "our production has fallen by only 8 per cent, so that there is no great danger in that direction." But the grand admiral decided to go and see the damage for himself. The sight that met his eyes in Hamburg was indeed dreadful, but what perturbed him far more was a message he received when he got there.

This told him that twenty-two U-boats had been lost at sea in the last ten days of July, yet, despite the most feverish researches by the experts, there was no reliable indication of the precise cause. To add to his worries the radar research section with Navy Group West, which had been carrying out experiments with *Metox* in conjunction with the A.O.C. Atlantic, had made an ominous discovery. Experiments had shown that, instead of giving warning of enemy radar impulses, the *Metox* search receiver was itself betraying the position of the U-boats.

The *Metox* emitted a strong radiation of its own which could be picked up within twelve miles at 1,500 feet, eighteen miles at 3,000 feet, and as far away as twenty-five miles at 6,000 feet. This shattering blow was swiftly followed by another, when a captured English pilot told the *Luftwaffe* interrogators at the camp at Oberursel that the R.A.F. hardly ever used their ASV since, by flying between 750 and 3,000 feet, they could pick up bearings of the U-boat receiver's own radiations at ranges up to ninety miles.

The Germans had at last solved the riddle of the mysterious loss of so many U-boats in the past months, and of the unexplained attacks by night and in fog. The U-boats might just as well have gone to sea lit up like Christmas trees.[2]

The Grand Admiral acted promptly. He immediately forbade any further use of the *Metox* and ordered his technical experts to check the report of the radar research station. This was soon confirmed in every detail. On August 19, he had a private audience with Hitler and told him everything. No word of reproach passed Hitler's lips as he listened to the dismal story of the past months; his only comment was that whereas these setbacks had revealed the cause of losses, the latest discoveries had done much to increase their knowledge of radar and its workings. Then Dönitz sent for his flotilla commanders; knowing that in the fateful month of May he had lost one of his two sons in a U-boat, they appreciated how he must be feeling as they listened to his orders. The *Metox*, he said, was being replaced by a new receiver, known as the "Bug"; at the same time, through tremendous efforts, Speer had managed to provide the first eighty-five T5 torpedoes well in advance of schedule. Special courses would be started at once to train officers and men in the use of this anti-destroyer weapon and of the new radar search receiver.

The atmosphere at U-boat headquarters was pregnant with expectation as the first boats sailed from Lorient on August 15, each carrying four T5s in addition to its normal torpedoes. The A.O.C. Atlantic had made available every plane that he had and for the first time the Focke-Wulffs were carrying the new glider bomb for use against warships. In their very first attack the destroyer *Egret* was sunk and a cruiser damaged.

---

[2] It should be noted that the German fears were unfounded. No Allied aircraft ever used the radiations of the *Metox* to "home" onto U-boats. The search radar of the aircraft was far more effective for this purpose. ASV Mark III, using the 10-centimeter wave length, was in use by Coastal Command aircraft operating against U-boats in the Bay of Biscay in the summer of 1943, and the German *Metox* search receiver was incapable of registering this short wave length.

The British promptly countered by withdrawing their surface patrols further to the west. During the last ten days of August, U-boat losses went back to normal and there were very few reports of attacks from the air, despite the unabated scale of the enemy's patrols. The staff officers breathed again; the "Bug" seemed to be effective.

But before long it was evident that not even the "Bug" could be fully relied on and it was not until much later, when the Naxos was introduced, that the last doubts about the enemy's radar frequencies were cleared up. However, the figure of fifteen boats lost in the Bay of Biscay in July, 1943, was not repeated in succeeding months; it remained at an average of two per month until May, 1944.[3]

The veterans of earlier battles, now on the staff at U-boat headquarters in Berlin, were constantly thinking up new devices to outwit the enemy. Where previously the boats had fought their way to the Atlantic in groups, for example, they were now told to slip through the bay singly and wide apart; they were sent to distant waters, long unoccupied, where the patrolling forces were weak; they sowed new types of mines in harbor entrances and attacked shipping when and where they could. Over a period of several weeks the radio stations successfully transmitted a series of dummy signals to give the impression that attacks were building up against particular Atlantic convoys, when no attacks were in fact contemplated.

In September operations were resumed in the North Atlantic, and when once again a group of boats began to close in on a convoy, it carried the hopes and fears of the men back in Berlin. On the morning of the nineteenth a decrypted message from a British aircraft reached headquarters: "Have attacked westbound U-boat. Four hits, unconfirmed." This was the curtain raiser to a most important operation, for unknown to the Germans, the enemy had joined two convoys together, resulting in a double-strength escort for both. At noon on the first day "Mac" Kinzel in U 338 sent a signal in accordance with the latest operational directive; "Am remaining on the surface to attack." It was the last signal he ever made. With his loss, contact was broken, but it was re-established that evening by five other boats; and now came the vital moment for putting the T5 torpedo to the acid test against the escorts.

Bahr in U 305 was the first to prove its value. He was hang-

[3] U-boat losses in the Bay of Biscay fell as soon as they gave up sailing in groups on the surface. The U-boats were naturally safer against air attack when submerged, but their passage time was thereby greatly increased.

ing on to the perimeter of a convoy when the sonar operator reported the sound of a destroyer's propellers; coming to periscope depth, he saw the ship bearing swiftly down upon him. He waited until the target showed clearly in his sights and fired; then down he went to 550 feet as fast as he could dive. Moments later a loud explosion echoed through the boat, followed after some time by another as the destroyer's depth charges went up. Bahr came to periscope depth and in the deepening twilight he saw the destroyer—one of the *Churchill* class which the USA had handed over to Britain—lying with a heavy list to port; a plane was cruising round the ship. Just as he was about to give the destroyer the coup de grâce, a second warship hove in sight; swiftly he aimed and fired, then turned to deal with the new adversary. The success of the T5 in the first attack had given him confidence; when the range dropped to 1,500 yards he fired again from his after-tube—the new target was a *Jervis* or *Hunt* class destroyer. Suddenly there came sounds of confusion from below and at the same moment through his periscope he saw a streak of foam astern of him. The second T5 had stuck in the tube—and the enemy ship was already close upon him! It was only when the range was already down to 500 yards that the torpedo suddenly loosed itself from the tube, and understandably the diving officer lost no time in taking the U-boat deep. While they were still diving, the sound of a second explosion reverberated through the boat; when eventually *U 305* surfaced again, the sea was empty.

Willberg, a reserve lieutenant commanding *U 666*, was also attacking this convoy. During the night he fired a T5 at an enemy destroyer which was racing down upon him with searchlights on and shells from her guns bursting round his conning tower. He dived but had barely reached 60 feet before the boom of the exploding torpedo was plainly heard. He surfaced again, to find clear evidence of his success floating round him; later on he was able to report to Berlin that he had sunk two destroyers. By the following morning Berlin had received fifteen signals reporting the firing of T5s, resulting in the sinking of seven destroyers for certain and three more unconfirmed; but the U-boats had not been able to reach the convoy. Then the fog descended and it was not until the following evening that the Wolves were able to resume the attack. That night they reported sinking five ships and five destroyers before fog had again forced them to break off; the total score after ninety hours of fighting was nine ships of 46,000 tons sunk and twelve destroyers, with three more probably sunk.[4] Two U-boats had failed to acknowledge signals from headquarters—but the T5 had won its laurels.

During the summer of 1943, some twenty ships had been sunk by German torpedoes on either side of Madagascar; and in August *U 181* returned from the Far East after completing the longest patrol of the war, having been at sea continuously for 220 days. Her captain, Lüth, was later awarded the diamonds to his Knight's Cross. Commander Junker in *U 532* had sunk five ships between Chagos Island and the south coast of India, and Lüdden in *U 188* had sunk three off the south coast of Arabia and in the Gulf of Oman. Henning in *U 533* was lost; but by November, four boats of the *Monsoon* Group had reached the base at Penang. In the Gulf of Guinea, Lauzemis in *U 68* claimed three ships, as did Henke in *U 515;* he was later taken prisoner and shot while trying to escape. *U 516* sank five ships of 30,000 tons off Panama before being forced to return through damage received in action. On her way back, she and *U 129* were due to refuel from *U 544.* As the two boats neared the meeting place, *U 129* heard a rapid series of depth charges exploding and the sound of destroyer propellers. Nothing was ever heard or seen again of *U 544.*

The bitter fight went on. Now it was no longer courage or ability or experience that decided the battle; the difference between success and failure, between life and death, depended in these days upon certain intangible high-frequency impulses and their reflection on a radar screen. As regards radar search receivers, the 'Bug" Mark I had been succeeded by the Mark II and then by the *Borkum* and the first rather primitive *Naxos;* and before the year ended the Germans learned what had long been expected—that the enemy was operating on very short wave lengths. They learned this from what came to be known as the *Rotterdam* device, called after a piece of badly smashed equipment that had been salvaged from a crashed British bomber in Rotterdam in the winter of 1942, and slowly and painfully reassembled.

Time after time, in response to Captain Meckel's urgent questioning, the Admiralty experts had refuted the possibility of enemy aircraft being equipped with a high-frequency short-

---

[4] The claim was grossly exaggerated. Records indicate that only three destroyer types were sunk and one damaged. Six merchant ships were lost out of the convoy. At this stage in the war no U-boat could risk waiting about to confirm the result of air attack on convoy escorts.

wave radar device. "Even if it were possible in theory," they insisted, "—and we don't think that it is—it would be highly improbable from a practical point of view. Short wave lengths are quite ineffective and in any case we reckon that it would be far too difficult to fit such short-wave gear into aircraft." Now, when their opinion was shown to be so utterly wrong, they gave the reasons for their previous standpoint: "German shore-based radar stations carried out experiments with short waves before the war at Pelzerhaken in the Bay of Lübeck, but the results obtained were so poor compared with the longer wave lengths that they were abandoned. No one could have foreseen that the Allies would achieve such great success with the short wave." Such admissions were of no help to Meckel. A conservative outlook and a lack of originality of thought are factors that one always has to reckon with; in this case they had been dearly paid for.

The Germans now knew the real reason for the heavy U-boat losses since 1942, and particularly in the catastrophic month of May, 1943. They had at last solved the riddle of why the *Metox, Grandin, Wanze* and *Borkum* gear had not recorded every enemy radar impulse; why boats were still attacked at night and in fog, even after they had switched off their detectors; and why the enemy had been able to divert his convoys from their patrol areas even before the U-boats had located them.

The lesson they had learned was bitter enough for U-boat crews and shore-based staff alike, but it was better by far to have learned it than to endure further months of mystification. In future the boats would be able to pick up impulses on any frequency, by using the *Wanze II, Borkum* and *Naxos;* that knowledge in itself was a great relief. Later they would receive the improved "Fly" and "Midge" gear, which could record every impulse from the high-pitched tone of the high frequency waves to the lowest notes of the longer wave lengths. Moreover, in November they would get the 3.7-cm.-A.A. guns that had been ordered in 1942; by mid-December all the boats had them, so that once more they had a chance of defending themselves against the armored four-engined bombers.

New German planes were also making their appearance; in November came the first Ju 290s—four-engined aircraft fitted with ASV, which could pick up an enemy convoy and "home" the U-boats on to it. But the old days of success were never to return. In February, 1944, it was decided to abandon any further attacks on convoys west of England; for even the grand admiral had to admit that, although no other arm of the fighting forces was doing so much damage to the enemy at so little cost, his U-boats were no longer capable of achieving their aim. The principles that he now laid down were of the greatest significance: "The boats must continue to operate, in order to maintain the threat to the enemy's supplies and to tie down his forces; but all commanding officers must understand that in the present phase of the campaign it is not victory, but the survival of boats and their crews, that must take priority. We shall need them later on, and when our new boats are ready, they will have fresh chances of success. Until then our policy must be to avoid all unnecessary risk."

3

TRANSITION PERIOD

(March–May, 1944)

The earlier intention of the German Admiralty to produce the first thirty boats of Type XXI by the autumn of 1944 had evoked severe criticism from Dönitz, who asked Speer whether he could not improve on this date. The minister's suggestions were revolutionary; he proposed—this was in August, 1943—that the first prototype should be completed and delivered by April 1, 1944—eight months earlier than the Admiralty's delivery date; and that building in series should begin at once *without testing the prototype,* each boat being built in sections at inland factories and delivered on the coast ready in all respects for final assembly. When Schürer, the famous U-boat designer of two wars, offered no objection, the grand admiral gave his approval and things began to move with a speed only equaled by that with which Todt had caused bunkers to be built on the Biscay coast. Responsibility for the execution of this program was vested in Herr Merker, the energetic managing director of the Magirus factory; it was a great responsibility, for never before had the ship-building industry undertaken assembly of prefabricated parts —least of all for complicated U-boats of an untested type.

Despite many difficulties, Merker delivered the first Type XXI punctually on April 1; by July it was due to be followed by thirty more. It was also hoped to deliver the little Type

XXIII of 200 tons from April onward at the rate of twenty boats a month. Delivery dates were problematical, when air raids were constantly destroying workshops, but Merker kept his promise. It was found, however, that several factories had been working to excessive tolerances for the assembly sections, and consequently the first half-dozen XXIs were unfit for war operations and were relegated to the U-boat school. But these and other teething troubles were ironed out one by one under the guidance of Admiral Topp, head of the building committee, and the schedules were maintained; so well, indeed, that despite the growing Allied air attacks, a higher tonnage of U-boats was delivered in the course of 1944 than had been completed in the raid-free year of 1942. Between January and March, 1945, with large areas of Germany already in enemy hands, more than 28,000 tons of U-boat construction was completed each month, as compared with 30,000 tons for the whole of 1941. But despite every effort to repair damage, despite all improvisation, the unceasing bomber raids caused the program as a whole to lag three months behind the planned schedule. No amount of inspired guidance from the top, no self-sacrifice by the workers themselves, was sufficient to deny this achievement to the enemy. The first fifty Type XXIs, scheduled for July 1944, were not launched until October of that year.

While the first of the new boats was being exhaustively tested in the Baltic by Captains Topp and Emmermann, the U-boat Command was evolving regulations for their tactical use. The "operational directives for Types XXI and XXIII" were as revolutionary in character as the new boats themselves. Hitherto attacks had, whenever possible, been delivered either on the surface under cover of night, or submerged to periscope depth by day; with either method, the captain relied upon his own eyesight. But in these new boats the human eye was to be replaced by a number of hypersensitive instruments which would record the enemy's bearing and course, thus supplying data for the attack. No longer would the captain alone observe and calculate the attack data; his post at the periscope, or at night upon the bridge, would no longer be the nerve center of operations. Instead, the "Balkon" hydrophone equipment would detect the enemy at ranges up to fifty miles; then, when the range had closed to between five and eight miles, the underwater supersonic detector, or S-gear, would come into play, supplying the captain with precise information as to the range, course, speed, numbers and types of target. The standard type of torpedo, fired singly or in pairs, and running on a straight course or with a preset gyro angle, was equally outmoded. The new boats would send a pattern of torpedoes crisscrossing the track of the convoy, while the U-boat herself would keep at about 150 feet depth, close to or right under the ships of the convoy, where the escorts could neither detect her nor depth-charge her, for fear of damaging the ships they were protecting.

These torpedoes, which would be fired six at a time, possessed characteristics undreamed of by earlier U-boat commanders. The LuT [1] torpedo was designed to weave a number of loops at right angles to the line of advance of the convoy; experiments in the Baltic had shown that each torpedo so fired had a 95 per cent chance of hitting a ship between 180 and 300 feet in length, regardless of the inclination of the target to the line of fire. Besides the LuT, there was now the improved antidestroyer torpedo, the T11, which could no longer be "foxed" by acoustic buoys [2] towed astern of the enemy destroyers; for this torpedo steered itself automatically toward propeller noises or, if these ceased, toward the noise of the auxiliary machinery.

On their speed trials along the measured mile off Hela, the new U-boats developed a submerged speed of 16½ to 17½ knots over a period of 60 to 80 minutes, which was not far short of their designed speed of 18 knots for 100 minutes. At silent-running speed they could remain fully submerged for 80 to 100 hours without using the snort. Tests were also very promising with the little XXIIIs—the modern version of the old "canoes"—which with a crew of thirteen carried only two torpedoes for coastal operations.

Meanwhile the Walter-boat—using hydrogen peroxide—had not been abandoned. Two ocean-going experimental boats of Type XVIII—*U 796* and *U 797*—were in course of construction, while four smaller ones of Type XVII—*U 792* and *794, 793* and *795*—had been put into service between November, 1943, and February, 1944. The last two, built by Blohm and Voss, made particularly successful trials; in March, 1944, the grand admiral embarked in *U 793* in the Baltic when she reached a submerged speed of 22 knots in a trial run. Later *U 792* attained a maximum submerged speed of 25 knots, and both the boats displayed excellent depth-

---

[1] LuT: abbreviation for *Lage-unabhängiger Torpedo*, or a torpedo that could be fired regardless of the inclination of the target at the moment of firing.

[2] Known as "Foxer" gear, a device to attract sound-seeking torpedoes and thus direct them from the towing ship.

keeping qualities. As a result of these trials a modified type, XVIIB, was ordered, but as with other new designs, there were delays and the first of these—*U 1405*—was not commissioned until December, 1944.

In May, 1944, building also began on a series of one hundred Walter-boats of Type XXVIW, displacing 850 tons and capable of maintaining a speed of 25 knots under water for ten to twelve hours. This was a tremendous advance, never before contemplated. With such a high-speed submerged endurance, a U-boat could not only close convoys from considerable distances but would easily outpace any A/S frigate or corvette. The swift variation in the speed and depth of the submerged U-boat would make it extremely difficult for a hunting destroyer to pin-point the target for an accurate depth-charge attack.

The Walter turbines in these boats had to be placed in a gasproof chamber at the afterend, which meant doing away with the usual after torpedo tubes. To make up for this, six torpedo tubes were built into the midship structure, so that with the four bow tubes the U-boat was capable of spreading a carpet of ten deadly fish in the path of an advancing convoy.

In short, the transition from the submersible to the fully operative underwater craft, though dogged by many obstacles, was now within sight of accomplishment.

4

END OF THE WOLF PACKS

(March–May, 1944)

Out of every hundred boats that put to sea after the crisis of May, 1943, thirty-five might never return. Although the rate of loss showed a slight decline at the beginning of 1944, life in the U-boats had by then become predominantly a struggle for survival against an enemy who ruled both sea and sky. It took from ten to twelve perilous days, creeping slowly through the Bay of Biscay, usually submerged—sometimes for twenty hours on end—before they reached the Atlantic battle zone; and the crews knew that only three or at the most four boats out of every five could expect to return.

The chances of success had steadily decreased since the day

when the search-group tactics were abandoned, the wolf packs were dissolved and the boats were sent out singly, each to its own independent area. As long as they had no adequate protection against radar location, their chances of survival must decrease still further.

In January, 1944, a new radar device which operated on a medium wave length had been recovered from a crashed enemy bomber. It was essential to provide a radar detector that could operate on this wave length, and in March the U-boats began to receive an apparatus with the code name of "Midge." This was only one of a long series of radar search receivers which were produced in the desperate race to keep abreast of new enemy techniques. The series had begun with the *Metox* or *Grandin* of unhappy memory, had continued with the "Bug I" and "Bug II," the *Hagenuk, Borkum, Naxos,* "Fly" and "Midge" to the combined *Tunis* and *Gema.* Finally there was the *Hohentwiel*—a search radar of the kind suggested by Captain Meckel as far back as 1942; this was eventually installed in U-boats in March, 1944.

The struggle was becoming more and more a test of nerves, in which the U-boat men had only their own high morale to make up for the inadequacy of their technical equipment. They could not be sure of a respite even when traveling submerged, for nearly every week the enemy added something new to his nerve-shattering collection of acoustic devices. Apart from the "Foxers," which emitted their own peculiar sound, there was the pinging and howling of the sonar impulses, tapping blindly round the hull, now fading away, now increasing to menacing strength. There was the "circular saw," which began with the deep hum of a bumblebee and rose to the thin high-pitched whine of a mosquito, then steadied on a metallic note which jarred the nerves of the men in the depths who, lying in their bunks to conserve oxygen, wondered what new sort of deviltry this noise could signify.

Whenever the boats returned to port, the commanders had new experiences to relate. One of them reported that the enemy was using a new type of noise-making buoy which imitated propeller sounds and sonar impulses. It looked, he said, like a black box with a spike on top and was obviously designed to scare U-boat men. Another reported a new type of explosive locating device, while a third told how he had been attacked by an aircraft using rockets. The enemy's latest sound gear was clearly much more powerful than the earlier models, for one U-boat had been located at a range of between 10,000 and 15,000 yards; the new and bigger depth charges, too, had damaged one U-boat's pressure hull at a depth of 650 feet. It was later established that this was the "killer" depth charge, which contained 1,000 pounds of explosive.

The U-boats now used their radio only when absolutely essential or when directly ordered to do so. As a result the U-boat Command, now transferred to a new headquarters code-named *Koralle* at Bernau near Berlin, received only the briefest reports and was often better informed by the radio intercept service than by its own boats. For the first time since 1939, it was really difficult to form an accurate estimate of the situation at sea; for days on end headquarters would remain ignorant of whether a boat was still "alive," because she had had no chance of reporting or of answering signals.

The boats were now widely scattered over the Atlantic, for the enemy must be kept aware of their presence, so as to compel him to expend his forces on convoy-escort work. The chances of attacking were becoming rare and since it was vital to conserve their numbers, they were told to avoid operating in areas where enemy patrols were known to be particularly strong. There was good reason for conserving strength at this time. A considerable number of VIIc boats had been dispatched to the Mediterranean [1] since the previous autumn; and since January, 1944, thirty boats had been diverted from the Atlantic for operations against the Murmansk convoys; while from February onward there was growing evidence that the enemy was mounting a large-scale invasion of the Continent, and precautionary measures had to be taken accordingly.

But where would the enemy land? The U-boat Command ordered a score of boats under Commander Schütze to Norway, as a precaution against a possible invasion of Jutland. When the tension heightened in March, fifteen Type VIIc's were ordered to stand by in the Biscay ports as the *"Landwirt* Group," which was strengthened by all boats arriving from home ports and those which had completed repairs in the Western dockyards.

At about this time the boats began to receive a new type of extensible snort to replace the earlier folding model. The object of fitting this equipment was not to restore the ag-

---

[1] Between September, 1943, and May, 1944, twenty-three U-boats attempted to enter the Mediterranean; thirteen succeeded, six were lost in the attempt and four abandoned the attempt.

gressive powers of the existing boats but to increase their chances of survival, and to relieve their feeling of helpless insecurity at sea. The installation of snort in the boats was, however, a slow process, for the overworked yards were no longer capable of meeting these new demands. Due to the bombing of supplies in transit and the growing disruption of communications in France, only about ten of the Atlantic-based boats could be so fitted during the month of May.

The experiences of the early snort boats hardly inspired confidence. The very first, *U 264* commanded by Lieutenant Looks, was sunk by a British destroyer in February, and the captain and chief engineer of a second which was also lost had been very critical of the device; although a special snort school was formed at Horten in the Oslo fjord, the commanders still regarded it with the deepest suspicion.

The snort head was fitted with a covering of foam-rubber intended to absorb the enemy radar impulses, and also with a search radar aerial for use while "snorting"; but all in all, there was not much fun in "snorting." If the snort dipped under in a seaway, the valve closed automatically and at once the diesels would suck all the air out of the boat, the consequent vacuum unpleasantly affecting eyes and ears. If the snort stayed under too long and the water pressure in the air pipe exceeded the pressure of the diesel exhaust gases, these gases were blown back into the boat, where their high content of carbon dioxide brought on every sort of symptom among the crew, from headaches, exhaustion and aching limbs to vomiting and even total collapse. It was Schröteler in *U 667* who eventually found the answer; he claimed to have spent nine days submerged on the homeward run without once surfacing. The important thing, he said, was to cut off the diesels immediately when the boat dipped, thus avoiding the danger from the exhaust gases. It was also essential to adjust routine in the boat to the requirements of "snorting"; if this was done, all would be well.

There were still a few boats operating in distant waters, and these accounted for most of the successes that were still attainable. *U 66*, under her third commander, Seehausen, sank five ships in the Gulf of Guinea. But when three more boats were dispatched to the same patrol area, they found the seas empty of traffic. Since the Allies had opened up the route through the Mediterranean, the alternative way round the Cape of Good Hope had lost much of its importance.

Some startling intelligence was now received which indicated that the enemy was endeavoring to locate submerged U-boats by means of buoys dropped by aircraft, called "Sono buoys." It appeared that these buoys automatically transmitted the result of their sonar impulse return to the aircraft. Soon after the first report of this device was received, a decrypted signal was picked up from an enemy aircraft in the Caribbean, which reported "sound contact" with a U-boat. This could only have been achieved by an intermediary device such as a sono buoy, as aircraft had no means of directly locating a submerged U-boat. U-boat commanders at once received orders to withdraw at high speed upon locating any such buoys.

No matter how far afield the U-boats ranged, their appearance was soon followed by a reinforcement of the enemy's A/S forces; there was evidently no area which he could not swiftly cover with a tightly drawn net of patrols. On March 12, Pich in *U 168,* Junker in *U 532* and Lüdden in *U 188* were due to rendezvous between Madagascar and Mauritius, to refuel from the tanker *Brake.* The secret meeting place lay well away from the shipping lanes—yet scarcely had *U 188* interrupted her refueling owing to the approach of bad weather, when her lookouts sighted an aircraft followed by a smoke cloud. The U-boat crash-dived and lay for forty long minutes soundlessly in the depths, while faint propeller noises could be heard in the sound gear on the same bearing as the smoke cloud. Then salvos of shells began to fall around the tanker and the U-boat men counted 148 explosions mingled with 14 heavy detonations, some of which shook *U 188* herself. For nearly an hour the noise went on, to be followed suddenly by the sounds of cracking and groaning as the *Brake* sank, and then another half hour of lesser bangs. At last all was still again, and Lüdden came cautiously to the surface. All he could see was a broad odoriferous streak of oil, a few pieces of floating wreckage, and in the distance the tanker's boats, heavily laden with survivors. The sun had gone down and night came with tropical swiftness as Lüdden hastened to pick up the survivors; later he handed them over to Pich in *U 168*.

In April, 1944, three boats bound for West Africa together with *U 66* were due to refuel from *U 488*, the last of the U-tankers; her captain, Studt, had last made a report on March 30, but in those days there was nothing abnormal in a boat remaining silent for three weeks. *U 66* was due to refuel on April 26, and Seehausen brought her to the meeting place on the twenty-fifth; finding strong patrols of carrier-borne aircraft, he stayed deep. That night he heard the sudden crash of several depth charges, followed by sinking noises; the next day *U 488* failed to appear. *U 66* slowly began her homeward run, surfacing for only a few hours at night to charge batteries. Her fuel tanks being almost empty, replenishment was essential. On April 29, Henke in *U 515* was sent orders to steer toward *U 66* but Henke failed to acknowledge the signal. As was learned later, his boat had been sunk by four destroyers and aircraft from the carrier *U.S.S. Guadalcanal,* he and some of his crew being taken prisoner. Thereupon Lauzemis in *U 68* was ordered to go to *U 66; U 68* failed to reply. *U. 188* was then ordered to the rescue, for *U 66*'s position was getting desperate. The following night, Lüdden in *U 188* heard heavy depth-charging close to the appointed rendevous; the next day he waited in vain for *U 66* to appear.

Because of these bitter experiences it was decided to initiate trials in the Baltic with underwater refueling between U-boats.

In the north a few U-boats were beginning to creep in, one at a time, to the English coast. No boat had been seen there for many a long day and their sudden reappearance would, it was hoped, upset the enemy's calculations. At the same time, four or five weather-reporting boats were stationed to the west of Britain, in the same waters where, a few years previously, the great U-boat "aces" had fought their nightly battles with the convoys. Now the U-boats could barely hold their own against the overwhelming number of hunters.

At the end of May the first snort boats returned to their bases after a week's patrol in the English Channel. Although they had no sinkings to report, they had at least achieved something which could be reckoned a success; they had proved that they could remain right under the enemy's nose in the shallow coastal waters—and at the moment that was more important than any victory, for it foreshadowed the possibility of the Wolves being able, with the help of the snort, once again to harry the enemy's lines of communication.

The sinking figures so far were certainly very disappointing. According to British statistics, thirteen ships totaling 92,000 tons had been sunk in January, eighteen of 93,000 tons in February, twenty-three of 143,000 tons in March, nine of 62,000 tons in April and only four ships of 24,000 tons in May; altogether sixty-seven ships totaling 414,000 tons in all operational areas from the North Cape to the Indian Ocean, from the Bay of Biscay to the Caribbean, as well as a couple of destroyers—an average of thirteen ships, or little over 80,000 tons, per month. That meant that during these five months, only one ship had been sunk every other day; it was painfully clear that the enemy was easily gaining in the race between new construction and losses of merchant ships, whereas the U-boat losses, though less than in the summer of 1943, were still very high.

5

INVASION

(June–August, 1944)

For a long time Stalin had been urging his western Allies to establish a second front—not in Africa or Sicily or Italy, but in Western Europe; but so far the Allies' strength had not been equal to this demand, for the U-boats had taken too heavy a toll of their shipping. By the end of May, 1943, the German Admiralty experts estimated that the enemy had lost 30 million tons of shipping from all causes, but mainly from U-boats; they reckoned that 15½ millions of that tonnage could have been replaced by new construction, so that the Allies still needed to make up 14½ million tons. Since then, however, the discontinuance of operations by German surface warships and the very limited success of the *Luftwaffe* against enemy shipping had, by relieving the pressure on Allied air and surface escorts, forced the U-boats back on the defensive; while at the same time a mighty fleet of *Liberty* and *Victory* ships and special landing craft was coming off the American launching ways in an ever-growing stream. Enemy losses had been made good to the point where a major landing on the Continent was feasible; and since February, 1944, reports from every source made it abundantly clear that the enemy was indeed preparing such a landing in the west.

The grand admiral had no doubts about the seriousness of the situation. On what proved to be his final visit to the Biscay bases, he revealed his thoughts to the U-boat crews. "If we cannot succeed in throwing the enemy back into the sea and he manages to reach the Ruhr, we shall have lost the war," he said. "Every unit and each man among you must understand that only the utmost determination will enable us to win through this decisive phase of the war. We know that the enemy is utterly resolved upon the destruction of the German people. We can expect no mercy. The Fortress of Europe must be defended to the last."

At the beginning of that fateful month of June, twenty-two U-boats forming "Middle Group" were lying at Bergen, Stavanger and Christiansand, in expectation of the enemy assault; none of them had the snort. The *"Landwirt* Group," now grown to thirty-six boats, was distributed among the Biscay bases—fifteen at Brest, of which only seven had the snort, and the remaining twenty-one at Lorient, St. Nazaire and La Pallice. They were kept at six hours' notice, fully armed and fueled and stocked with food. All leave had been canceled; everyone knew what was in the wind. For weeks Allied bombers had been blazing a wide and deadly trail across France toward Paris, preparing the ground for the victories to come. Railway stations and bridges, marshalling yards, crossroads, airfields—the whole system of communications throughout Northern France was exposed to a whirlwind of destruction.

Hitler had long since forbidden the grand admiral to fly to France on visits of inspection. The staff cars of the senior officer, flotillas (West) had often covered hundreds of miles in convoy, racing at breakneck speed from airfield to airfield, wherever the grand admiral's plane was expected to land, but all that was over now. For the officers at the French bases there were no more shooting parties after deer, hares, pheasants or pigeons, for in Occupied France their lives were no longer safe. Neumann, Adjutant to the Senior Officer, had recently been held up in broad daylight by Frenchmen armed with submachine guns, who relieved him of his shotgun and sent him home; he was lucky to escape with his life, for the maquis were as ubiquitous as they were confident. No German dared show himself in the forests between Lorient and Vannes, nor in many other parts of France. The German garrisons were no longer strong enough to restrain the partisans, who were armed with weapons dropped for them by parachute nearly every night from Allied aircraft.

Then came the invasion. The first indication of it was a number of "blips" appearing on the screens at coastal radar stations, and some reports from patrol ships in the channel. It was obvious that something was afoot on the English coastline—something more than the usual assembly of big bomber forces over the channel for a raid on Germany. Indeed it proved to be the mightiest armada that had ever put out from the shore of England. The invading forces were led by innumerable mine sweepers; then came the destroyers—one hundred of them—then merchant ships, cruisers, special landing craft, troop transports by the thousand; and in the background appeared the dim outlines of powerful battleships. Five thousand fighters and three thousand bombers, most of them flying fortresses, roared overhead, and in their van, transport aircraft towed an endless stream of gliders.

The first warning reports reached the German Command at about one o'clock on the morning of June 6; they came in from Calais, from the mouth of the Seine, from le Havre and from Cotentin. There were reports of isolated landings by parachutists west of Caen at the mouth of the Orne; near St. Mère Eglise north of Carentan; to the east of Cotentin and at the mouth of the river Vire. The main body of the invasion was still on passage; it had only just been located and had so far given no indication of its precise destination. Supreme Headquarters believed that the landings of parachutists and gliders in the Cotentin peninsula were merely supply drops for the maquis or perhaps a feint attack; the main assault was expected at Calais. But Admiral Krancke in Paris immediately interpreted this activity as the beginning of the main invasion.

Soon afterward the first heavy combined attack from aircraft and warships fell upon the mouth of the Orne in the Bay of Carentan; simultaneously, troops began to disembark from a swarm of landing craft on the beaches at Carentan, St. Mère Eglise, Vierville, Arromanches and Courcelles. At 0305 the U-boat Command received from the German Admiralty the first news of events in France: "Large numbers of parachutists and gliders are landing in Western Normandy." Five minutes later the alarm went out to the "Middle Group" of U-boats in Norway; half an hour later it was sent to the *"Landwirt* Group" in the Bay of Biscay; it was also flashed to some U-boats that had just sailed from Norway, instructing them to stay where they were and await further orders. Two hours later, five snort boats in the Atlantic were ordered to return at full speed to Western France, where they were to rearm and proceed to sea again immediately. Eight boats with snort from Brest and another from Lorient were ordered into action to the north of Cherbourg. Those boats in Brest which had no snort were ordered to attack British supply convoys between the Lizard and

Hartland Point; the rest of the snortless boats from Lorient, St. Nazaire and La Pallice were ordered to make reconnaissance patrols in the bay, while the "Middle Group" in Western and Southern Norway were brought to immediate readiness.

It was still dark when the U-boats sailed. Their orders read: "Full action. Proceed at maximum speed on the surface, repel enemy aircraft." They knew what that meant. As the clouds rolled away, the unwelcome moon shone brilliantly down upon them; they knew what that meant, too.

The log of *U 415*, commanded by Lieutenant Werner, gives a picture of what followed:

0140. Bright moonlight, good visibility. Escort is dropped off Brest, course 270°, full speed.

0145. The next astern, *U 256*, is attacked by aircraft. We also open fire. *U 256* shoots down one plane. Radar impulses all round us, strength 3–4.

0220. Impulses cease to starboard. Presume plane approaching. Sunderland attacks from 40° to starboard. I open fire. He drops four bombs ahead of me which explode beneath the boat. Simultaneous attack from another four-engined plane, a Liberator, from starboard. Some hits on the bridge from aircraft shells. No bombs dropped. Both diesels stalled from damage from the Sunderland's bombs. Boat thrown upward and dips stern so deep that water comes through the conning-tower hatch. Order all hands on deck. The speed of the attack and the damage sustained prevent me from making a signal. Dinghy and lifebuoys made ready. As the boat is still afloat, I order all ammunition to be brought to the bridge and stacked round the guns. The boat is now lying stopped, with helm jammed hard-a-starboard.

0228. Fresh attack from starboard by Sunderland which attacks with gunfire and drops bombs from low altitude. Bombs fall amidships, to port and starboard. A Liberator then attacks from port and opens fire. Our guns set this aircraft on fire and it crashes into the sea astern of us. As all attacks are delivered from ahead, the 3.7-cm. gun can only be brought to bear as the planes are flying away from us. Both twin machine guns score hits on fuselage and engines in all attacks. Very good shooting. Our "Bug" and "Fly" gear are both shot away. . . .

After some time, Chief Engineer reports boat can dive on one electric motor. I order hands below again. Set course for base. . . .

The U-boats on their way to the channel shot down four big enemy planes, while reports of more than fifty attacks from the air poured into the U-boat Command within twenty-four hours. Five boats, one of them fitted with snort, were so badly damaged that they had to return to Brest. Ketels in *U 970* was lost and so was Baden in *U 955*, inward-bound from the Atlantic; two more boats were lost on the morning of the eighth and two others so damaged that they had to turn back. By the tenth no less than ten of the boats from Brest which had no snort were once more lying under the shelter of the bunkers, while another had failed to return altogether.

By June 12, it was safe to assume that the enemy had no intention of landing elsewhere in Normandy, and the *"Land-wirt* Group" was ordered to return to Brest, although the "Middle Group" off Norway remained at sea until the end of the month, as Supreme Headquarters was still expecting a major enemy landing between Trondheim and Lindesnäs. When no such landing had occurred by the end of June, Admiral U-boats kept a bare half-dozen boats at sea as his "eyes and ears," and ordered the rest to be decommissioned and their crews sent to Germany to man the new Type XXIs. Of the seventy-five boats which had been got ready for the invasion, barely a dozen remained available to attack the invaders' supply lines. All of these were fitted with the snort, but they soon discovered that the enemy could get a radar reflection off the snort head; nevertheless the first captains to return from the invasion area on June 22 showed surprising confidence. Stuckmann in *U 621* had sunk a tank landing ship and von Bremen in *U 764* had sunk a destroyer north of Jersey; on the whole the snort had proved itself. Equally satisfactory experiences with the snort were reported by four boats which sailed from Brest for Cherbourg carrying 8,000 rounds of armor-piercing A.A. and 350,000 rounds of machine-gun ammunition, although they were unable to enter harbor and discharge their cargoes, for when they arrived on the twenty-third, Cherbourg was already besieged and they had to return to Brest.

By the end of June, according to British statistics, the snort boats had sunk five ships totaling 30,000 tons and two frigates, and had damaged a 7,000-tonner and a third frigate. Poor reward as this was for the loss of five hundred valuable U-boat men, it would have cost far more to destroy the troops and supplies carried in those five ships once they had been landed.

On land things were not going well; the enemy had not been thrown back into the sea. Every day his beachhead grew wider and deeper, filling up steadily with new divisions, tanks, lorries and ammunition—all landed over the artificial harbors made out of giant pontoons sunk off the coast. At times it became almost impossible for the U-boat Command to control the boats at sea, since incoming reports were too few to enable *Koralle* to build up a clear picture of the situation; and the U-boats were frequently unable to come up close enough to the surface to receive the long-wave transmissions destined for them. For the first time in five years of war, the U-boat Command found itself entirely dependent upon reports from the intercept service and from commanders returning from patrol.

In view of the snort boats' experiences in the English Channel, only experienced commanders were allowed to be sent there in future; the veteran captains returning to port drew vivid pictures of the almost insuperable difficulties of waging war in the invasion area. They explained how the whole routine of life on board had had to be adapted to what they called the "snort rhythm." The main meal of the day, with properly cooked food, could be prepared and eaten only while snorting; and only then could running repairs be carried out. By this means they could conserve the precious oxygen which was needed for the rest of the day when they dived deep.

The log of Schröter, commanding *U 763*, gives a picture of the difficulties and hazards in which a U-boat commander could easily find himself during this phase of the operations. On July 6, he was being persistently hunted by a group of A/S ships in a position which he calculated was "south of the Isle of Wight." By midnight he had counted 252 depth charges at varying distances from his U-boat. For over twenty-four hours he had had no chance of surfacing to ventilate the boat and as a result his men were getting very exhausted. By the following day *U 763* had successfully eluded her pursuers, but she now encountered an even greater danger:

7.7.1944.
1200. After 30 hours of pursuit I am very worried about our position. During all that time we could take no proper echo soundings to check our position. We must have covered a considerable distance on varying courses and in varying currents. By dead reckoning we should be 20 to 30 miles to the north of Cherbourg . . .
1654. Boat has touched bottom in 20 fathoms.
1902. Boat is lying uneasily on the bottom in 20 fathoms, despite her bows-down trim. In view of the shallow water

ought we not to be further south? But there the current can be as much as 9 knots . . . Boat no longer aground. Have come to periscope depth, course 330°. Land in sight bearing 300° to port.

2258. Dusk. Visibility very bad to starboard and no visual bearings can be taken. There are no stars. Comparison with the chart seems to indicate that the current has carried us between the Channel Islands. By keeping the echo sounder going and making use of the northerly set, I am trying to steer northward using snort. Visibility is poor ahead of us.

0041. The soundings do not seem right. An attempt to get a fix by radio beacons produces only one position line—from Brest. It runs across our presumed position as indicated by the echo soundings. So long as there is sufficient water under the keel and adequate visibility, surfacing won't help. I am carrying on with the snort, so as to be able to check my position at first light at periscope depth.

0356. Almost no wind. Moonlight. Visibility poor. Surfaced. Four destroyers are lying astern of me—range 4000 to 5000 yards. Land in sight on both quarters. To port I can also see the outline of several merchant ships. I steer northwest on the supposition that the land to starboard is the Cotentin peninsula, occupied by the enemy.

0433. Aground in 17½ fathoms. Now that I have time to digest what I have seen, I realize that the boat must have grounded on the English coast. But where are we? From the projected line of bearing from Brest radio-beacon and from the chart, it looks as though we are off Spithead, improbable as that may seem. . . .

Scröter was right. He was neither thirty miles north of Cherbourg, as he had at first thought, nor between the Channel Islands, but actually in the famous fleet anchorage at Spithead. Until morning he kept still as an oyster. Then he began to thread his way cautiously between a mass of old ships in ballast, hurrying harbor craft, hospital ships and landing craft, until he suddenly found himself in very shallow water. The echo sounder was registering less than ten fathoms when the bows touched bottom, and now he was in danger of being left high and dry—or at any rate partly out of the water—when the tide fell. That would be the end, and the crew would almost be able to walk ashore to England— "for a counterinvasion," as the sublieutenant perkily suggested.

But the captain was in no laughing mood. Laboriously he worked his boat into deeper water, where she could lie in ten fathoms to await the next high tide. When at last the moment came and the chief engineer could lift the boat gently off the bottom, *U 763* proceeded submerged, keeping to the starboard side of the channel while several incoming landing craft and two destroyers passed her on an opposite course.

During July there were always three or four snort boats operating in the channel. Creeping along under the coast to avoid radar detection, they "snorted" their way to their patrol areas and sank whatever came within range of their torpedoes, which was little enough. On July 5, Sieder in *U 984* sank three ships totaling 21,550 tons and a frigate out of a convoy of troop transports north of Barfleur, and damaged a 7,000-tonner. Including the sinkings in more distant waters, the month closed with losses, as admitted by the British, of 63,000 tons. In the third week of August two more boats returned from the Seine area where they had sunk a tank landing ship and damaged two others totaling 17,000 tons. "There's plenty of traffic there," said the commander of one of them with a wry smile, "the prospects are not bad but the enemy patrols are exceptionally strong." Mahrholz, commanding *U 309*, spent only a week there and then had to return as his crew were worn out. Extracts from his log read as follows:

12.8.1944.
0345. In company with *U 981*, set course for rendezvous with escort off La Pallice.
0415. *U 981* has struck a mine. As everything was out of action on board her, I sent a signal: "Urgent. *U 981* has struck mine, unable to dive, all machinery out of action, request immediate assistance, am remaining on spot, *U 309*."
0620. Attacked by Halifax aircraft. Am lying stopped near *U 981* as she cannot move. Aircraft fly over us three times. Three parachute flares dropped . . . *U 981* under way again on her motors. Resumed slow speed on motors, course 90°, passing along the line of buoys. . . .
0624. Bombs dropped on *U 981* . . . further attack by Halifax. A.A. fire from both U-boats scores hits. Another mine explodes under *U 981*. Further attack on *U 981* by twin-engined plane. *U 981* suddenly goes full speed ahead on both diesels and hauls out of the line.
0643. Dinghies made ready on upper deck. The other boat begins to sink by the bows. Crew jump overboard. I immediately close the spot and take 40 survivors on board. The captain and twelve men are missing. . . .

While the enemy was making his preparations for the decisive thrust on land, he had also been busy strewing mines from aircraft by night on the approaches to the U-boat bases.

Reports from returning U-boats showed too that the enemy had reverted to the old anti-submarine device developed in the First World War—the explosive A/S trawl. This heavily weighted net could be dragged along the sea bottom in depths up to 160 feet; when the steel meshes scraped along a U-boat's hull an explosion would follow.

Between the ninth and thirteenth of August strong bomber formations attacked the U-boat bunkers. In Bordeaux they scored twenty-six direct hits with 1,000-pound bombs—with no result whatever! Twenty feet of reinforced concrete with a superimposed burster course ten-foot thick were more than enough to ward off the bombs. One bunker at Brest actually was penetrated when the enemy used five and six-ton bombs; the hole measured thirty feet across, but the damage inside was slight. The bunkers were secure against any attack from the air—but not from the land.

After the American armored columns had broken through at Avranches, Brest prepared to make its last stand. A stream of retreating formations poured into the fortress and its bunkers, and it was only with difficulty that work on the U-boats could be continued. Of the two flotilla commanders in Brest, only Commander Winter stayed on. Captain Lehmann-Willenbrock took over *U 256*, which had been paid off owing to severe damage; she was quickly put into running order, fitted with a lash-up snort and sailed with a scratch crew made up from reserve crews and technicians. Weeks later, when he had already been given up for lost, Lehmann-Willenbrock brought his rickety craft safely into Bergen. There *U 256* was finally paid off.

The break-through at Avranches meant the loss of the U-boat bases at Brest, St. Nazaire and Lorient. Such boats as could move were sent southward to La Rochelle, whither the senior officer U-boats, West, had also been transferred. Seven out of the fifteen boats were lost through air attack while on passage; the crews of those boats unable to sail were told to make for Germany as best they could, there to man the new XXIs. Some of the Norway-based boats were sent to the Baltic to strengthen the defenses of Libau, while the snort boats from Bordeaux and La Pallice were ordered to the Bristol and North Channels, where they hoped to find targets in the Western Approaches.

In the third week of August Schröteler in *U 667*, who had been off the northwest coast of Cornwall since the beginning of the month, reported the sinking of 15,000 tons of shipping and a destroyer, while five other boats on passage from the channel to Norway announced the destruction among them of five ships of 22,800 tons and a destroyer and the damaging of another ship. One of these boats, *U 480 (Förster)*, had her hull coated with "Alberich," a rubber skin designed to absorb the radar impulses. Her victims included the s.s. *St. Enogat* and *Orminster* and HMS *Loyalty*. Although continuously hunted for several hours by a group of A/S vessels, her "Alberich" covering protected her. On January 6, she sailed again from Bergen for her former beat in the channel; fighting continuously against the vigilant patrols, she survived for six weeks before being sunk by the depth charges of two destroyers.

By the end of August, thirty snort boats among them had completed forty-five patrols in the channel; in two months they had sunk twelve escort vessels and twenty ships of 112,800 tons and damaged one patrol vessel and seven ships of 44,000 tons. This meant that they had prevented over 100,000 tons of cargo, including dozens of supply trucks laden with war material, from reaching the battlefield; on the other hand, two thirds of the channel U-boats had failed to return and not more than 250 out of the 1,000 men in them had been rescued.

More and more of the Biscay-based boats were being transferred to Norway; as the American armored columns drove deep inland and threatened even La Pallice and Bordeaux, the last of the Sea Wolves abandoned their lairs on the Biscay coast. Four of them, unable to get new batteries, were blown up, among them some famous veterans of the old days—Niko Clausen's *U 129* (Clausen himself was long since dead), Hardegen's *U 123* which had participated in *Paukenschlag* off New York, *U 178* which Willem Spahr had brought back from East Asia, and Lüdden's *U 188*. The last of the boats sailed from Bordeaux on August 25. Some of the flotilla personnel were sent to strengthen the garrison of La Rochelle, others began the long march toward Germany together with 20,000 soldiers, dockyard workers and garrison clerks, who had been integrated into regiments. Their road lay across a France overrun by enemy tanks and in a state of wild confusion. Only a few of them managed to get home; nothing more was heard of the rest until after the war. Among those who ended up in a POW camp somewhere in France was the former captain of *U 108* and commander of the Twelfth Flotilla, Klaus Scholz.

While Commander Winter stayed on in Brest, Kals remained in Lorient, Piening in St. Nazaire and Zapp at La

Rochelle. Their U-boat crews played a worthy part in the defense of the ancient fortresses, fighting on shore as resolutely as they had fought on sea. One day a general visiting the front line came upon a 20 mm. A.A. gun mounted out in the open without any camouflage, while its crew of U-boat men stood round it quite unprotected. "Why don't you dig yourselves in?" he asked them. "Well, Sir," answered the captain of the gun, "there was no way of digging ourselves in when we were fighting at sea."

The senior officer U-boats, West, left La Rochelle for Norway at the same time as his U-boats, but he had orders to go by air. At home, hasty arrangements were being made to provide berths for all these returning boats, as Norway could take only about one third of them. The home dockyards, already strained to the limit, could not take on the additional repair work, while the boats themselves had to steam from six hundred to one thousand miles further to reach their operational areas, and when they got there, they had to spend whole weeks on end below the surface, breathing through their snorts. Had the days of the wolf packs really existed? Had there really been the great campaigns in American and African waters, in the Caribbean and the Gulf of Mexico—or had it all been a dream? To put to sea under the prevailing conditions was a far greater ordeal than anyone had foreseen; but though the strain under which the U-boat men worked was great, their spirit remained unshaken.

6

THE NARROWING RING

(September, 1944–April, 1945)

By the middle of September, 1944, all U-boat attacks on the invasion fleets had ceased. The last boat to leave the Sixth and Seventh Flotillas' base at St. Nazaire was Tinschert's *U 267*, which sailed before the end of the month. Although Lieutenant Graf von Matuschka in *U 482* reported sinking 23,000 tons of shipping and a destroyer in the North Channel, it was clear that the Allied ring was closing in and driving the U-boats back into their former battlegrounds.

Scarcely one of the old combatants was still active; some had been captured, while such of their boats as had not been sunk had long since been absorbed into the training flotillas. The war which had begun off the coasts of Britain had returned to those coasts, and there it would stay until such time as the new boats now on the building ways could once more carry it into the Atlantic Ocean.

When Colonel Graf von Stauffenberg made his attempt on the life of Hitler on July 20, the U-boat men remained unaffected. It was enough for them to know that Dönitz had taken no part in the plot; they were fighting men who had taken an oath of loyalty and what went on at the higher levels was no concern of theirs. Dönitz had bluntly refused to have anything to do with the conspiracy. His one aim—and that of all the German forces in the west—was to defeat the enemy. He knew that the elimination of the Head of the State at this critical juncture could only result in a weakening of Germany's position generally. He remembered all too well the slogan of 1917 and 1918: "Get rid of the Kaiser and all will be well." Such propaganda in respect to his present leader left him unimpressed; he knew that the Allies were demanding unconditional surrender and he did not believe that Hitler's disappearance from the scene would make them abandon that demand. He knew all about the top secret "Eclipse" directive captured from the British, which foreshadowed the geographical dismemberment of Germany, and this knowledge only strengthened his conviction that it was better to concentrate all available forces against the external enemy. If only the invaders could be thrown back, he still hoped that time would allow the new U-boats to resume the offensive and compel the enemy to sue for terms; now that the older types of boats were being fitted with the snort, they also were beginning to revive the offensive.

And so the fight continued, with the IXc boats off Newfoundland, the American coast and the St. Lawrence; and the VIIc boats off the coast of Britain, the Firth of Moray, the Minch, the North Channel and Iceland. These operational positions were occupied more or less continuously until the surrender in May, 1945. In the meantime, as the steady withdrawal of the German front line in France made it more and more difficult to maintain land communications, the commanders of Army depots and Naval bases began to call upon the U-boats for help. All through September and October exorbitant requests came pouring into *Koralle*. The naval officer in charge, Loire, asked for supplies, particularly of fuel, to be sent in by U-boat; Navy Group Command West asked for three months' rations for the eighty thousand men garrisoning the Atlantic fortresses; Dunkirk wanted ammunition; the quartermaster general of the Army called for U-boats in the Baltic to insure supplies for Army Group North; Naval Command Norway requested the allocation of five boats to escort troop convoys to Germany and to drive off enemy forces dominating the Arctic Strait. The U-boat Command was quite unable to fulfill any of these demands.

In October the Thirteenth Flotilla in Trondheim and the Eleventh in Bergen became the new headquarters for the former Biscay-based U-boats, of which twenty-eight were now on their way back from operations, two on their way out and only six actually on patrol. This was a smaller number than at any time in the last three years, and half-a-dozen boats were detached from "Middle Group" in order to maintain pressure against the enemy. Of these, Voigt in *U 1006* was lost, Rabe in *U 246* returned to harbor after being depth-charged, while Pulst in *U 978* reached the channel, and subsequently reported the sinking of three ships.

In the Mediterranean the loss of the last three U-boats had terminated all activity there, and the Flag Officer, Admiral Kreisch, and his staff returned to Germany. So ended the German U-boat campaign in the Mediterranean, which had been marked by many important achievements, though the cost was high.

In the autumn and winter the successes of the snort boats were surprisingly high. According to British statistics, seven ships of 30,000 tons were lost in November from U-boat attack; in December the score was nine ships of 59,000 tons. The Coastal Command bombers could not maintain their usual rate of U-boat sinkings, for the boats no longer came to the surface but stayed down deep and used the snort sparingly. The A/S vessels had their difficulties, too, for the U-boat was hard to find while deep, and even harder to detect in the shallow coastal waters where the sonar impulses became confused. The U-boat Command only learned of their operations through enemy signals decrypted by the intercept service, and through reports from the German garrisons on the Channel Islands of explosions observed to seaward at night or of wreckage found on the beaches. The curve of U-boat losses fell away sharply to 10.5 per cent—eighteen boats in four months. Losses had not been so low for years, not even in the second half of 1942, while the tonnage sunk per boat per day at sea was once again as high as in the old days.

There was still some activity in the more distant waters, too. *U 862* under Timm sailed from Penang to the coast of Australia, sinking a *Liberty* ship south of Sydney on Christmas Eve, 1944, and another ship seven hundred miles west of Perth at the beginning of January, 1945; at about the same time Hilbig in *U 1230* landed two secret agents near Boston, U.S.A. An average of two boats were operating regularly to the south of Newfoundland, off Nova Scotia and the New England coast; one of them—Roth in *U 1232*—sank six ships and a destroyer out of two convoys, while other boats sank four escort ships and torpedoed several freighters, of which two were later confirmed sunk. Just before Christmas, Altmeyer in *U 1227* and Hechler in *U 870*, on patrol off Gibraltar, sank two tank landing craft and a corvette out of one convoy and three ships and a French corvette out of others in the next three weeks.

The U-boats in Japan and at Penang received orders to sail for home not later than the middle of January; as they had no snort and only a few were fitted with effective radar detector gear, they were instructed to cross the dangerous area south of Iceland at the darkest time of the year. Four of them were lost, two being sunk by Allied submarines. Oesten in *U 861* deceived the enemy spies by numerous false starts and other stratagems, and finally won his way to the open sea quite undetected. Without snort or radar equipment, he brought his boat across thousands of miles of ocean, to arrive in Trondheim safe and sound in the spring. This was at a time when even in South African waters the sinking of a single ship was sufficient to bring powerful enemy forces out in retaliation. One such force, consisting of two aircraft carriers, four frigates, two Indian and one English A/S vessels, two corvettes and a squadron of land-based planes, only sank their quarry, a U-cruiser, after the planes had spent 871 flying hours covering thousands of miles of sea.

In Northern Europe the first of the new Type XXI boats, *U 2511*, had completed her shakedown under Commander Schnee with the veteran Lieutenant Suhren as his chief engineer. On express orders from the grand admiral the training had been expedited, and others of the type were soon to follow.

The general situation in Germany had begun to deteriorate alarmingly. The Ardennes offensive of December—the Army's last hope—had failed, and blow succeeded blow. In January the Russians broke through at Baranow and established a bridgehead at Wriezen—less than twenty miles from *Koralle*.

The grand admiral promptly dispersed the Naval High Command and ordered the operational staffs to withdraw to Sengwarden, near Wilhelmshaven. The U-boat Command returned to the same barracks they had occupied at the beginning of the war. The ring was closing; for the first time in six years of war the head of the U-boats was separated from his staff, and no longer in direct control of U-boat operations. He remained in Berlin with only a few of his officers.

The failure of the Ardennes offensive had put an end to his hopes of reviving the campaign with the new types of boats, but he was encouraged to continue operations by the successes which the existing boats had recently achieved without undue loss to themselves. He could not hope to exert really effective pressure on the enemy until the new boats were ready, but the XXIIIs would be available in February and the XXIs in March; meanwhile agents' reports as well as the enemy's press showed that the Allies were alive to the need for further antidotes to counteract the revival of U-boat activity. A series of very heavy air raids on U-boat bases and repair yards heralded a new phase in the Allied offensive; the long-promised "Roof over Germany" of thousands of German fighter aircraft was not forthcoming and a number of XXIs were damaged or destroyed in their pens. Nevertheless the first of the little XXIIIs sailed for the coast of England in February, 1945, while simultaneously some fifty snort boats were dispatched toward Cherbourg, Portsmouth, Ushant and the southwest coast of Britain; to the Isle of Man, Liverpool and the Skerries; to the North Channel and the Clyde, North Minch, the Pentland Firth and the Firths of Moray and Forth. When they got back, their commanders talked confidently of future operations, for they had learned how long they could stay at sea by using the snort and how it improved their prospects of success. Such confidence was not entirely shared by the Command staff. Agents' reports mentioned fresh mine fields off the English coast; the enemy was suspiciously quick to react to German radio transmissions at sea. No clear picture of the situation at sea could be gained, since the U-boat commanders did not dare to use their transmitters to report; some of them had been at sea for over two months, and that in itself gave cause for anxiety.

Becker, commanding *U 260*, reported that he had struck a mine while navigating at 250 feet—60 feet above the sea bed. His boat had been so badly damaged that he had been forced to surface and he and his crew had landed on the

coast of Ireland after scuttling her. The reports of new mine
fields were evidently correct.

Once again a sharp rise in losses forced the Command to
withdraw the U-boats from the coast, to send them out further
to the west or, when necessary, to bring them home altogether.
For the last time half a dozen of the larger boats were formed
into a group, called "Sea Wolf" and sent westward in the
hope of finding some convoys whose escorts might perhaps
be much reduced, after the lull in the Atlantic. At the same
time eighteen so-called "Seals"—a new type of midget submarine with a two-man crew, developed under the super-
vision of Vice Admiral Heye, were sent out from bases in
Holland on their first operation. These were tiny craft, less
than 30 feet long, powered by a lorry-type diesel engine and
the electric motor from a torpedo and carrying two torpedoes
outside the hull. The range of the boats depended upon the
stamina of the captain and his engineer, who operated them
in a semiprone position. On their first mission they were over-
taken by a sudden storm which put them to the severest test,
but they made two very important discoveries. They were so
small that they were almost invisible on the surface and undetectable submerged; and the explosion of a depth charge
merely tossed them to one side without damaging them. Their
radius of action exceeded everybody's hopes; out of ten which
sailed on one mission, the last one returned after six days at
sea, during which its crew of two had scarcely been able to
move from their cramped positions.

As the German armies fell back in the west, the "Beaver"
was equally in demand. This was a one-man U-boat driven
by a small gasoline engine and electric motor, which also
carried two torpedoes outboard. Its endurance was so limited
that it could only expect to reach its target but not to return.
Yet there was no lack of volunteers, including women, for
service with Commander Bartels, the "Beaver" squadron commander. Naturally the offer from the women was refused.
Like the German fighter pilots who were beginning to ram
enemy planes in the air, the midget U-boat men also set forth
knowing that there would be no return.

From mid-January onward, the grand admiral took part
almost daily in the Führer conferences at Supreme Headquarters. He now assumed responsibility also for the transport
and distribution of coal throughout Northern Germany. There
was no end to the problems which were heaped upon him:
organizing sea transport, training and equipping the newly
created Naval Infantry Brigades, supplying anti-aircraft guns

for the transports, dealing with bottlenecks in the supply of coal and oil, the movement of troops and supplies to and from Norway, the evacuation of refugees from the crowded harbors of Danzig, Gotenhafen, Pillau, Swinemünde and Kolberg; the transfer of wounded from the Eastern front, the evacuation of Memel, the U-boat war itself, the laying of mines in the mouth of the Scheldt, minesweeping in the Baltic, where Russian submarines were beginning to appear; the threat of an English invasion of Jutland and Zeeland, the operation of ice-breakers on the Oder and in the Frisches Haff, the evacuation of the Army of Courland, anti-aircraft defenses for Stettin, Swinemünde and the hydroworks at Poelitz; lack of ammunition here, lack of weapons there; manpower allocations for the Army; warding off the encroaching hand of Dr. Goebbels, the Reich Commissioner for Defense; evacuees, casualties, lack of oil and of coal—and always the air raids.

Göring required naval troops to relieve his parachutists at Stettin, but this was out of the question; the only men available were highly qualified technicians without any sort of training in land warfare. Any further allocation of ships for the evacuation of Courland could only be made at the expense of Norway; it would take thirty-five ships ninety days to remove the 300,000 men of the Courland Army and the labor battalions. The personnel at the Admiralty had been reduced from 8,000 to 2,800 men, leaving only the essential departments still functioning. Another 4,000 Navy men were assigned for duty as shock troops. There were 35,000 refugees in Stettin and another 22,000 on the way, and all of them had to be evacuated—60,000 refugees were brought out of Kolberg in ten days. The coal situation in Norway was desperate—only two trains were running each day, their engines burning wood. The transport of coal at home was equally difficult owing to the blocking of the Rhine and the destruction of the inland waterways, such as the Dortmund-Ems canal.

The score per U-boat in December was 9,000 tons; in January the figure rose to 11,000 tons. This was as high as in the most successful phase of the war, but the boats were too few in number and their passage from base to patrol area took too long. In the first months of 1945, 237 U-boats were under repair or in the process of completion; they included 111 old ones, 84 Type XXIs and 42 Type XXIIIs. Sixty new boats were being commissioned every month, but at the same time air raids on the U-boat yards had destroyed 24 boats and damaged another twelve since March 30. The *Admiral Scheer* had capsized, the cruiser *Admiral Hipper* had caught fire, the *Emden* was damaged.

And so the tale of woe continued. On April 12, 1945, the grand admiral obtained Hitler's approval to move to North Germany if Berlin should be abandoned; but for the time being he remained at *Koralle,* working to save what he could from the catastrophe that was about to engulf all Germany.

Franco had warned Churchill in vain that the Allies' policy of utterly destroying Germany would bring the Russians to the shore of the Atlantic. When the British Premier suggested to Eisenhower that Allied forces should land in the Balkans and occupy Vienna and Budapest, the American supreme commander had replied that he had no such directive. It would not be wise to arouse the Russians' misgivings. Then came the second landing in Southern France and since then the Great Powers had divided Germany up between them at Yalta.

At Teheran, Churchill had tried without success to win over Roosevelt from his illusions, but the American President's conviction as to Germany's collective war guilt was too deep rooted. Despite protests in the United States, Morgenthau's plan of destruction became the official policy of America. Germany was to be dismembered, her people put to the fire and the sword, her soil turned to desert. Stalin heartily endorsed the plan.

After the terrible martyrdom of Dresden, when millions of refugees poured along the roads to the west, Churchill appealed to Eisenhower to allow Montgomery to occupy Berlin—but Eisenhower "had no directive." On April 12, Roosevelt died and hope flickered anew in the German people. Had not Frederick the Great himself been saved in the hour of defeat by the death of his bitter enemy, Catherine of Russia? Would history repeat itself? Would they be rescued at the eleventh hour? But no, it was not to be. The narrowing ring of fate came ever closer—Berlin would soon be isolated.

7

LAST DAYS AT SEA

(May, 1945)

Dönitz had hoped, as we know, that the advent of the new U-boats would radically alter the course of the war, but "Fortress Europe" fell before they could make their presence felt.

Only one of the XXIs—Schnee's *U 2511*—reached the Atlantic. In mid-March two Type XXIIIs, Rapprad's *U 2324* and Heckel's *U 2322*, sailed from Christiansand for the east coast of Scotland; this was their second patrol. Barschkies in *U 2321* sank a freighter south of St. Abb's Head and by May 6, more XXIII's had sailed on missions in the same area and off Lowestoft. But that was all.

When they returned, the captains were full of praise for their new commands which, they said, were ideal for short patrols in coastal waters. They could reach a speed of 13 knots submerged, they were easy to handle and answered their controls very well under water. Their small size rendered them less susceptible to location by sonar or to depth-charge attack.

While still on passage through the North Sea from Bergen to the Atlantic, Schnee picked up the singing of an A/S group, but unlike the older boats which were forced to remain almost immobile, the XXIs relied upon their speed to escape. Schnee altered course by no more than 30 degrees and the electric motors began to hum as the speed indicator rose steadily, until it was hovering round the figure 16. At 16 knots *U 2511* shot away from her pursuers, moving under water as fast as the corvettes could steam on the surface. She maintained that speed effortlessly for a whole hour without unduly taxing the capacity of her batteries, while the pings grew steadily weaker and finally faded out.

A sudden feeling of triumph and confidence animated captain and crew. For the first time in years the U-boat men felt superior to their adversary as, with a couple of turns on a wheel, they eluded their pursuers. With renewed enthusiasm they fell to discussing the U-boat tactics of the future. Their admiral had given them complete freedom of movement; they could go where they wished. Schnee had resolved upon a surprise attack on Panama, where he could be sure of finding plenty of targets; he could expect to be there within a matter of weeks.

Suddenly, while "snorting" on May 4, he received Dönitz's cease-fire order. What now? They had often discussed in the wardroom what to do if the war should end while they were still at sea. One of the officers had suggested that they should remain at sea while their supplies lasted; there would be little enough to eat at home in such a time of crisis, he argued, and a few weeks' "rest cure" would do them good. Another jokingly proposed that they should make for Argentina [1] and sell the U-boat there for what she would fetch; they all laughed at this. There was an undercurrent of truth in it all; life in defeated Germany would hold few attractions during the next few years. Schnee now consulted his friend Suhren, the chief engineer, and together they decided to return to Bergen.

A few hours after they had begun their return journey, the soundman reported propeller noises. As Schnee brought his boat cautiously to periscope depth and gazed through the eyepiece, a string of oaths came from his lips. A 10,000-ton cruiser escorted by four destroyers was coming straight toward him! It might have been a torpedo practice setup in peacetime! Schnee's hunting instincts battled with his better judgment. If only he had not received that cease-fire order! Suddenly he made up his mind and proceeded to carry out an attack on the cruiser, quite undetected by the four destroyers. Only when the moment came to fire the torpedoes, he substituted a curse for the order to fire and took his boat deep once more.

That was the first and only attack ever made by a Type XXI in the Second World War. Too late!

The cease-fire order was followed by a signal to the U-boats at sea:

My U-boat men! Six years of war lie behind us. You have fought like lions. An overwhelming material superiority has driven us into a tight corner, from which it is no longer possible to continue the war. Unbeaten and unblemished, you lay down your arms after a heroic fight without parallel. We proudly remember our fallen comrades who gave their lives for Führer and Fatherland. Comrades! Preserve that spirit in which you have fought so long and so gallantly, for the sake of the future of the Fatherland. Long live Germany!

Your Grand Admiral

A later signal reminded the captains how important it was to observe the conditions of the armistice, and canceled the order to withdraw to Norway. Detailed instructions were given for the U-boats to make for British or American ports; they were to proceed on the surface, displaying a large black or dark blue flag. When Schröteler, commanding *U 1023,* received this order out in the Atlantic, he carefully considered how to act. He was the senior of all the commanders then at

---

[1] *U 530* and *U 977* actually escaped to Argentina, where they arrived in July and August, 1945.

sea, and he knew that his juniors would all be wondering how to meet the situation. Someone would have to take the first step. In drafting his signal, he hoped that it would provide an example to the rest: "To Grand Admiral. On snort patrol lasting 46 days have sunk one 8,000-ton ship and one destroyer. Have damaged one 10,000-ton merchant ship. All torpedoes fired. With the fullest confidence in you, we are now about to obey the most painful order of all. Schröteler—*U 1023*." Then he surfaced and made for an enemy port.

Of the forty-three boats that were at sea when the armistice was signed, twenty-three made for British ports, three went to America, four to Canadian ports, seven to Norway or Kiel. One boat ran aground off Amrum, another struck a mine in the Elbe, a third and fourth were beached or scuttled off the Portuguese coast and two sailed for Argentina. The Captain of *U 1277*, Stever, who scuttled his boat off Oporto, was later severely punished by a British court-martial.

8

THE LAST MISSION

(April–May, 1945)

In the summer of 1944 the grand admiral had been in favor of fighting on, for at that time the acceptance of the terms of unconditional surrender demanded by the Allies would have caught millions of German troops still deep in Russian territory. All of them, unable to withdraw, would have fallen into Russian hands; everyone knew what that meant—not least the grand admiral who, like Hitler, refused to countenance the sacrifice of these millions of fighting men.

Even in summertime the feeding of millions of prisoners had proved to be an almost impossible task, as the German High Command had learned after the early successes against Russia in 1941; if the same problem had to be faced in winter, the result would be the death of thousands from starvation and cold, for which no one was prepared to take the responsibility. Dönitz knew that the enemy would never negotiate for peace on the basis of a compromise, so that Germany's only hope of gaining time was to fight on until the coming of warmer weather ensured that living conditions behind barbed wire would be tolerable. Meanwhile the most important task was to rescue as many as he could of the troops and refugees from the grasp of the Red armies advancing from the East.

To achieve this he requisitioned every ship that would float, sending them back and forth in an unending stream. He continued to direct this operation even after he had transferred to Camp *Forelle* near Plön, whither Hitler sent him to act as Supreme Commander of the "Northern Area," in the event of Germany being split in two; Kesselring was given a similar directive in the south. Dönitz reached Plön on April 21 by devious roads, and the scenes of misery he witnessed on his hazardous journey strengthened his determination to resist. A thick file on his desk contained harrowing reports of murder, rape and arson—depositions by refugees and eyewitnesses in localities which had been temporarily recaptured from the Russians, all of which emphasized the need to keep the way to the west open as long as possible.

As a fighting man, Dönitz never imagined in those troubled days that the mantle of Hitler might soon fall upon his shoulders; not even when, on April 23, Göring was stripped of all his offices and branded as a traitor, because he had thought fit to take over on the assumption that Hitler was no longer in power in Berlin. Dönitz had visited Hitler for the last time on April 20 accompanied by his adjutant, Lüdde-Neurath. This is how the latter described the Führer on that occasion: "His voice and his eyes are as impressive as ever. His intellectual powers seem unimpaired, nor is he crazy in the accepted sense of the word. But physically he gives the impression of a broken man, utterly worn out, bent and wracked with nerves."

On April 28 the grand admiral arrived in Rheinsberg, the new headquarters of the Supreme Command, to confer once more with Jodl, Keitel and Himmler. Jodl's appreciation of the situation made it abundantly clear that there could be no point in continuing the struggle; even the defense of the "Northern Area" could no longer serve any useful purpose. Dönitz set his face resolutely against any suggestion of isolated operations which might endanger the efficacy of the all-important rescue work. For this reason he maintained that Hamburg must not capitulate independently, as had been suggested, for the road to Schleswig-Holstein must be kept open for the refugees.

Since Göring's "treachery," it was no longer clear who was to be Hitler's successor; the grand admiral thought it would be Himmler, the most powerful man in the country—an opinion which was clearly shared by Himmler himself, and which he did not hesitate to stress at Rheinsberg. Dönitz was thus all the more astonished to receive a radio message on April 30 from the Reich Chancellery that Himmler was guilty of "treachery by initiating negotiations through Sweden." The directive ordered the grand admiral to deal with the head of the SS "with lightning speed, and ruthlessly." That was easier said than done; at that moment all power lay in the hands of Himmler, not Dönitz. In any case the grand admiral did not entirely trust this report, which was first picked up from an enemy broadcast; while Himmler, whom he met that same afternoon in Lübeck, at once strongly repudiated any suggestion that he had put out feelers to the enemy. In any event Dönitz felt that his duty lay not in suppressing traitors but in terminating a hopeless war with speed, decency and the minimum loss of life.

He had already decided what to do, as far as he himself and his Navy were concerned, as soon as it became clear that complete military collapse was inevitable. Once he had been released from his oath of loyalty by Hitler's death, he would capitulate on behalf of the forces under his command, but would himself seek death in a final attack. This would eliminate any suggestion of personal cowardice and would atone for the stain of any arbitrary capitulation by him and his troops. His most intimate friends—his son-in-law Hessler, Godt the colleague of many years, his adjutant, Lüdde-Neurath, to whom he revealed this intention—knew that these were no idle words. Hessler and the U-boat Command, which had been withdrawn from Sengwarden to Plön, now transferred to Flensburg while the grand admiral himself remained at *Forelle*. It was here on April 30, on his return from the meeting with Himmler at Lübeck, that he received the unexpected news. Only Speer was with him when Lüdde-Neurath came in with the fateful message: "Personal for Grand Admiral Dönitz. In place of the former *Reichsmarschall* Göring the Führer has nominated you as his successor. You should at once take all necessary steps required by the present situation. (signed) Bormann."

The three men looked at one another; Speer made a feeble attempt to offer congratulations. One thing was clear to them all—this was the end. Hitler was either already dead or about to die. The telegram was obviously authentic, for it had come by the one remaining channel that possessed the special secret cypher. The grand admiral was completely taken aback by this turn of events. As always when he needed to reflect, he stepped out into the open air, and went for a walk by the lakeside with Lüdde-Neurath. When they returned, Speer had already drafted a reply to Hitler's message.

The grand admiral was under no illusions. There could be only one logical conclusion to his nomination—to do that which Hitler himself was not prepared to do: to surrender. He had been given this task because, as a fighting man without political interest, the enemy would be prepared to negotiate with him. But could he—indeed, *should* he—accept Hitler's inheritance? The war was totally lost, the defeat was absolute. Must he, before the whole German people, put his name to this most terrible of all capitulations? He was faced with the most difficult decision of his whole life; the message from Berlin had given him freedom of action but had also placed upon him the full burden of responsibility. He was well aware of the dissension which was dividing the German people at that moment. In the West one cry was, "Make an end of it, finish the war now! It is criminal lunacy to prolong it for a single day." But in the East millions were expecting the fighting to be continued at least until they could escape from the clutches of the Russians. The grand admiral made his decision in favor of the people in the East and millions of refugees and troops were to be grateful for it. The same day he sent for Jodl, Keitel—and Himmler, to clarify the internal situation of the country.

When Himmler arrived late in the evening with an escort of heavily armed SS officers, there were U-boat men hiding behind every bush with tommy-guns at the ready. These were survivors of a new boat that had been bombed and sunk; under their captain, 'Ali' Cremer, they had seized some three-wheeled delivery vans and, armed only with antitank grenades, had destroyed a number of British tanks at the gates of Harburg before fighting their way through to Plön; there they formed the "Dönitz Guard Battalion" and made themselves responsible for the grand admiral's personal safety. Dönitz himself had placed a cocked pistol underneath some papers on his desk, while Lüdde-Neurath tried to engage Himmler's companions in conversation in the wardroom. The interview took place in the grand admiral's study.

Dönitz laid Bormann's telegram before the unsuspecting Himmler who read it, went pale and remained silent. At length he stood up. "I congratulate you, *Herr Grossadmiral*."

Then after a pause he added hesitatingly, "You will allow me then to be the second man in the country."

"That is not possible."

"Why not?"

"Insofar as is practicable, I intend to form a nonpolitical government. There would be no room in it for anyone as politically prominent as yourself. You would be unacceptable to the enemy in any negotiations."

For over an hour the argument between the two men continued. At this period the grand admiral was still ignorant of concentration camps or mass murders; to him, Himmler was "basically a decent fellow, who has as good a control over his SS as I have over my Navy." He tried in vain to make Himmler understand that any German Government entering into negotiations for surrender would be hopelessly handicapped if he, Himmler, were in it. Himmler, though uncomprehending, at last gave way and at two thirty in the morning he left again with his escort.

On the morning of May 1 another radio message arrived from Bormann: "Testament now in force. I will come to you as quickly as I can. Until then I recommend that this news should not be published." So Hitler was dead! The message did not say how he had died, but the German people must not be left to learn the news from the enemy and so Dönitz immediately made it public. On the same day he made an appeal to the nation. "My first task is to save German lives. . . . In the difficult days to come I shall try, so far as lies in my power, to create bearable living conditions for our gallant men, women and children. For this I need your help. Give me your confidence, for your way is my way. . . ."

So far as lay in his power . . . He was under no illusions as to the dubious nature of this "power," nor was he by any means sure that the enemy would recognize him as Hitler's legal successor, or whether indeed any German Government would exist after the surrender.

On the afternoon of May 1 came a third telegram from Bormann: "The Führer passed away yesterday at 3:30 P.M. His will dated April 29 nominates you as President of the Reich, Dr. Goebbels as Reich Chancellor, Bormann as Minister for the Party, Seiss-Inquart as Minister for Foreign Affairs. . . ." The grand admiral's first reaction to this situation was one of consternation but, as always, he was prepared to deal with it. "You should at once take all necessary steps," the first signal had said. That meant complete freedom of action; and with Hitler dead he was no longer bound by any oath of loyalty, but answerable only to his own conscience.

He was not prepared to obey this posthumous directive, which restricted his powers and saddled him with men whom he could not tolerate. He therefore suppressed that last telegram and imposed upon all communications personnel concerned with it a special oath of secrecy. Aware that in the forthcoming negotiations he would need the services of an experienced foreign minister with some prestige abroad, he had already instructed Lüdde-Neurath to summon Baron von Neurath, the former foreign minister. On learning of this move, von Ribbentrop asked for an audience and was duly received by the grand admiral, who explained why he could not make use of Hitler's foreign minister in this capacity; he ended by asking von Ribbentrop, who was clearly hurt, to make his own recommendation. The next morning the telephone rang; it was von Ribbentrop coolly recommending himself! He was promptly removed from office.

Events now moved faster than ever. On May 2 the British were already in Lübeck, barely an hour's drive by tank from Plön; when talking over the telephone to Lieutenant Maus near Draeger, Lüdde-Neurath could plainly hear the clatter of tank tracks over the wire. There was no time to be lost and the grand admiral hastily withdrew to Flensburg. In Italy, Army Group Southwest had surrendered; the Americans had reached the Baltic at Wismar. Dönitz was faced with the question whether it would not be more honorable and logical to fight the war to the bitter end, rather than surrender. "As far as he himself was concerned," said Lüdde-Neurath afterward, "death would have been the simplest way out. He had nothing more to lose. Both his sons had been lost at sea, his life's work—the U-boat Service—was destroyed, his own property had vanished." But he regarded Hitler's heritage as a liability from which he must not shrink. Even at the expense of his personal honor he must do what his conscience told him was right for the Armed Forces and right for the German people.

On May 3 von Friedeburg opened negotiations with Montgomery for the capitulation of Northern Germany; on the fourth he conferred with the grand admiral at Flensburg and then flew back to sign the instrument of surrender, which came into effect on the morning of the fifth. The most important thing about it was that not only the Netherlands and Denmark, but also the German Navy were included in the terms of surrender; contrary to tradition, no scuttling was to be allowed. This was a bitter pill for the grand admiral, but Montgomery had hinted that he would sanction the continuation of ship movements from the east, and that any individual soldiers who wanted to surrender on the demarcation line would be sent to British prison camps. With a heavy heart Dönitz issued a direct order forbidding the destruction of weapons and the scuttling of ships; in the main this order was obeyed in the Navy out of personal loyalty to the commander in chief. Montgomery's demand was the subject of heated discussions in Dönitz's own private circle, but he was determined not to expose the German people to any suggestion of a breach of the armistice terms such as might be alleged if, for instance, the U-boats were scuttled in the few hours before the cease-fire became effective.

The code word for the premeditated scuttling of German warships was "Rainbow." The order to cancel "Rainbow" loosed a flood of questions and protests. Had the grand admiral really given the order? If he had, it could only have been under duress—certainly not willingly! Did he really think the order would be obeyed? Lüdde-Neurath's telephone never stopped ringing; he could only repeat the same answer over and over again. "No, that is the truth, 'Rainbow' has been canceled. . . . Yes, I am certain of it . . . the grand admiral's orders. . . He still needs the ships. Withdrawals from the East are being continued."

Late that night, when the grand admiral had gone to bed and Lüdde-Neurath was making some last entries in the War Diary, the door burst open and a group of officers, including an admiral, a holder of the oak leaves and a crowd of U-boat commanders, stormed in. "Where is the grand admiral? We must speak to him at once!"

"The grand admiral is asleep," said Lüdde-Neurath, placing himself in front of his chief's bedroom door, "you cannot speak to him now."

"What does this mean, 'Rainbow' has been canceled? It's all nonsense! He must explain it himself. It's unheard of! The capitulation doesn't come into effect until tomorrow."

They were exactly the same arguments that Lüdde-Neurath had been answering over the telephone for hours past.

"Gentlemen," he said, "I can guarantee it. The grand admiral has indeed ordered the cancellation. He has given you the reason often enough—he needs the ships."

"The ships, yes, but not the U-boats. You can't evacuate people in U-boats."

"But be reasonable, for God's sake!" Lüdde-Neurath burst out angrily, "what else can the grand admiral do? He is Head of the State now! He is responsible for everything—not just for the Navy. The negotiations with the British are going well. Is he now to upset them by sending out the order for 'Rainbow' and so breaking the armistice terms?"

"And we?" answered one of the junior U-boat commanders sharply. "What are we supposed to do? Hand our boats over? What does he think about that?"

"He thinks more about it than you evidently realize, I can assure you of that. Anyway, if I were a U-boat commander, I would not hesitate, but would act as I thought fit."

They stared at him in silence. Suddenly one of them turned and made for the door; now he realized what was needed! The others followed close upon his heels. There was unanimity of feeling, for within a very short time the U-boat radio transmitters began to buzz throughout Northern Germany; "Rainbow! *Rainbow!* RAINBOW!!!" Bosuns' pipes shrilled through the barracks and men awoke to the shouted order, "All hands turn out! 'Rainbow'!" Crews sleeping on board the U-boats were awakened by the same call from their captains. Hurriedly putting their personal belongings on shore, they cast off and then all along the coast, at Flensburg, Eckernförde and Kiel, in Lübeck-Travemunde, at Neustadt, Hamburg and at Wilhelmshaven, the long dark shapes slid away from the jetties as, for the very last time, the diesels spluttered into life. In great numbers the Sea Wolves sailed on their final mission: out into the Bays of Lübeck and Eckernförde and the estuaries of the Elbe, the Weser and the Jade. Still flying the ensigns under which they had fought for six long years, they blew themselves up and sank. When the capitulation of Northern Germany came into force on the morning of May 5, 215 U-boats already lay on the sea bed off the North Sea and Baltic harbors. There was every type among them: XXI and XXIII, the famous old VIIc and IXc, U-cruisers, special minelayers, Walter-boats, "canoes." The enemy did not take general reprisals for this arbitrary act of scuttling as Dönitz had feared, but the engineer officer who scuttled two Walter-boats at Cuxhaven was brought before a British court-martial. Although he had acted in good faith on receiving the code word "Rainbow," he was sentenced to five years' imprisonment.

The signing of the armistice with Montgomery meant that the first part at least of Dönitz's program had been successfully carried out. By day and by night the transports steamed back and forth in the Baltic, bringing tens of thousands of refugees and troops out of the east to the safety of Schleswig-Holstein and Denmark. Well over two million souls had been brought thus to safety since the evacuations began in January; despite the loss of the *Gustloff*, *Steuben* and *Goya* with twelve thousand people aboard—sunk by Russian submarines—the total losses were less than one per cent of the whole. Even the U-boats were pressed into service as transports to bring women, children and wounded men back from Memel, Pillau, Danzig and Gotenhafen, after those ports had been cut off from outside help.

On May 11 the Allied Control Commission, consisting of the American Major General Rooks and the British Brigadier Foord, arrived in Flensburg and set up headquarters on board the *Patria*. On May 22 Dönitz, von Friedeburg and Jodl were ordered to report on board. On hearing of the order, the grand admiral merely said, "Pack your bags." He had been expecting such a move for days. None of the high authorities —not even Churchill—had taken the slightest notice of him or his government. On the morning of May 23 he arrived punctually on board the *Patria*. There was no one to receive him at the head of the gangway—only a crowd of photographers. His arrest was clearly imminent. Major General Rooks intimated that he had orders to arrest both the Government and the Supreme Command. He asked if Dönitz had anything to say, but the grand admiral answered coldly that this was no time for making speeches, then stood up and left the room.

Mass arrests followed. Von Friedeburg poisoned himself before he could be taken. On the evening of May 23 the arrested men were flown to Luxembourg, where they were lodged in the Palace Hotel at Bad Mondorf, which had been converted into a prison.

The Dönitz Government, last symbol of the unity of the German Reich, had been eliminated.

9

FINALE AT NUREMBERG

(1945–1946)

Grand Admiral Dönitz selected the Fleet Advocate, Captain Kranzbühler, to act as counsel for his defense at Nuremberg. The two men had known each other for many years, and now in one of the cubicles in the visitors' room at the Palace of Justice, they stood face to face, separated by the iron grill that prevented even a handshake. The admiral spoke somewhat as follows: "In asking you to act as my counsel, I do not imply that you should undertake primarily the defense of my person, in regard to which I have no qualms, but rather the defense of the German Navy, and in particular of the U-boat Service. At first I had it in mind to have nothing to do with this farce, whatever the consequences might be to myself. But then I realized it would be better to stand up to my accusers, sooner than be defamed without the opportunity of answering the charges. For we *have* an answer, and this is probably our last chance of stating it in public. They will try to brand us before the whole world as a bunch of murderers. But we owe it to our fallen comrades to ensure, as far as this lies in our power, that their reputation remains unsullied. The German people, too, must hear what we have to say in answer to these accusations, and they must know that their fighting men were not a horde of common criminals."

For months past, the team of prosecutors had been searching through a mountain of captured German documents to procure the necessary evidence. Every facility was available to them; if necessary they could detail a special aircraft to fly some wanted file from Washington within twenty-four hours. On the other hand the defense at first had literally nothing to work on. Before the war had ended, Dönitz had expressly forbidden the destruction of the German naval archives, for he considered that anyone should be free to learn from them, and that there was nothing to hide. The victors had captured these archives which were now housed at the Admiralty in London. Eventually Kranzbühler succeeded in obtaining approval from the Tribunal and from the British Admiralty to send his assistant, Captain Meckel, to London. There Meckel worked for three whole weeks, spending each night in a P.O.W. Camp and traveling each morning to the Admiralty with his escort, a Navy sublieutenant. Unremittingly he ploughed his way through endless files, making notes and extracts and taking photostat copies, working against time, for he knew that there would be no other chance of obtaining the vital documentary evidence.

Meanwhile Nuremberg saw the arrival of large numbers of witnesses for both prosecution and defense, the latter being lodged in the courthouse prison. For the defense of Dönitz they included Rear Admirals Wagner and Godt, and Captain Hessler, Dönitz's son-in-law. Godt had earlier been flown to the United States, where pressure was put on him to give evidence against Dönitz. His interrogators told him that as his chief could not now be saved, it would make no difference whether Godt spoke for or against him. It was even put to him that he might save his own skin if he gave the evidence the prosecution desired. Godt, however, was indifferent to these suggestions, and eventually he was sent back to Nuremberg and placed at the disposal of the defense.[1]

The Indictments commenced on October 18, 1945, and the presentation of the case by the prosecution in January, 1946. Meanwhile Dönitz was receiving a stream of letters from his old Sea Wolves, expressing their loyalty and faith in him and asking what they could do to help. One of these letters bore the signature of sixty-seven former U-boat commanders, headed by Captain Winter, who had commanded the First Flotilla at Brest; it was used as evidence for the defense, and ran as follows:

> From press and radio we learn that Grand Admiral Dönitz is being accused of having ordered the slaughter of survivors from torpedoed ships. We, the undersigned, declare upon oath that the grand admiral never issued any such order, either in writing or by word of mouth. The order that was issued instructed the U-boats, in the interests of their own safety, not to surface after torpedo attacks, as they had done in the early part of the war. Because of the greatly increased danger from the enemy's A/S forces, surfacing after attacks would probably lead to the destruction of the U-boats. This was an unequivocal order, and was never construed by us as authorizing the killing of survivors. We, the undersigned, declare that the German Navy was taught by its leaders to respect the written and unwritten laws of the sea, and we have always regarded it as a point of honor to uphold these laws and to conduct the war with chivalry.

The period in May covering the hearing of the cases for Dönitz and Raeder was notable for the consistency of the evidence given by the witnesses for the defense. But the prosecution showed that it had in no way been impressed by this evidence, when the American Chief Prosecutor, Justice Jackson, winding up his case, pointed an accusing finger at Dönitz, and uttered the following words: "Dönitz, Hitler's legatee of defeat, promoted the success of the Nazi aggressions by instructing his pack of submarine killers to wage the war at sea with the lawless savagery of the jungle. . . ." and so on.

The months dragged on as the trials slowly moved toward

---

[1] This was done at the request of the tribunal. Godt, himself, was not tried as a war criminal.

a climax. At last on August 31, 1946, Dönitz was called on to make his final statement before the Tribunal.

"Firstly," he said, "you must assess the legality of the German submarine campaign as your conscience dictates. I regard this mode of warfare as legitimate, and I have acted according to my own conscience. The subordinates, however, who carried out my orders, acted in good faith and without a shadow of doubt as to the necessity or legality of these orders. In my view no subsequent judgment can deprive them of their faith in the honorable character of a struggle for which they were ready to sacrifice themselves until the end.

"Secondly, much has been said here of a conspiracy which is alleged to have existed among the defendants. I regard this assertion as a piece of political dogma, which can never be proved, but only believed or rejected. But large sections of the German people will never believe that such a conspiracy could have been the cause of their misfortune. Let the politicians and jurists argue about it. They will only make it harder for the German people to draw a lesson from this trial, which is of decisive importance for its attitude toward the past and its shaping of the future—the acknowledgment that the Führer principle as a political principle is wrong. This principle had proved itself in the military leadership of every army in the world, and therefore I believed that it was right also in political leadership, especially for a people in the hopeless position of the German people in 1932. The great successes of the new government and a feeling of happiness such as the entire nation had never known before seemed to prove it right. But despite the idealism, the decency and devotion of the German people, the Führer principle must be wrong, since human nature is evidently incapable of exploiting its inherent power without abusing it.

"Thirdly, my life has been dedicated to my profession and thereby to the service of the German people. As the last Commander in Chief of the German Navy and as the last Head of the State, I consider myself answerable to the German people for all that I have done or have left undone."

A whole month elapsed before the trial culminated in the pronouncement of the judgments. The increased stress was evidenced by the greater security measures. Extra guards were established at strategic points inside the prison, while armored cars patrolled the streets outside, which were cordoned off, with troops held in readiness. The principal seats in the courtroom were reserved for the highest-ranking Allied officers, while senior officers were accommodated in the gallery, with the press and photographers in the hall below.

The defending counsel were ordered to assemble in a special room, where they were searched for hidden arms before being escorted two by two into the courtroom. The findings of the court occupied a day and a half, the individual judges of the four nations giving lengthy descriptions of developments in Germany since the First World War, with frequent reference to the accused and the role they played. As for Dönitz, he was found not guilty on Count One of the Indictment—that is, conspiracy to wage aggressive war, but guilty on Counts Two and Three; that is, guilty of planning, preparing and initiating wars of aggression, and guilty of violation of the laws or customs of war. But in pronouncing the verdict, the judge expressly stated that the sentence of Dönitz was *not* assessed on the ground of any breaches of the international law of submarine warfare.

Finally, on the afternoon of October 1, 1946, the court assembled to pronounce the sentences. Tension was at its height. Could the grand admiral be condemned to death on Counts Two and Three? The courtroom began to fill again, the prisoners' benches were empty, the press and cameramen were excluded. It was also observed that the distinguished Allied generals who had been present that morning during the judgments were now absent, except for two Russians and Admiral Sir John Cunningham. While the Allied generals were evidently unwilling to hear the sentence of death passed on their wartime opponents, the presence of the British First Sea Lord gave hope of a less drastic fate for the German admirals.

A deathly silence pervaded the courtroom as the President of the Tribunal called the name of the first accused: "Hermann Wilhelm Göring!" Flanked by two white-helmeted military police, the defendant entered the courtroom, moved toward his seat in the dock, and settled the earphones on his head. In a quiet, even voice Lord Lawrence pronounced the sentence. "On the counts of the Indictment on which you have been convicted, the International Military Tribunal sentences you to death by hanging." Without a word the former *Reichsmarschall* removed his earphones, stepped back, still flanked by his guards, and left the courtroom. Rudolph Hess was then called, and the President, using the identical procedure, announced the sentence of life imprisonment. Hess was followed at brief intervals by seven further defendants, each of whom was to hear those grim words "death by hanging." Now it was the turn of Dönitz. As soon as he had fixed his headphones, the President spoke: "Defendant Karl Dönitz, on the counts of the Indictment on which you have been convicted, the Tribunal sentences you to ten years' imprisonment." There was a moment's pause; then the grand admiral made his exit, and so he passed from the glare of the contemporary scene into the somber, pitiless twilight of Spandau.[2]

Thus the curtain fell on a drama unparalleled in the history of war. This book has attempted to describe the life and activities of one important arm of the German fighting services in the Second World War. The consequences of that war have profoundly influenced the lives of millions, and it will be for a future historian to assess not only these consequences, but also the ultimate effect of the victors' unprecedented decision to indict the war leaders of their erstwhile antagonists.

[2] Dönitz was released from Spandau in 1955.

APPENDIX I

Designation of Allied Convoys
Mentioned in the Text

Each convoy was allocated letters and figures. The letters indicated the route and the figures the number of the particular convoy on that route.

GUS	North Africa—USA
HG	Gibraltar—UK
HX	New York, Halifax, etc.—UK
OB	Liverpool—Western Approaches
OG	UK—Gibraltar
ON	UK—North America
ONS	UK—North America (slow)
OS	UK—West Africa
PQ	UK—North Russia
QP	North Russia—UK
SC	Halifax—UK
SL	West Africa—UK
UGS	USA—North Africa

APPENDIX II

Types and Details of U-Boats used by the Germans in the Second World War

Type	Description	Year of Commissioning	Number Built and Commissioned	Armament, Max. Speed Surfaced/Submerged	Remarks
I	800 ton Atlantic U-Boat	1936	2	6 torpedo tubes; 14 torpedoes; one 10.5cm gun; one 20mm flak; 18/8 knots; crew 43	
II	250–300 ton coastal U-Boat	1935–1940	50	3 bow torpedo tubes; 5 torpedoes; one 20mm twin flak; 13/8 knots; crew 25	Known as "canoes"
VII B VII C VII C	600 ton Atlantic U-Boat 750 ton Atlantic U-Boat 770 ton Atlantic U-Boat	1936–1937 1938–1942 1940–1945	10 25 659	4 bow, 1 stern torpedo tubes; 12 torpedoes; one 20mm twin flak; 17/8 knots; crew 44	The VII C was the standard type of Atlantic U-Boat which was responsible for most of the Allied tonnage sunk
VII C/42 VII D VII F	1,000 ton U-Boats	1941–1943	12	as for Type VII C.; 18/8 knots	For various special purposes, transport, minelaying, etc.
IX	1,000–1,100 ton U-Boat	1938–1945	155	4 bow, 2 stern torpedo tubes; 19 torpedoes or 66 mines; one 37-mm flak; two 20mm twin flak; 18/7.3 knots; crew 48	Various improvements added in later designs of this type. (IX B, C and D) Known as "sea cows"
IX D	1,600 ton U-Cruiser	1942–1944	31	4 bow, 2 stern torpedo tubes; 24 torpedoes; one 37mm flak; two 20mm twin flak; 19/7 knots; crew 57	Used in remote operations
X B	1,760 ton minelaying U-Boat	1941–1943	8	2 stern torpedo tubes; 30 mine shafts; 15 torpedoes, 66 mines; one 37mm flak; two 20mm twin flak; 17/7 knots; crew 52	Used also as tankers
XIV	1,700 ton supply U-Boat	1941–1943	10	one 37mm flak; two 20mm twin flak; 15/6.2 knots; crew 53	